Talk: The Science of Conversation

Talk: The Science of Conversation

Elizabeth Stokoe

ROBINSON

ROBINSON

First published in Great Britain in 2018 by Robinson

3 5 7 9 10 8 6 4 2

Copyright © Elizabeth Stokoe, 2018

The moral right of the author has been asserted.

A CIP catalogue record for this book
is available from the British Library.

ISBN: 978-1-47214-084-5

Typeset in Minion Pro by SX Composing DTP, Rayleigh, Essex SS6 7EF
Printed and bound in Great Britain by Clays Ltd, Elcograf S.p.A.

Papers used by Robinson are from well-managed forests
and other responsible sources.

For Eunice

CONTENTS

1: The conversational racetrack   **1**

   'Hello!'   3

   'Um, hello . . . ?'   18

   The conversational racetrack   30

2: Here comes the science   **32**

   Scriptwriters are conversation analysts 38

   The building blocks of talk   43

   How to build a successful invitation   45

   Interruptions, dating, and a roll-on deodorant   53

   The science of conversation   62

3: You are the turns you take   **63**

   First moves and '*first movers*'   65

   How turns build people   71

   You are the words you *say* you are   87

   Conversation Analytic Personality Diagnostic   92

   Talk builds people   99

4: Sticks, stones, and . . . talk   100

Do actions speak louder than words?   101

Is communication 93 per cent body language?   115

Do women and men talk differently?   119

Do different 'cultures' talk differently?   129

Are 'ums' errors?   132

Why are there so many myths about talk?   137

5: Every word matters   139

Word selection matters   141

The trouble with 'women'   144

How words change outcomes   151

'Some' or 'any'?   155

Getting people to donate to charity   159

'Talk' or 'speak'?   162

'Are you willing?'   166

Talk matters   174

6: Are you being served?   176

How to get help   177

Service in seconds   182

Service burden   195

Recruiters and the recruited   210

Thank you for not helping   216

7: How to have better conversations 217

The problem with communication skills 220

The future of talk 239

Five ways to have better conversations 241

Appendix 255

Acknowledgements 257

References 261

Index 269

1
THE CONVERSATIONAL
RACETRACK

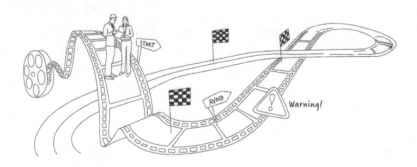

This book will change the way you think about talk. It will show you how to lift the lid on the engine that drives our everyday lives. It will show you why there is a big pay-off to understanding talk scientifically.

Of course, when we try to understand something like talk scientifically, it is not the same as trying to understand something like a black hole. Talk, as a phenomenon of social life, exists only to be understood.[1] It is designed by humans for humans to get every facet of life accomplished. We build, maintain and end our personal and professional relationships through talk. We buy and sell. We get and give help. We are excited, persuaded, irritated, embarrassed and consoled in response to things others say to us. Talk is the tool we have to do all of these things.

Talk is also our resource for fixing things that go wrong. When we characterise some aspect of our talk as 'communication breakdown',

---

1 Edwards (2012).

we are probably referring to feeling trapped in a conversation, or that we are struggling to get heard, or as though we are on the back foot. This book will show you how to unpack and understand talk and what to say to anticipate, resist, avoid – or further aggravate – these problems.

Scientists strive to understand black holes, even though they do not exist in the first place to be understood by humans. Talk, on the other hand, exists *only* to be understood by humans. In that sense, a book about the science of talk should be an easy read; the conceptual gap between the audience and the phenomenon is small. On the other hand, it might be a challenge to convince you that we need a scientific approach to the study of something that seems, on the surface, so easy to understand. Can we really gain anything by analysing something that we 'just do'? The chapters in this book will show you that the answer is 'yes'. And it will show you that the science of conversation is not just interesting, or fun. It is crucial.

Along with many other academic colleagues around the world, I have spent the last twenty years working as a conversation analyst, studying recordings of real talk from real people talking to each other in real time. While the linguist Noam Chomsky once described conversation as a 'disorderly phenomenon', it is, in fact, highly organised. And we are quite unaware of how systematic our talk is, and how different words lead to different outcomes. So while we all keep talking, we are not good at understanding precisely what went wrong in an encounter, or what went right. Analysing real talk in the wild – and in slow motion – shows us the incredible power talk has to shape our daily lives.

Think about the last time you went on a rollercoaster.[2] You might have seen – even if you did not purchase it – the snapshot of yourself as you zoomed down the steepest incline. Rollercoaster snapshots reveal how you looked at a particular moment, even though you are unable to remember or reproduce it later. Similarly, we are not capable of recalling and reproducing – with the exact words, the

---

2   Albert et al. (2018).

exact intonation and the exact facial expression – what we said at, say, thirty-three seconds into a particular conversation. Studying talk scientifically allows us to freeze-frame that moment and scrutinise it to see *how* it worked, *what* worked and what did *not work*.

In this opening chapter, we investigate what happens at the start of encounters. Talk can run smoothly or awkwardly from the very first 'hello'. We can predict what is likely to happen next from the first words uttered. This is because all conversations have a landscape; a conversational racetrack. We start at the beginning of an encounter with another person or people and, along the way, complete projects. We anticipate and avoid or crash into hurdles. Conversations become tense, difficult or all-out war. An opening 'hello' can even be, quite simply, a matter of life and death.

'Hello!'

The discipline of conversation analysis was invented by three academics in the 1960s: Harvey Sacks, Emanuel Schegloff and Gail Jefferson.[3] Sacks was killed in a car crash in 1975 and, like celebrities who die young or in mysterious circumstances, there is something of a rock 'n' roll mystique about him. There are also many arguments over his legacy and competitive in-groups and sub-camps typical of any academic field.

This book is not the place for lengthy accounts of the discipline, but it is worth knowing that each of these three figures holds a special position in the hearts and minds of conversation analysts around the world. And, as an advocate for conversation analysis to a likely non-specialist audience, and for context, you might be surprised to learn that conversation analytic research is among the most cited in academia, even compared to 'hard science' disciplines.[4]

---

3 Sacks et al. (1974).

4 An article in *Nature* entitled 'The top 100 papers', listing the most-cited research of all time, identified papers in the 'hard' sciences with citations ranging from 305K to 12.2K, at the time of publication in 2014. The foundational piece by Sacks, Schegloff and Jefferson currently has over

Before we see our first example of two people starting to talk, let me explain briefly how their talk will be presented. As with all the other data analysed in this book, recordings of real (generally anonymised) interactions are transcribed using a technical system developed by Jefferson.[5] The system is the first stage of analysis and cannot be reproduced by a machine – even though speech-to-text software will produce reasonably accurate verbatim transcripts (see 'The future of talk', in Chapter 7).

The 'Jefferson system' is designed to represent not just *what* is said but *how* it is produced, placed, timed and so on. It includes information about intonation, lengths of pauses and gaps within and between turns at talk, the onset and end of overlapping talk, and the precise moment when who is speaking changes. It also tells us how speakers build *actions* through talk – the component activities that comprise complete encounters. At first, the transcripts might seem overly technical. But this is how people talk – keeping in the detail of how talk works, rather than stripping it away to the words alone. It's what actually happened.

For the first few extracts in this chapter, though, I will present a verbatim version of the transcript alongside the technical version, to enable you to become familiar with the system. A key to all of the symbols appears at the end of the book. You can also listen to some of the examples I present online,[6] where they feature as part of a lecture or presentation.

Our first example is an ordinary domestic telephone call between two American friends, Hyla and Nancy. Hyla is calling Nancy; this is a telephone line without caller ID.[7] Her dialling is the summons that

---

16K cites in March 2018; Schegloff has 76K citations; Jefferson 45K and Sacks 50K. For a relatively unknown discipline, its impact is actually rather massive!

5   Jefferson (2004).

6   Listen to Hyla and Nancy (and other examples from the book) at www.carmtraining.org/talk/extras.

7   Comparing mobile calls to landlines without caller ID, 'answers to the summons of a mobile call treat the summons as being personalised in giving information on the caller, and allowing the answer to be designed accordingly' (Arminen and Leinonen, 2006).

starts the conversational ball rolling. It is the first action that must be completed for any further talk to happen.

Example 1: Hyla and Nancy

'Jefferson' transcript			Simplified transcript		
01		((telephone rings))	01		((telephone rings))
02	Nancy:	H'llo:?	02	Nancy:	Hello?

Take a look at Nancy's answering turn, 'H'llo:?' The punctuation marks help researchers, and you, understand exactly *how* she said it. For instance, the colon indicates that the 'o' sound is slightly elongated. The question mark indicates 'questioning intonation'. You might be surprised to learn that 'questioning intonation' does not always accompany the spoken production of a question. In fact, questions are more often delivered with *falling* or 'closing' intonation, indicated by a full stop. This is one of many communication myths that we will bust in this book.

Systematic patterns exist in the way conversation starts, and not just on the telephone. This is because although the *means* of communication might be different (e.g., language choice, modality, gesture, sign language, written, spoken), and the exact words used also vary (e.g., 'hello', 'hiya', 'yo!'), the *actions* being done remain the same.

Watch how Hyla and Nancy's conversation unfolds.

| 03 | Hyla | Hi:, | 03 | Hyla | Hi |
| 04 | Nancy | HI::. | 04 | Nancy | Hi! |

When Hyla says, 'Hi:,' she delivers a *greeting* but also communicates *recognition* of her friend's voice. The comma indicates what conversation analysts call 'continuing intonation' – think how it sounds to read items on a shopping list or the digits in a telephone number.

At line 04, Nancy gives a second greeting, but it sounds very different to her answering-the-phone 'H'llo:?'. This time, the 'HI::.' is louder, brighter, and more animated. It conveys recognition of Hyla's voice.

Next, Hyla and Nancy exchange 'how-are-yous'.

| 05 | Hyla | How are yuhh.= | 05 | Hyla | How are you? |
| 06 | Nancy | =Fi:ne how're you. | 06 | Nancy | Fine, how are you? |

Hyla and Nancy exchange 'how-are-yous' rapidly, and reciprocally. The speed of exchange is represented by the equals signs ('='), which indicate that the two turns are 'latched' together. The quick pace of their turn-taking is also indicated implicitly, because when gaps occur between turns – as we will see in later examples – they are measured and included in the transcript.

On the face of it, this is utterly mundane. There's no science here! Well, actually there is. Conversation analysts have shown that, across settings including phone calls, face-to-face encounters, Skype calls and even instant messaging, conversations recurrently open with three rapid, reciprocal, component pairs of actions:

1. The summons and answer (the opening at lines 01–02).

2. The greetings and identification (for Hyla and Nancy, just the sound of the voice is enough for identification at lines 03–04).

3. The initial enquiries (the 'how-are-yous' at lines 05–06).

This sequence of actions is pretty robust across opening sequences, whether on the telephone or face to face. In Example 2, Dad and Liz are Skyping. The pound signs indicate 'smile-voice' – how people sound when they smile as they talk. You can watch this clip online.[8]

Example 2: Dad and Liz

01	Dad	£Hi Liz, how're you.£	01	Dad	Hi Liz, how are you?
02	Liz	£I'm fine thanks.=	02	Liz	I'm fine thanks.
03		how're you.£	03		How are you?

In Skype conversations, the 'summons and answer' sequence still occurs because someone still has to 'go first' in any interaction. However, the identification part may be redundant, because we generally know who we will talk to when we initiate a video chat. Of course, I can use my partner's mobile phone or Skype account to make a call, and the recipient may not expect to see or hear me when they answer the summons.

Example 3 comes from a written exchange between two friends on a social media messaging app.[9]

---

8   Listen to Dad and Liz (and other examples from the book) at www.carmtraining.org/talk/extras.
9   Meredith (2014).

Example 3: Isla and Joe

01	Joe:	hey isla
02		how are you?
03	Isla:	hey you :-)
04		i'm not too bad thanks :-) :-)
05		you?

The same components are in place: 'summons and answer'; 'greetings and identification', and the reciprocal 'how-are-yous'. They take a bit longer, because writing is slower than talking. But otherwise, the same actions happen.

Example 4 is from a conversation between two office workers from different departments of the local council.

Example 4: Katy and Darcy

01	Katy:	Katy Green, good morning, c'n I he̲:lp you,
02		(0.3)
03	Darcy:	He̲:llo Katy good morning t'you.=it's Darcy:.
04	Katy:	.pt £Hello Da̲:rcy, how're you.£=
05	Darcy:	=A̲'right thank you?='re you [m'duck,]
06	Katy:	[Myeah] not too bad.

In this recording, the square brackets at lines 05 and 06 represent overlapping talk. So as Darcy says 'm'duck' – one of many terms of endearment used in the UK, such as 'love', 'hen' or 'pet' – Katy begins to respond to Darcy's 'how-are-you'.

There are several features that you may not initially notice in this example, but that are important when it comes to understanding the more complex conversational openings we come to later. So, first, note that the way Katy answers the phone tells us that this is not a domestic setting, but a workplace. Second, Katy's next turn, at line 04, is delivered with 'smile-voice', *after* she knows who she is speaking to. She does not smile when she answers the phone.

Third, Darcy and Katy do not know each other well enough for Darcy to simply respond 'Hi' at line 03, as we have seen in previous examples: she returns Katy's greeting fully and identifies herself explicitly. But Darcy and Katy *do* know each other well enough to now move into a reciprocal 'how-are-you' sequence.

The equals signs at lines 03, 04 and 05 indicate when speakers rapidly add another part to a turn that is potentially already complete. Conversation analysts refer to the 'point of possible completion' that happens when a speaker has done something that can be responded to by the next speaker, such as asking a question. These are usually grammatically complete, too. Points of completion are also indicated strongly by intonation. As you read this book, read out loud, if you can. Each time a full stop happens, your intonation should fall. In the Jefferson system, full stops indicate 'closing intonation' and that a 'unit' of a turn has been completed.

It is worth pausing here, to point out that in everyday written text, full stops ('periods' in the USA) are not, however, intonation markers! They are grammatical markers, placed at the end of grammatical sentences. That is something that all readers of this book will know, whether intuitively or explicitly. Jefferson borrowed and reassigned the full stop and other conventions of written text (colons, commas, question marks, etc.) to talk's intonational patterns. Of course, *both* transcription and everyday written punctuation are technical and precise – we are just more used to the conventions for written text.

Returning to Darcy and Katy's conversation, at line 03, Darcy's turn is complete as she says 'good morning t'you.' but she rapidly adds a second 'unit' to the end of her turn: '.=it's Darcy:.' What a simplified verbatim transcript would not show is Darcy's tacit analysis of her response to Katy. The rapid addition of a second unit reveals Darcy's ongoing monitoring of the unfolding interaction. She needs to identify herself. This is not my analysis of what Katy and Darcy are doing, it is *Darcy's*. My job is to reveal their analysis to you.

Think about when a friend invites you for dinner. They may say something like, 'Do you fancy dinner on Friday? Or Saturday?' The addition of 'Or Saturday' shows their ongoing monitoring of your lack of immediate response. The idea that taking a turn in a conversation requires 'processing time', producing pauses, is another myth about talk that we will bust in this book. In fact, we can and do respond very quickly within milliseconds. Indeed, speakers are actually monitoring reactions while their own turn is in progress, which is what enables such rapid interchange to take place. And the fact that we (can) respond quickly provides us with the evidence that delays, gaps, silences indicate an upcoming problem. Of course, we can respond quickly with turns that start with built-in delay-tactics (e.g., 'Um:::::'). But a delay in responding to an invitation indicates an upcoming turndown. Because they are fast to recognise a possible turndown, your friend quickly adds another option, to which you can hopefully say 'yes' . . .!

This is the tacit knowledge that people have for interacting. We reveal it as we construct our turns, word by word, turn by turn, although we cannot articulate what we are doing. But, without knowing it, we anticipate hurdles on the racetrack of conversation, and try to avoid them.

Finally, look closely at the overlapping talk at lines 05 and 06. The overlap shows that Katy has heard enough of the second unit of Darcy's turn to know what action Darcy is doing even though it is not complete: she is doing a reciprocal 'how-are-you'. This sort of overlap is very common in interaction: people can sufficiently anticipate the action that is coming to begin to respond without leaving any gap between turns.

You might be thinking that everything you have read so far is worthy of an entry in a *Private Eye* 'Pseud's Corner' jibe – and, in fact, an early observation from Sacks, Schegloff and Jefferson, that 'one speaker speaks at a time and speaker change recurs', actually was! It is certainly common to hear people describe or reflect on conversational components like 'how-are-you' sequences critically, as a bit of pointless 'filler', said 'just to be polite', in a meaningless and 'non-genuine' way. I will show that these sorts of comments misunderstand the importance of starting to unpack the basic machinery of talk as a precursor to persuading you of some crucial insights into how talk works.

You might also be thinking that there are numerous instances where conversation openings are quite different. And, of course, they are. Here are four quick examples.

Example 5: Calling the doctor's

01		((ring))
02	Recep:	>Good< mornin:g, surgery: Cath speaking,
03		(1.6)
04	Patient:	Hello have you got an appointment for Frida:y
05		afternoon or teatime please.

Example 6: Salesperson calling a business

01		((ring))
02	Business:	Good afternoon,=Advance Services Management,
03		(.)
04	Sales:	Hi.=↑Can I::- (0.5) ↓speak with John Stornoway
05		please.

In Example 5, a patient phones her local surgery. The parties greet each other ('>Good< mornin:g,' and 'Hello'), but, in this opening moment, only the receptionist provides identification of both the surgery and her first name. Who the patient is becomes relevant later; for now, the main action is requesting an appointment. There are no 'how-are-yous' – potentially tricky in this setting! Example 6 has two people at work calling each other, but, unlike Katy and Darcy, they do not know each other.

Example 7 is a domestic phone call, but Lesley, who answers the ringing phone, is being called by someone who wants to make a delivery to Lesley's house. Example 8 is another of Katy's calls, but this one is to her daughter at home. As with all our examples, use the transcription key presented in the Appendix to unpack the technical aspects about which you want to learn.

Example 7: Lesley and Mr Harris (simplified transcript)

01   ((ring))

02   Lesley: Hello:?

03   (0.3)

04   Harris: Hello Missus Field it's Jamie Harris here from Castle

05   Kerry's [(Group)]

06   Lesley: [O h h e l l o,]

07   Harris: Hello Missus Field .hh uhm .t.h Would you be

08   available for supply on Thu::rsda:y.=

Example 8: Katy and her daughter

01		((ring))
02	Daughter:	hHello:?
03	Katy:	.pt Hi £sweetie.£= it's only me,
04	Daughter:	h[Hi::]
05	Katy:	[.pt] did'ya get in an' unlock the ala:rm?

There are reciprocal greetings – spot Lesley's second one at line 06 in which she also shows she recognises Mr Harris and has expected him to call. See also that Mr Harris recognises Lesley from her answering 'hello'. As the caller, he is in a position to know who is likely to answer the phone. However, he identifies himself using his own name and the name of the business. He does not expect Lesley to recognise him from his voice alone; they do not have the kind of relationship where Mr Harris could simply say 'Hi!' next.

Example 8 neatly demonstrates how we calibrate the purpose of our call by including or dispensing with things that would ordinarily happen in the conversation. While mother and daughter exchange greetings, there are no 'how-are-yous'. Why not? Dispensing with 'how-are-yous' helps us know the kind of conversation we are in. This is going to be a quick call to check on the important activity of getting into the house and disabling alarms. So by asking a question about the house's alarm in the slot usually filled with a 'how-are-you', Katy indicates to her daughter what type of call this will be.

Call openings vary, then, depending on contingencies like who is calling whom; whether or not speakers know each other; the urgency of the situation; and so on. These are not random, messy variations, but systematic ones, by which we construct and recognise the particular nature of each type of call. It is the fact that we do this

– making our actions recognisable for each other – that makes those same actions and methods recognisable for conversation analysts.

We conclude this section on 'Hello!' by focusing again on the three actions done in openings: the summons and answer; greeting and identification, and 'how-are-yous'. Example 9 is another call in which we encounter Hyla, this time talking to her boyfriend, Richard. Their opening shows the irresistibility of completing these three actions, which further undermines the notion that they are pointless 'filler'. They are doing something important in an interaction: framing it, establishing its footing and the relationships involved.

Harvey Sacks made a classic observation about 'how-are-yous' in a paper called 'Everyone Has to Lie'.[10] He was referring to the kind of social situation that *requires* a 'fine, thanks, how are you' response, not a long (happy or sad) answer to the question. Not everyone is the right person to receive the 'true' answer (e.g., 'I'm feeling lousy'; 'I'm so excited!'), but neither is every slot in a conversation the right place to say it. In Hyla and Nancy's call, it later turns out that Hyla is not fine – after the opening 'how-are-yous' she goes on to recount to Nancy her problems with Richard. But everybody has to lie.

The call between Hyla and Richard has an extended opening. There is a lot of laughter and breathiness in the call; Richard arrived home to hear the phone ringing inside the house and has raced in to answer it. The transcript represents the laughter and breathiness. I hope that, by now, you can see how impoverished a verbatim transcript would be, when compared to this technical version. Imagine if you were not permitted to use emoticons or emojis when writing text messages or using instant messaging services. Imagine I presented an analysis of text-based interaction and deliberately removed these features. Representing talk with this technical system is not just good science. It's an ethical decision. This is how people actually talk, and I want to show you what really happened when Hyla called Richard.

Our target three actions – the summons/answer; greetings/identification; and 'how-are-yous' – are highlighted.

---

10   Sacks (1975).

Example 9: Hyla and Richard

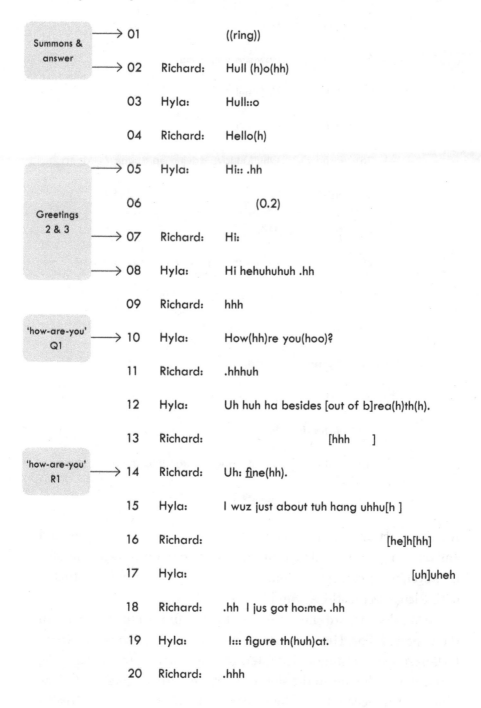

Summons & answer	→ 01		((ring))
	→ 02	Richard:	Hull (h)o(hh)
	03	Hyla:	Hull::o
	04	Richard:	Hello(h)
Greetings 2 & 3	→ 05	Hyla:	Hi:: .hh
	06		(0.2)
	→ 07	Richard:	Hi:
	→ 08	Hyla:	Hi hehuhuhuh .hh
	09	Richard:	hhh
'how-are-you' Q1	→ 10	Hyla:	How(hh)re you(hoo)?
	11	Richard:	.hhhuh
	12	Hyla:	Uh huh ha besides [out of b]rea(h)th(h).
	13	Richard:	[hhh]
'how-are-you' R1	→ 14	Richard:	Uh: fine(hh).
	15	Hyla:	I wuz just about tuh hang uhhu[h]
	16	Richard:	[he]h[hh]
	17	Hyla:	[uh]uheh
	18	Richard:	.hh I jus got ho:me. .hh
	19	Hyla:	I::: figure th(huh)at.
	20	Richard:	.hhh

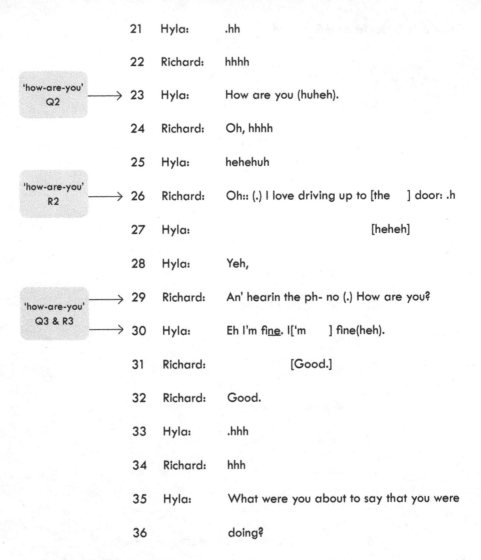

	21	Hyla:	.hh
	22	Richard:	hhhh
'how-are-you' Q2 →	23	Hyla:	How are you (huheh).
	24	Richard:	Oh, hhhh
	25	Hyla:	hehehuh
'how-are-you' R2 →	26	Richard:	Oh:: (.) I love driving up to [the　] door: .h
	27	Hyla:	[heheh]
	28	Hyla:	Yeh,
'how-are-you' Q3 & R3 →	29	Richard:	An' hearin the ph- no (.) How are you?
→	30	Hyla:	Eh I'm fi_ne_. I['m　] fine(heh).
	31	Richard:	[Good.]
	32	Richard:	Good.
	33	Hyla:	.hhh
	34	Richard:	hhh
	35	Hyla:	What were you about to say that you were
	36		doing?

All three actions are present in the call, with the summons and answer and greeting and identification done rapidly and sequentially. However, the greetings are done a second and third time, punctuated with Richard's breathiness and Hyla's laughter.

Hyla asks Richard 'how are you' for the first time at line 10, in the expected slot. His response is more heavy breathing, to which Hyla responds with more laughter. Her laughter is, in fact, helping Richard out. She fills in the slot for his turn with laughter, as well as providing an account for why he cannot talk – he is 'out of brea(h) th(h).', she says. Eventually, Richard produces the standard 'fine' response at line 14.

Hyla and Richard's opening sequence is extended with more talk; Hyla reports that she nearly hung up the call; Richard accounts for why he took so long to answer. It is interesting that Hyla asks a second 'how-are-you' at line 23. This time, Richard gives an ironic response: 'Oh, I love driving up to the door and hearing the ph-'. But see what he does next! He cuts off this response, which is starting to sound like a complaint about Hyla making him run to the house. He then says 'no', explicitly verbalising the fact that he 'will not go there'; he will not keep complaining. In so doing, Richard halts the development of a possible argument before it has started. Instead, he asks a reciprocal 'how-are-you'. He uses his tacit knowledge of *what should happen next* to avoid potential conflict, and Hyla gives the standard response.

Hyla and Richard show us that the ordinary words and phrases, like greetings and 'how-are-yous', are a useful resource. They start an encounter. They can be extended to help someone who is out of breath. More importantly, though, the fact that Hyla and Richard do and redo these actions shows that they are an interactional *imperative*. They simply have to be done. People show us this all the time. Speakers monitor each other's turns for their appropriateness of action and position.

The interactional imperative holds for written talk too, as we saw earlier in Isla and Joe's messaging app conversation. Here is Isla talking to another friend. When Jane opens the conversation in a non-standard way ('urgh'), Isla responds a minute or so later with a comment about Jane's inapposite conversation opener.

Example 10: Isla and Jane[11]

01	Jane:	urgh
02		(82.0)
03	Isla:	what a greeting!!

These early conversational actions, whose patterns are robust across settings of all kinds, can also be usurped as resources for conflict and argument, as we will see in the next section.

'Um, hello . . . ?'

So far, the conversations we have encountered have been friendly, or affiliative. They have started smoothly, with the speakers more or less in alignment. In this section, we move on to examine some rather more problematic – and even life-changing – conversational openings.

We start with a call between boyfriend and girlfriend, Dana and Gordon. They are students who are home for their holidays and living with their respective parents.

Example 11: Dana and Gordon

01		((ring))
02	Gordon:	Hello:,
03		(0.7)

Let us stop here, before Dana has even spoken. Lines 01–03 are all we need to see to know that there is trouble ahead. This is because of what happens at line 03; or rather, what does *not* happen. Dana does not issue a reciprocal greeting. Instead, there is a silence of 0.7

---

11 Meredith (2014).

seconds. This might not seem like long, but it is. And it is just this kind of detail that allows us to zoom in on parts of the conversational racetrack where there might be either smooth progress – alignment – or trouble – disaffiliation.

It is worth restating that the silence of 0.7 seconds is not required for Dana to *think* about what her response should be. Go back to Hyla and Nancy's call – Example 1. Between their turns at talk there was no gap, and no overlap. Their turns were produced in rapid succession – but not automatically.

Conversation analysis is not a branch of behaviourism. Saying 'hello' does not guarantee a 'hello' in response. In fact, a missing 'hello' can indicate mishearing, rudeness, or some other potential communication problem. But the take-home message is that because conversations *do* regularly open like Hyla and Nancy's, something interesting is happening when the pattern breaks.

Returning to Gordon and Dana's conversation, here is Dana's delayed response.

04   Dana: Hello where've you been all morning.

So, Dana returns the greeting at the start of her turn, but immediately opens up a new action: a question. And it is a challenging question. It is not just an information-seeking question; it has got some bite in it. It is a complaint. She is Gordon's girlfriend and so is somewhat entitled – her question presupposes this – to know where he is. She should not have had to try to get him 'all morning'. Of course, 'all morning' is not meant literally. But Dana uses this rather extreme – but very ordinary and recognisable – way of describing her sustained attempts to speak to Gordon. Including – or not including – 'all morning' makes a difference. Every word matters, for the things we are doing with our turns at talk.

It turns out later that Gordon had phoned Dana's house, very late and drunk, the previous evening. Now Dana is in trouble with her mum. What possibilities does Gordon have for responding to Dana's question? He could say, 'What do you mean, where have I been all morning?', or 'We're not joined at the hip', or something else that meets the challenge head on, attacking Dana or defending himself. And then the couple might head straight into an argument.

Another option is to push back on the trajectory started by Dana's question, which is what Gordon does.

05   Gordon: .hh HELLO!

Gordon responds with a bright-sounding 'Hello!', very much like Nancy's 'Hi!' of recognition in Example 1. In so doing, Gordon recruits his tacit knowledge of what kind of turn typically fills this slot in an encounter. In other words, Gordon recruits the conversational racetrack.

This is not the end of Gordon's turn, however. It unfolds in a way that further marks Dana's question as, literally, out of turn.

05   Gordon: .hh HELLO! Uhm (0.6)

Note two tiny details that only a Jefferson transcript can magnify: an 'Uhm' and a 0.6 second pause. Sounds like 'Uh', 'um', 'uh:::::' can be subtly altered in myriad ways with intonation. They are not random, or meaningless, or speech production errors. They can be systematic, cropping up in exactly the *same* types of conversational environments. For instance, a little 'uh' sound frequently crops up when speakers are confronted with an inapposite or unexpected prior turn – which Dana's is. And this analysis is supported by the fact that what Gordon did first *was* what Dana could expect – he gave a 'hello' of recognition.

These three items at the start of Gordon's turn, the bright 'hello!', the 'uh' and the 0.6 second pause, all push back on Dana's first turn – her first move. The idea that Dana is a 'first mover' – the kind of person who opens an encounter with such a challenging first turn – is something that we will return to in Chapter 3. We will see how we use talk to assess everything about a person from their personality and disposition to their motivation, emotions and attitude. Talk is often the only evidence we have to make such assessments. We are the turns we take.

Only after these three items have been produced does Gordon answer Dana's question. For those who are enjoying getting into the detail, there are other tiny perturbations in his turn: an in-breath right at the start (.hh) – this is what 'take-a-deep-breath' looks like! And he makes a lip-smack sound (.pt).

05   Gordon: .hh HELLO! Uhm (0.6) .pt I've been at a music workshop

And after answering the question, Gordon once more reveals his tacit understanding of what should happen next.

06   Gordon: How are you.

So Gordon initiates the third part of a typical opening sequence: the 'how-are-you'. Now, if Dana was satisfied with Gordon's answer at line 05, and ready to get on with the conversation, we would expect to see her respond with 'Fine' (or a variant) and a reciprocal 'how-are-you'. However, this is what happens next.

07   (0.5)

By now, you should know enough about conversation analysis to interpret a delay of 0.5 seconds as an indication that Dana is 'not fine'. We can now predict that she is not likely to move into a reciprocal pair of 'how-are-you' turns with Gordon. Are we right?

08   Dana: I'm okay,

Yes! We can predict the future when we study talk scientifically. Dana's intonation makes her response sound anything but 'okay,' (but everyone has to lie . . .). There is no smile-voice. The 'continuing intonation' on 'okay,' suggests there is more (about Dana) to come. And she does not ask Gordon how he is.

Dana has given Gordon enough evidence for him to pick up on the fact that something is wrong. So now he has another option. Should he ask Dana 'what's up?' That could, of course, open up a can of worms. So instead, he treats Dana's 'I'm okay,' as a straightforward and positive response to his question.

```
09 Gordon:     Good,
```

The ongoing saga of Dana and Gordon has grabbed the interest of online commentators who have seen my talks with this clip presented with audio. People have tweeted to ask, 'Whatever DID happen to Gordon and Dana?', or commented that 'Gordon can do better. IMHO'. And consider the following comment from a YouTuber.

Example 12: YouTuber

```
01   YouTuber:   Hello

02               (0.7)

03   YouTuber:   EPIC!! LMAO!!
```

Audience responses such as these provide evidence that these openings are useful for explaining what conversation analysts do. And they show how accessible, recognisable and reproducible talk is – after all, it is what we all do . . .

Example 13: Lyrics from 'Telephone Line', 1976, Electric Light Orchestra

```
01   Caller:   Hello:

02             (2.5)

03   Caller:   ~H-~ how are yo:u,
```

If a silence of 0.7 seconds is enough to indicate trouble for Gordon, a silence of 2.5 seconds is enough for Jeff Lynne's caller to know they are in a very poor situation. The caller moves to ask 'how-are-you', when no response is forthcoming. The ~tilde~ sign represents 'wobbly voice', a feature added to the Jefferson system by Alexa Hepburn,[12] who is an expert in transcribing crying and other emotional sounds.

Dana and Gordon's call is important because it explains some fundamental things about talk. First, it shows how two people can have quite different agendas, or projects, in their encounters. Dana's project was to get to talk to Gordon about the trouble she is in with her mother, caused by him. Gordon's project was to avoid having that conversation!

Next, the 0.7-second silence before Dana uttered a word shows that we can pinpoint moments of trouble very precisely. This sort of precision has big pay-offs when it comes to understanding what works and what is less effective in, say, professional or workplace encounters. For example, we can search for silences and find out what happened previously to produce it; what particular word, question, description or phrase. Examples throughout the book will show that a question, an explanation, an offer, an assessment, an invitation – and lots of other actions – can be pinpointed as failing by looking at what happens in the very next turn.

There are other ways that call openings tell us there is trouble ahead, or they can misfire completely. In Example 14, Frannie has called her friend Shirley at work. She has been transferred to Shirley's line by a receptionist. These are the first turns exchanged between the pair.

---

12 Hepburn (2004).

Example 14: Frannie and Shirley

01		((ring))
02	Shirley:	District Attorney's Office.
03	Frannie:	Sh̲irley:¿
04	Shirley:	Frannie¿=
05	Frannie:	↑What i̲s tha dea̲::l.
06	Shirley:	Whaddayou ↑mean.

Shirley answers the phone in 'work mode'. Stating 'District Attorney's Office' is a self-identification in a way that 'hello' is not.[13] In the ensuing turns, the punctuation marks and arrows indicate a level of emotional delivery that is hard to represent on paper. But it should be clear that dispensing with greetings *and* 'how-are-yous' are signals for turbulence ahead. Shirley uses her friend's name with a sharp tone in her first turn, rather than 'hello'. People often think that using names 'builds rapport' between speakers. This is another communication myth we will bust later in the book.

If you are reading this book looking for communication tips, then one option Shirley has to respond is to do what Gordon did: give a bright 'Hello!' She could do what typically happens next, at the start of the conversational racetrack. But Shirley responds using the same format and vexed intonation as Frannie. The two are in perfect alignment, with conflict their joint project. And look at the next two turns: Frannie makes a 'first move' like Dana's – a challenging question. But rather than push back on the challenge as Gordon did, Shirley responds defensively. This is not communication breakdown. It is the flawlessly produced, precision-timed, start of a fight.

Example 15 comes from a business-to-business cold call. The salesman, Jack, is calling Max for the first time: they have never

---

13 Schegloff (2002).

spoken before. Jack's project is to try and make an appointment to meet Max with a view to selling a contract for telephone lines.

Example 15: Business-to-business cold-call sales

01		((ring))
02	Max:	Hello Max speaking,=How can I help.
03		(.)
04	Jack:	Hello Max, it's Jack from Ocom.=£How're you doing this
05		morning.£

Like Katy and Darcy in Example 4, we can easily identify this as a workplace call, not a domestic call. Max's answer to the summons contains exactly the same components as Katy's: a *greeting* (Katy said, 'Good morning'); an *identification* (Katy said, 'Katy Green'), and a *question about help* (Katy said, 'c'n I he:lp you,').

There is a micropause (line 03) after Max answers the phone. The first part of Jack's response is similar to Darcy's: a return greeting and identification ('He:llo Katy good morning t'you.=it's Darcy:'). However, things start to go wrong immediately afterwards. Note the full stop after 'Ocom.', and an immediately latched next unit of subsequent talk: '=£How're you doing this morning.£'.

This is very similar to what happens in Katy and Darcy's conversation – except that Katy, not Darcy, does the first 'how-are-you'. Not only that, Jack's 'how-are-you' is delivered with premature 'smile-voice' – remember, Katy only used 'smile-voice' once she knew who she was talking to – and when she realised she *knew* the person she was talking to!

Jack's turn is problematic because it is said in the wrong place with the wrong intonation. It is this kind of turn that people can quite rightly criticise as 'filler' or 'non-genuine'. But don't take my word for it. This is Max's analysis too, as we can see in his response.

If Jack and Max knew each other, like Katy and Darcy, then we would expect Max to reciprocate a 'how-are-you'.

```
06              (.)

07    Max:   Good thanks,

08              (.)

09    Jack:   Not too bad,
```

Max answers the question, but does not ask Jack how he is. This does not matter for Jack, who simply takes the next turn as if he has been asked a 'how-are-you'! This is one of the strangest snippets of conversation I have ever analysed, in which a salesperson embodies the problems of cold-calling and scripted interaction so transparently.

Things go from awkward to worse as Jack tries, unsuccessfully, to engage Max in conversation. We will return to the cold-callers in Chapter 7 when we take up the issue of 'rapport' and examine how (not) to build it. We will think about how communication training to 'build rapport' is something of an oxymoron; if you have to train for it, you probably do not have it – as Max and Jack neatly show us . . .

Sometimes what happens in call openings can be, quite simply, a matter of life and death. Example 15 comes from a famous conversation analytic paper called 'When words fail'.[14] The authors analysed a call to emergency services. The case was an early example of what is commonplace now – the intense public scrutiny of a telephone call between a member of the public and a member of an emergency service, in which communication failure results in dramatic service failure.

The case in question took place in Dallas, Texas, in which a caller ended up arguing for seven minutes with an ambulance dispatcher while his stepmother lay dying. Here is the very start of the call.

---

14 Whalen, Zimmerman, and Whalen (1988).

Example 16: Emergency call

01	Dispatch:	<u>Fire</u> department
02		(0.8)
03	Caller:	Yes, I'd like tuh have an ambulance at forty one
04		thirty nine Haverford please
05		(0.5)
06	Dispatch:	What's thuh <u>p</u>roblem sir?
07	Caller:	I: don't know, n'if I knew I wouldn't be ca:lling
08		you all

I will not reproduce the whole three-minute call here. Suffice to say that the caller's first request does not sufficiently convey urgency to the dispatcher, who asks for more detail at line 06. The fact that the caller treats the dispatcher's question as problematic, and even offensive, enables us to see how quickly an encounter can escalate into conflict. It shows us, as the authors say, 'how this sort of thing can happen'.

In a follow-up call, the caller's roommate makes a different request: 'Hello uh: I need an ambulance (for) someone that appears tuh (.) have almost stopped breathing?' However, by the time the ambulance arrives, the outcome is fatal.

Example 17 is similarly dramatic. It is the start of a call between a person in crisis, Kevin, threatening suicide, and a police negotiator, Steve.

Example 17: Crisis negotiation

01		((ring))
02	Kevin:	Hell<u>o</u>?
03	Steve:	.ptk hello Kevin=it's Steve. Thanks for: uh >putting your
04		phone< back on, .hhh uh: I'd ↑l<u>i</u>ke to talk to you a bit
05		more about this pee cee <u>North</u>.=cos it's obviously-
06		it's- I mean it's something that's very important to
07		you.=It's important to <u>me</u>:.
08		(.)
09	Steve:	To find out what's going <u>o</u>n.
10		(0.2)
11	Steve:	.hhh
12	Kevin:	((hangs up))

You have probably noticed that this call opening is a failure. Our evidence is that the person in crisis says only an 'answering' hello before hanging up. He does not do a second 'greeting' hello and there are no 'how-are-yous'. What becomes clear, in analysing conversations from negotiation to selling, is that 'fake' rapport and scripted talk is easy to spot and almost always fails to do the job it is designed for.

Several components of Steve's turn do not work: thanking Kevin for putting his phone on, saying what he would like to do, saying what is important to Kevin, and saying that Kevin is important to Steve. There is also very little space for Kevin to say anything. However, Steve makes a second attempt at opening a conversation with Kevin, which is successful. It looks very different.

Example 18: Crisis negotiation

01   Kevin: Ye=h<u>e</u>llo:.

02   Steve: Hello Kevin=it's Steve.

03   (1.0)

04   Steve: .hh Kevin- (.) can you tell me: a bit more about pee cee

05   <u>N</u>orth so I can do something ab<u>ou</u>t it.

06   Kevin: <u>Ri</u>:ght. (0.3) six months ago: (0.2) there was a::- Big Power

07   had a call injunction to come in the house ((continues))

Steve's second attempt erases much of the 'rapport-building' content we saw in his earlier conversation. He also asks a 'closed' question – never recommended in communication guidance – replacing his open-ended request to talk in the first attempt. Yet despite being asked a 'yes/no' question, Kevin starts talking. Steve also focuses his question on action, and what can be done, rather than talking things through.

By comparing Steve's failed and successful attempts to get Kevin to talk, we can identify what works. As we will see, throughout the book, what works is often not what we probably think will work. A closed question, without an attempt at rapport, is effective in this negotiation with a suicidal person in crisis.

This is what I do as a conversation analyst. I collect lots of instances of, say, negotiation openings, analysing each word by word, turn by turn. I can then map different types of turns and patterns to different outcomes. Outcomes may be built into the very encounter being studied. They happen *inside* the encounter. A person says yes or no; buys something or does not; gets an appointment or does not – commits suicide, or does not . . . Talk is not trivial, easy or mundane. It is crucial.

The conversational racetrack

Conversations are encounters with a landscape, with a start and an end like a racetrack. We start at the beginning with our recipient or recipients and, along the way, complete various projects, like we saw Hyla and Nancy, and Dana and Gordon do. We design and build openings with summons and answers, greetings and identifications, and 'how-are-yous'.

Think about the encounters you have with friends, partners, the checkout person at the supermarket, your children's schoolteacher, the doctor, a first date. Each of these has a landscape with projects, or actions, that comprise the complete encounter. Some actions will be the same, like greetings, openings and closings. Others will be particular to the setting, like diagnoses, flirts, storytelling, complaints, requests or instructions. We may move smoothly along the racetrack from one project to the next, like Katy and Darcy, or bump along the sides of the racetrack, on the rumble strips, like Max and Jack.

Years of popular psychology have taught us to think about life and behaviour in terms of gender, culture, personality and other variables. We tend to think we are individuals who behave according to our intentions, in idiosyncratic ways. This book will show you that we are far more interesting than this. It will also show you that we are pushed and pulled around by words, phrases, intonation – *by talk* – far more than we realise.

Conversation analysts study conversational racetracks of all kinds, from people on first dates to police interrogations of suspects; from doctors and patients in hospital to aeroplane cockpit communication. By zooming in on the projects that comprise complete encounters, and by analysing many instances of, say, a patient asking for an appointment, or a police officer asking a suspect what they did, we can understand how different ways of asking questions lead to different outcomes – patients get an appointment or do not; suspects give full accounts or do not. This book will guide you along many racetracks. You will see how to avoid an argument like Gordon did;

how to avoid sounding scripted or fake like Jack did: how to use the ordinary resources of words to get things done.

The next chapter will take you deeper into conversation analysis. It will introduce you to some of the technicalities involved in analysing talk. So sit back, relax . . . here comes the science.

2

HERE COMES THE SCIENCE

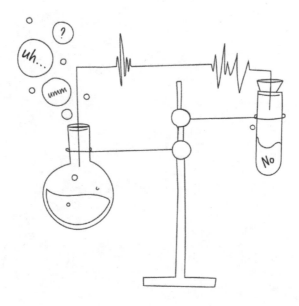

As talkers, we know – tacitly at least – pretty much everything there is to know about talking. We know how to build a turn at talk. We know when to take a turn and when someone else is likely to finish *their* turn. We know how to keep the floor and what it means to inter-rupt. We know how to fix a misspoken turn. And we know how to use the gaze of our eyes, the position of our bodies, and the material environment to augment or replace speech.

When we participate in conversation, we analyse *everything* our interlocutors say so that we can take a turn. We are doing a kind of analysis all the time, without being conscious of it. We assess constantly what people say to us, mulling our assessments over privately ('I wonder what he meant by that . . .?'). We talk to our friends about what people say to us and to them ('I think she was just being friendly'). And we challenge people directly ('What did you mean by that?'). We can spot when others fish for compliments or are disingenuous; we can tell people that they missed someone being hypocritical or flirting with them.

But we do not know how talk works *scientifically*. And some of what we *think* we know about talk is wrong. We will examine common myths about talk more fully later in the book. One example is that silence does not do anything. Or that silence is just what happens when our brains take time to process what someone has just said to us. Both of these assertions are far too simple. As talkers, we already know this. Our knowledge of silence is built into idiomatic phrases like, 'your silence speaks volumes'. We say this to tell the person we are talking to that we are interpreting their lack of response as problematic in some way. But we do not treat silences – generally – as a processing delay.

Indeed, the fact that silence can indicate trouble ahead can be found in both real and scripted talk. In *The Duchess*, a film based on a biography of aristocrat Georgiana Cavendish, the Duchess is talking to Charles Grey (of Earl Grey tea fame, and who was Prime Minister of Great Britain in the early nineteenth century), with whom she is having an affair. Georgiana is played by Keira Knightley, and Charles Grey by Dominic Cooper. I have transcribed the performance from the film's audio track. So the silence at line 02 is how the scene was actually delivered.

Example 1: Scene from *The Duchess*

01   Georgiana: Do you thi:nk of me when we're not together.

02   (2.0)

03   Charles: .hh (0.2) You ought to <u>know</u> I do:.

04   Georgiana: You hesitated before you replied.

Just before we analyse those two seconds of silence, this is what the audio track looks like when it is represented in the software editor I use to transcribe the recording.

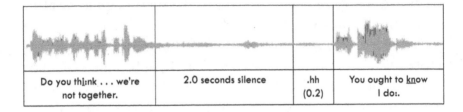

Do you thl:nk . . . we're not together.	2.0 seconds silence	.hh (0.2)	You ought to <u>know</u> I do:.

The sound wave forms peaks and troughs as words are uttered. The long silence is easy to spot, though there is some background noise in the second half of the silence. We can also hear Charles take a breath and pause before he delivers the words of his turn, though this is hard to spot simply by looking at the wave pattern.

The sound wave gives an indication of a speaker's loudness, but not their intonation or pitch. Some analysts find it difficult to 'hear' the pitch of talk accurately (it helps if you are musical!) – does the pitch of the final word of a turn rise or fall? Other software can reveal how speakers shift pitch up and down as they talk, producing images like the one below, of Charles's turn, 'You ought to know I do:.'

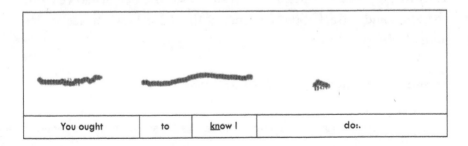

You ought	to	<u>know</u> I	do:.

There are no extremes of pitch movement in his turn, but you should see that it rises slightly when he says 'know' and falls at the end – represented in the transcript by underlining on 'know' and a full stop at the end of 'do:.'.

Returning to the conversation itself, Georgiana asks her lover a question. It is a 'yes/no' question (sometimes referred to as a 'closed' question), designed to get 'yes' or 'no' (at least!) in response. These options are not equivalent. In this context, 'yes' is clearly a better response.

However, before Charles responds with either 'yes' or 'no', what happens next is . . . silence. After a two-second delay, he says, 'You ought to know I do.' His response implies that Georgiana did not need to ask this question. She should take for granted the fact that he thinks of her when they are apart. Yet Georgiana's next response, 'You hesitated before you replied', highlights the negative implications of delaying a response.

The conversation analyst Emily Hofstetter uses a similar example from the blockbuster film *Frozen* to show the conversation analytic skills of one of the film's main characters, Olaf the snowman. In the scene Hofstetter describes, Princess Anna is talking to an iceman, Kristoff, about her hair changing colour from brown to white, becoming frozen.

Example 2: Scene from *Frozen*, from EM does CA[15]

01	Anna:	Does it look bad?
02		(2.0)
03	Kristoff:	No!
04	Olaf:	You hesitated.

---

15 www.youtube.com/watch?v=pLSmv9KJcdw

In Example 1, 'yes' is what conversation analysts refer to as a 'preferred' response; in Example 2, the 'preferred response' is 'no'. This is a structural, not a psychological, kind of preference – to do with the systematic ways in which people respond to questions, invitations, requests, offers and other conversational actions. We will explore the technicalities of 'preference' later in the chapter.

For now, though, notice that, like Georgiana's question, Anna's question is also a 'yes/no' question. Here, Anna is probably hoping for a 'no' – which should also be said immediately! And notice that it is only after a two-second silence that Kristoff replies. At this point in the film, Olaf pops up into the scene, to say to Kristoff, 'You hesitated.' Olaf's interpretation is the same as Georgiana's.

Hofstetter uses this example to explain a number of technical features of conversation analysis. We will also examine some of these later in the chapter. But it is clear that each of these silences are doing something other than allowing Charles, and Kristoff, time for cognitive processing. Their delays predict something about their upcoming responses. Pointing out the hesitations implies that Kristoff's response, while it is the 'right' one, is less genuine or sincere. He says 'no' because it is right or expected, not because he means it! And this suggests that genuine responses happen rapidly.

The very fact that scriptwriters write these scenes – to be enlivened by actors and to be comprehensible for the audience – tells us something fundamental about the systematic nature of talk. It is no coincidence that our examples above contain two-second delays. It is unlikely that the actors were told to 'pause for two seconds'. But their tacit knowledge of how long a hesitation is – a clear, impossible-to-miss hesitation – has resulted in almost identical performances.

Let us have a look at some unscripted dialogue, now, from the television show, *Location, Location, Location*.[16] In the programme, the hosts are two property experts, Phil Spencer and Kirsty Allsopp. They help house-hunters find a property to buy. Phil and Kirsty show

---

16 *Location, Location, Location*, Surrey, 04:10 11/09/2017, Channel 4, 55 mins. https://learningon-screen.ac.uk/ondemand/index.php/prog/01585721

the house-hunters several properties in different locations during the course of each episode.

In Example 3, Phil is asking a couple, Suzie and Andy, if they know the town where the next property to be viewed is located.

Example 3: *Location, Location, Location* **(simplified transcript)**

01	Phil:	Do you know Hersham?
02	Suzie:	Yeah we [do.
03	Andy:	[Yeah we do yeah.
04	Suzie:	Yep.
05	Phil:	Is that a good thing?
06		(2.0)
07	Suzie:	No! ((laughs))
08	Phil:	Silence! ((laughs))
09	All:	((Laughing))
10	Phil:	Not a good thing!

Suzie and Andy respond rapidly and positively to Phil's first question, 'Do you know Hersham?' with a series of 'yeahs'. But a now-familiar two-second delay follows Phil's follow-up question, 'Is that a good thing?'

Now, this conversation represents just a tiny fragment of what it takes to buy a house. But a 'yes' to Phil's second question would indicate Suzie and Andy's positive disposition towards the town where the house is located (never mind the house itself). In other

---

(accessed 02 Jan 2018).

words, a tiny 'yes' at this moment would mean that the parties take one step further along the conversational racetrack. Saying 'no' halts this progress.

So, like our earlier examples, a two-second delay tells us pretty much all we need to know about the likely direction of a response – before it is even uttered. Phil understands this too – he names the couple's delay ('Silence!') and makes explicit what saying nothing means ('Not a good thing!'). One word – 'no' – has big implications!

This chapter will examine the building blocks of talk using examples from familiar television programmes and films, as well as from real-life conversation in different settings, to explain how talk works. We will see what it takes to make a conversation move forward, what the common types of move in talk are, and how people do things with talk.

In the first chapter, we focused on how people do one type of thing – greet each other. In this chapter, we will see how people do other things – actions like inviting, requesting, complaining, interrupting – all using the machinery of conversation.

Scriptwriters are conversation analysts

Olaf from *Frozen* might well be a conversation analyst but, of course, his character is brought to life, not just by the magical powers of Queen Elsa, but by those who write scripts for film and television. One of the best sources of scripted interaction for helping us to understand the technology of conversation analysis, and the science of talk, is the American sitcom *Friends*.[17] The programme followed the friendships, families, romantic and career lives of six friends (including a brother and sister and two flat-sharing pairs) living in Manhattan, who often hung out at their local coffee shop, Central Perk. The programme ran for a decade between 1994 and

---

17 Created by David Crane and Marta Kauffman, and produced by Bright/Kauffman/Crane Productions, in association with Warner Bros. Television.

2004, with a huge audience and massive cultural impact (and plenty of scholarly analysis).

Love or loathe the programme, the scripts from *Friends* work well to help us understand the science of conversation. The scriptwriters juxtapose spoken turns in ways that throw into sharp relief the underpinning machinery of talk. Because a lot of the humour in *Friends* depends on clever conversational devices – not set-piece jokes or one-liners – audience laughter can be used as another useful tool for pinning down how talk works.[18, 19, 20]

Our first example comes from an episode in which two of the main characters, Monica and Phoebe, are about to start a conversation. The setting is the apartment Monica shares with another character, Rachel. In the transcript, audience laughter is treated as a participant.

Example 4: *Friends*: 'The One With Ross's New Girlfriend'[21]

01   Monica: Hey Pheebs.

02   (1.3) ((Phoebe looks at Monica as she crosses the room))

03   Monica: Y'know what I'm thinki:n'?

As the scene starts, Monica crosses the floor of her apartment to where Phoebe is sitting. She says hello to Phoebe, who raises her head in response. Monica asks Phoebe, 'Y'know what I'm thinki:n'?' What kind of turn is this? Well, by dint of its grammatical design, as

---

18 As Mills (2005, p. 14) points out, 'Laughter is important to the sitcom not only because it is the genre's intention, but because the use of studio audiences and canned laughter means that it is part of the text.'

19 Canned or real; it does not matter. See Medhurst and Tuck (1982).

20 Writing about *Mork and Mindy*, a sitcom about an alien (Mork) and his human companion, Goldman (1982) observes how Mork 'makes visible the normally hidden, socially constructed conventions that are the foundations for intersubjectivity. Through Mork's violations of conventional language use and the rules of cultural logic the veil of naturalness is raised from the processes of the social construction of reality.'

21 Written by Jeffrey Astrof and Mike Sikowitz.

written, this is a 'declarative'. Questioning intonation is used to turn declarative into an 'interrogative' – a 'yes/no' polar question.

In transformational grammar, there is a transformation called 'do-fronting' that converts declaratives into interrogatives. However, in talk, people are often elliptical; that is, they miss words out. So 'Y'know what I'm thinki:n'?' is readily heard as an abbreviated version of 'Do you know what I'm thinking?', restoring it as an interrogative.

In fact, this grammatical form is a vehicle for a particular function. It is not solely after a 'yes' or a 'no' in response. Monica's question is designed to lay the foundation for *something else* to happen. It is what conversation analysts call a 'pre' – a type of turn that sets up a future activity. So a pre-announcement, or a pre-telling, such as Monica produces, is designed to get a 'go-ahead' from Phoebe – something like, 'no, what?' If Phoebe gives her the go-ahead, Monica can report her thoughts on some unspecified topic.

Setting the stage for a future conversational action happens regularly. In a real-life telephone call below, Donny is calling Marsha.

Example 5: Donny and Marsha

01		((telephone rings))
02	Marsha:	Hello?
03	Donny:	H'lo M̲arsha,
04	Marsha:	Ye̲:a[h.]
05	Donny:	[It's D]onny.
06	Marsha:	H̲i Do:nny.
07	Donny:	Guess what. hh

Once they have said their hellos, and established that they know who each other is, Donny says, 'Guess what.' This is a 'pre' action, like

Monica's 'Y'know what I'm thinking?' Donny and Monica both seek a go-ahead from the person they are talking to.

Let us see what happens next, in both conversations.

07   Donny: Guess what. hh

08   Marsha: What.

09   Donny: .hh my ca:r is sta::lled.

In the ordinary telephone call, Donny gets a go-ahead from Marsha ('What.'). By doing this, she returns the floor to Donny, who then delivers some bad news about his car.

But something different happens next in our *Friends* example.

03   Monica: Y'know what I'm thinki:n'?

04   Phoebe: .pt ↑↑O:h: ↑okay. Hh

If Phoebe had replied to Monica in the same way that Marsha replied to Donny, with a 'What?', Monica would have her go-ahead. But Phoebe responds to the form not the function of Monica's turn, treating it literally as an invitation to guess what she is thinking.

Evidence that this is an odd thing to do comes from what happens next: the audience breaks into laughter.

04   Phoebe: .pt ↑↑O:h: ↑okay. Hh

05   (0.5)

06   Audience: HEH HEH HEH HEH HEH heh heh heh heh [heh

If Phoebe had given Monica a go-ahead, most likely the audience would not have laughed. So why *does* the audience laugh, at just *this* point? There is no obvious sitcom joke. The humour is generated by what happens at line 04; the audience recognises the correct function of Monica's 'pre' turn.

As the laughter subsides, Phoebe begins to respond to Monica.

06   Audience: HEH HEH HEH HEH HEH heh heh heh heh [heh

07   Phoebe: [How::,

08   it's been so: lo::ng, <<since you've: had sex>>

09   >you're wondering if they've changed it?<

10   Audience: HEH HEH HEH heh heh heh

The transcription symbols '<< >>' tell us that Phoebe slows down her pace of talking, quite dramatically, as she searches for an answer to Monica's question, 'You know what I'm thinking?' The laughter that follows Phoebe's suggestion – that Monica is wondering if sex is still the same – is about the ridiculousness of the hypothesis, and the obvious tease: that it's been so long since Monica had sex (the tease) that sex itself might have changed in the interval (the ridiculous extreme)!

In Donny and Marsha's conversation, Donny sets the scene for Marsha to offer help, following his car breakdown. Even though the *Friends* example is scripted, it turns out that Monica's 'pre' turn similarly lays the foundation for eliciting an offer from Phoebe to cut Monica's hair.

11   Phoebe: So what were you thinking.

12   Monica: Well, I was thinking that you gave the guys such great

13   haircuts I thought maybe you'd like to do mi:ne.

14   Phoebe: ((smiling)) £Oh!!£

15   (0.2)

16   Phoebe: >↓No.<

17   Audience: HEH HEH HEH heh heh heh

Phoebe finally gives Monica the go-ahead, and now Monica can say what was on her mind ('Well, I was thinking . . .'). She tries to elicit an offer of a haircut from Phoebe. At line 14, Phoebe shows that she knows where Monica's 'pre' turn was heading. While the audience does not laugh in response to Phoebe's smiley 'Oh!!', they *do* laugh after she delivers something that is definitely not an offer!

Monica did not ask Phoebe to cut her hair directly (e.g., 'Can you cut my hair?'); she made an indirect, rather than direct, request. However, Phoebe skips past this indirectness and turns Monica down baldly, with no explanation. In another context, this might start an argument or be treated as rude; here, the scriptwriters have produced a line designed for a laugh. We will return to how people request and offer help in Chapter 6, 'Are you being served?'

The building blocks of talk

In developing (realistic-*ish*[22]) dialogue for *Friends*, the scriptwriters show us their implicit knowledge about how talk works. To start with, they know that turns are organised into pairs. Monica's first turn – 'You know what I'm thinking?' – is the 'first pair part' of what conversation analysts call an 'adjacency pair'. An adjacency pair is a basic building block for talking. It provides the foundation for constructing 'sequences' of activity.

After one speaker has produced a 'first pair part', their recipient is expected to respond with a turn that delivers a second action. The second action is paired with, and fitted to, the first one – for instance, 'question-answer'; 'greeting-greeting'; 'invitation-accept-ance'; 'request-offer'. The second action is the 'second pair part'.

Once the first pair part has been produced, almost *anything* produced next comprises the second pair part. This includes silence and delay. The second pair part may be inspected for its timeliness ('your silence speaks volumes!'), whether or not it is fitted properly to the first ('I was asking for a go-ahead, not to play a guessing game!'),

---

22 Quaglio (2009).

and whether or not it helps the overall sequence progress smoothly or stall and falter.

Think about the last time you invited someone to do something. Without realising it explicitly, you analysed what your interlocutor said in response to your invitation, how they said it, and when they said it. You interpreted their response as an acceptance, a rejection, a stalling manoeuvre, an account for non-acceptance, or whatever.

This way of understanding social interaction is rooted in a style of sociology called 'ethnomethodology', from which conversation analysis evolved. Ethnomethodology, invented by Harold Garfinkel,[23] means the 'study of people's methods'. Garfinkel's central concern was to make common sense, or the 'seen but unnoticed' organisation of social life, visible for academic scrutiny.

Think about how you walk around a museum. Your pace will be rather different to that used in an airport. You notice if a small child runs in an art gallery, and hope that their parents fulfil their obligations to socialise their children. The instruction to 'stop dawdling' makes more sense on the walk to school than in a museum.

One way to make these invisible but powerful 'methods' evident is to examine what happens when tacit rules are breached. Garfinkel conducted what he called 'breaching experiments'. He instructed his students to talk to their friends and ask them to 'clarify the sense of commonplace remarks' (1967, p. 42). Example 6 is one student's reported conversation.

Example 6: Garfinkel's 'breaching experiment'

01	Friend:	How is your girlfriend feeling?
02	Student:	What do you mean, 'How is she feeling?'
03		Do you mean physical or mental?
04	Friend:	I mean how is she feeling? What's the matter with you?

---

23 Garfinkel (1967).

05   (He looked peeved).

06   Student: Nothing. Just explain a little clearer what do you mean?

07   Friend: Skip it. How are your Med School applications coming?

08   Student: What do you mean, 'How are they?'

09   Friend: You know what I mean.

10   Student: I really don't.

11   Friend: What's the matter with you? Are you sick?

In each turn, the student attempts to get their unwitting friend to make explicit what would normally be understood without such explicitness. Responses to students were often hostile, although they sometimes thought the student was actually trying to be funny. Like our example from *Friends*, then, when speakers do not respond in the way one expects, a possible outcome is laughter.

Garfinkel's breaching experiments allowed him to identify what it is that gives ordinary scenes their 'familiar, life-as-usual character' (p. 37). Taking this one step further, we would not be able to understand a 'breach' without understanding how systematic our everyday actions actually are. This rule applies to how we communicate, too.

How to build a successful invitation

Almost every social action we might conceive of requires communication – talk, writing, gesture, signing – to make it happen. Actions are accomplished in *turns*, one after another. Turns are built from individual words, formed into units. These units may be sentences, in the way we traditionally understand grammar and composition – though they may not be. And sequences of turns build conversational racetracks.

In conversation, people have to monitor each other's turns for when it might be relevant for them to take a turn. They have to figure out who should talk next, and when – and how – to take a longer turn than one unit of talk. Speakers have to understand ongoing talk and make a 'fitted' – that is, apposite – response. They must deal with trouble in speaking, hearing and understanding. Finally, and crucially, speakers build turns from a massive range of lexical and grammatical possibilities. One word can make a difference to the outcome of an encounter, as we will see later in the book.

The idea that people just take turns, one after the other, may sound simple. It is not. Think about what is required, word for word, turn by turn, to build a successful invitation. It is straightforward, right?

Example 7: A basic invitation

| 03 | A: | Want to go to the cinema? | First Pair Part |
| 06 | B: | Okay. | Second Pair Part |

To invite someone to go to the cinema, we need to build a turn of talk that does the action of inviting. There are many ways to do this. In the example above, Speaker A asks, 'Want to go to the cinema?' But other combinations of words and phrases, with varying intonation and other paralinguistic subtleties, will also deliver an invitation.

The design of an invitation – and any action – will depend on who you are asking, what kind of relationship you have with your recipient, what is at stake, how important an acceptance (or rejection) is, and so on. Conversation analysts have shown that these sorts of contingencies inform the design of the turn and are embedded in those designs.

If the person is your partner, for instance, just saying 'Cinema . . .?' may do the job. From 'fancy a movie?' to 'I wondered if you'd like to come with me to the cinema' – there are multiple options.

In Example 7, B responds positively to A. You may have spotted, however, that only lines 03 and 06 are included in the transcript – at least four turns are missing. The invitation and the acceptance are present – the first pair part and the second pair part. Together, two turns build a 'base' sequence – a base 'adjacency pair'. The base completes the core activity – the invitation – being done.

But much more can happen in what is still a simple action. Let us fill in lines 01–02.

01	A: What are you up to this evening?	First Pair Part – **pre** pair
02	B: Nothing much.	Second Pair Part – **pre** pair
03	A: **Want to go to the cinema?**	First Pair Part – **base** pair
06	B: **Okay.**	Second Pair Part – **base** pair

The meaning of 'preference', introduced at the start of this chapter, comes alive in the first two lines of this encounter. We are not talking about psychological or personal preference, though. Although we might think it is obvious that the 'preferred' response to an invitation is acceptance, it is not so obvious what the preferred response to a compliment is. 'Preference' refers to something *structural* about paired turns of talk. They keep the action moving forward. Put simply, 'preferred' responses take less conversational effort; 'dispreferred' responses take more.

If the preferred response to an invitation is acceptance, what are the best ways to ensure a positive outcome? The answer is to do a 'pre'. We encountered 'pre' turns earlier in the chapter, when Monica and Donny used them to get go-aheads from Phoebe and Marsha. Asking 'what are you up to this evening?' is a pre-invitation. If B says they are busy, then A knows issuing an invitation is likely to receive a rejection – a dispreferred response.

People design their talk to help those they are talking to *avoid* having to give such responses. Imagine how strange this conversation would be:

01	A:	What are you doing later?
02	B:	Oh, I'm going for dinner with Hugh.
03	A:	Want to go to the cinema with me?
04	B:	Huh?!?

Returning to Example 7, A has established some grounds for going ahead with an invitation, with a 'pre-sequence' comprised of another adjacency pair of turns. But there are still two lines missing before B accepts the invitation.

01	A:	What are you up to this evening?	First Pair Part – **pre** pair
02	B:	Nothing much.	Second Pair Part – **pre** pair
03	A:	**Want to go to the cinema?**	First Pair Part – **base pair**
04	B:	What's on?	First Pair Part – **insert** pair
05	A:	An Alfred Hitchcock film – *Vertigo*.	Second Pair Part – **insert** pair
06	B:	**Okay.**	Second Pair Part – **base** pair

B is available to go to the cinema. But B does not accept A's invitation before establishing that there is a film they would actually like to watch. B establishes this by initiating *another* adjacency pair of turns which *expands* the base sequence. In technical terms, this pair of turns is inserted between the *base* pair (lines 03–06).

Now we can see why B does not accept A's invitation until line 06. The sequence is nearly complete.

01	A:	What are you up to this evening?	First Pair Part – **pre** pair
02	B:	Nothing much.	Second Pair Part – **pre** pair
03	A:	**Want to go to the cinema?**	First Pair Part – **base** pair
04	B:	What's on?	First Pair Part – **insert** pair
05	A:	An Alfred Hitchcock film – Vertigo.	Second Pair Part – **insert** pair
06	B:	**Okay.**	Second Pair Part – **base** pair
07	A:	Shall I collect you at eight?	First Pair Part – **post** pair
08	B:	Great, thanks!	Second Pair Part – **post** pair

A and B take two final turns, expanding *past* the base sequence into a 'post' sequence, finalising arrangements for their cinema trip (lines 07–08). Now the core activity, with its pre-invitation sequence, its two expansions (inserted and post-sequences), is complete, across eight turns at talk.

A neat illustration of the concepts we have been introduced to, including 'adjacency pairs' and 'preference', is found in scripted dialogue too. This next example from *Friends* is also about invitations. Rachel has arrived in New York seeking her old friend Monica, after abandoning her wedding and leaving her fiancé at the altar. Monica's brother, Ross, also newly single, is moving into a new apartment. Ross asks Rachel if she wants to come to his apartment with two of the other friends, Joey and Chandler, to help him assemble his new furniture. Ross's 'pre-invitation' starts the sequence.

Example 8: *Friends:* **'Pilot'**[24, 25]

| 01 | Ross: | So Rachel what're you uh: what're you up to tonight. |

---

24 Some lines have been omitted from these scenes that are not central to the core 'invitation' activity.

25 Written by Marta Kauffman and David Crane.

The core activity in this scene is Ross's invitation to Rachel to help put together his furniture. When Ross asks, 'So Rachel what're you uh: what're you up to tonight.', we can recognise it easily as a 'pre-invitation'. It is laying the ground for a *possible* invitation, depending on Rachel's answer. If she is busy, Ross can avoid later rejection by not issuing the invitation in the first place. Or, more technically, he can ensure that the conversation avoids a failed base 'first pair part'. So, what is Rachel doing tonight?

02   Rachel: We:ll, I was ki:nda supposed t'be headed for Aru:ba

03   on my h:oneymoon.=so ↑no:thin(h)g. uh heh

04   Audience: HEH HEH HEH HEH heh heh heh heh heh heh

What are Rachel's options for responding to Ross's 'pre' turn? She could report that she has plans for the evening, blocking any forthcoming invitation. In the script, Rachel gives a 'go-ahead' response (she is doing '↑no:thin(h)g.'), but it is said ironically. She is doing nothing because she is not on her planned honeymoon. Ross's question now seems clumsy; he has asked her what she is 'up to' on the night of her abandoned wedding, while she sits in front of him in a wedding dress.

Having received Rachel's, albeit ironic, go-ahead, Ross goes ahead with his (pretty indirect) invitation.

05   Ross: If you don't feel like being alone tonight, uh Joey

06   an' Chandler are comin' over to help me put together

07   my: my new furniture.

08   Rachel: Well actually thanks: but I think I'm jus' gonna:

09   hang out (0.3) here tonight.=it's- (.) been a long

10   [day.

11   Ross: [Oh sure okay.=sure.

Ross's invitation takes into account Rachel's earlier reply that she is 'doing nothing'. In the first part of his invitation, he shows some consideration for her circumstances: 'If you don't feel like being alone tonight'.

Invitations can, of course, be accepted or declined. But these are not symmetrical, equally valued alternatives. To keep talk flowing smoothly, the preferred response to an invitation is to accept it. If Rachel accepted, the course of action initiated by Ross would be successfully accomplished – she would go to his apartment to help with the furniture.

But Rachel produces a dispreferred response – she says 'no'. Look at how many words it takes to say 'no'. If you do not understand that Rachel's words add up to 'no', remedial work is needed on your conversational skills. It is a good job you are reading this book!

Conversation analysts have shown that preferred responses are generally short and unelaborated. Dispreferred responses are more intricate. Dispreferred turns often occur after a delay (silence speaks volumes . . .!). They may start with words like 'well'. They may contain an appreciation (e.g., for the invitation). They may contain pauses and other signs of perturbation. They may also contain explanations, accounts, or excuses for why the speaker cannot produce the preferred response.

Rachel's response to Ross's invitation, as a declination, contains all the right features for saying 'no'. She starts with 'well'; her turn contains an appreciation of the invitation ('actually thanks:'), and it includes an account for saying 'no' ('it's been a long day.'). Because it contains all these features, Rachel has said 'no' in the regular way. There is no breach. It is not funny. The audience does not laugh.

As the scene moves on, Joey and Chandler ask Phoebe if she would like to help with the furniture. This time, when Phoebe says 'no', the audience laughs. Why?

12	Joey:	Hey <u>Phee</u>bs.=you wanna help?
13		(0.3)
14	Phoebe:	↑Oh:: ↑I wish I <u>c</u>ould but I don't want to.
15	Audience:	HEH HEH HEH HEH heh heh heh heh heh heh

Joey makes
an 'Okay'
gesture

Joey asks Phoebe if she would like to help – it is a 'yes/no' question. Saying 'yes' would mean giving the preferred response. It would most likely be done immediately, without elaboration, and it probably would not be funny. We can tell that Phoebe is going to say 'no' from the first part of her response '↑Oh:: ↑I wish I could'. This looks like it will be the start of a regular dispreferred turn, just like Rachel's, showing an appreciation of the invitation before turning it down.

It is the second part of Phoebe's response that gets the audience laughing. She says, 'I don't want to.' Although this does provide an explanation for saying 'no', it is not the sort of reason generally found in declinations. The standard way to say 'no' is to say that you cannot accept the invitation, not that you do not want to accept it. In ordinary conversation, such a turn might start an argument ('What's the matter with *you*?').

Reasons for declining invitations are generally situational or circumstantial, set against matters of volition or desire. But more simply, note that 'I *wish* I could' is *contradicted* by 'I don't *want* to'. So instead of providing a psychological disposition to accept, being thwarted by a circumstantial reason for having to refuse, Phoebe states a desire ('wish') to accept and contradicts it with a desire ('want') to reject. It is this bald contrast that the audience finds funny, as well as the unadorned nature of the rejection. Phoebe is flouting the whole normative business of providing circumstantial reasons for rejecting invitations that one would otherwise want to accept.

Alongside the audience's laughter is Joey's bemused, embodied 'okay' gesture. His response ends the sequence and is a light-hearted assessment of 'typical' Phoebe – typical Phoebe who baldly said 'no' earlier, when Monica asked her for a haircut. The scriptwriters often have Phoebe making these kinds of conversational breaches.

By writing this scene, and by laughing at the place designed for laughter, the scriptwriters, actors, audience and viewers show that they know a lot about talk already. We might not use technical terms like 'first pair part' or 'preference organisation' to describe talk, but we sense the way it is organised. And we know that talk gets things done.

Interruptions, dating, and a roll-on deodorant

Dawn, Ella, Marie and Kate are friends (in real life; this is not television). They are getting ready to go out to a nightclub.

Example 9: Real friends talking

01	Dawn:	We need to go: in >three quarters< of an hour.
02	Ella:	'Kay
03		(0.7)

Let us return to the start of this book, and this chapter, and to the idea that we all *talk*. So we already know a lot about talk. But the purpose of this book is to inform its readers about how talk works scientifically. A basic observation from the inventors of conversation analysis was that, in order to talk, one speaker speaks at a time and speakers change. We noted that this statement was reproduced in *Private Eye* as an example of pretentious academic nonsense.

In Example 9, one speaker speaks at a time and speakers change. Dawn is watching the clock; Ella shows that she is on board with leaving soon. This is a basic, two-turn sequence. They take turns; one at a time. After two turns, the activity is over. No one else responds. Dawn does not pursue a response from anyone else.

Next, Marie starts a new sequence. There is only one problem with going out; she is already feeling sweaty.

04   Marie: <Oh ↑↑ma::n >I 'aven't e'en< gone <u>OU</u>t and I'm sweating

05   like a, (0.4) [rapist,]

06   Kate: [Man.]

Something happens at line 06 that we have not paid much attention to so far. Two speakers talk *at the same time*. How does this happen? Is it a mistake? An interruption? In fact, it is an example of collaboration between friends.

Marie is searching for a word to complete her turn, that she is 'sweating like a . . .' Marie has not finished her turn: it is not complete in any sense – *grammatically* (it stops mid-air); *intonationally* (she does not sound like she has completed the turn) and in terms of the *action* being done (making an analogy is not complete). The pause of four-tenths of a second – which is still mid-turn – tells us that she is searching for a word. We have some grounds to say that this kind of silence is a processing silence. The right thing to do is wait for processing to happen.

So why does Kate start talking, when Marie is clearly not finished? Note the point where the overlapping talk starts. Kate starts talking at the point that she judges is enough time for Marie to find the right word to complete her analogy – in this case, four-tenths of a second. She sees her friend failing to come up with a word and so makes a suggestion: Marie is 'sweating like a . . . man'. But just as Kate says 'man', Marie finds the word she was looking for . . . 'rapist'.

You are probably thinking that this is a rather offensive way to complete the analogy. 'Sweating like a pig' is the common idiom.

Marie's turn – offensive or not; in regular use or not – is a first pair part. What kind of action is it doing? It could be a 'pre' – it could set the scene for help with her sweatiness.

```
07                  (0.8)

08   Ella:    hhTch.[Heh heh heh heh heh]

09   Dawn:         [ EE::www::gghh.      ]

10   Kate:         [Heh heh heh heh heh]

11   Marie:   I'm rea:lly [  ho:t!.     ]

12   Ella              [You two've ] gotta stop <with that phra:se,>
```

However, her friends' response – each of them doing a second pair part in overlap with one another – combines shock, horror and laughter. Their responses show disapproval, but in a light-hearted way. Notice – while we examine this conversation – that all four speakers talk at once. But this is not hostile interruption. Speakers can and do regularly talk at the same time, particularly when they are all working on the same action at the same time.

In the next first pair part, which keeps the talk moving forward, Marie says that she is 'really hot'. At line 12, Ella closes this particular topic by telling Marie (and probably Dawn) that they have to stop using 'that phrase'. We discover, here, that 'sweating like a rapist' is not a one-off expression but has evolved in the friendship group. We have some insight into the culture of the group.

Marie moves the talk on again, with another 'first pair part'.

13 Marie: ↑Has ↑anyone- (0.2) ↑has ↑anyone got any really non:

14   sweaty stuff.

Marie's turn is comprised of one unit of talk (called a 'turn construction unit'). It starts with, '↑Has ↑anyone-', which we can see from the rest of her turn is the start of a 'yes/no' question. No one can respond yet, though. No action has been completed. Marie pauses briefly, then starts again. These kinds of false starts and little glitches litter our talk.

Marie recycles the original start of the turn and then completes it. We know Marie's turn is complete for the following reasons. First, it ends with falling intonation (indicated with a full stop; it is a myth that questions always end with rising intonation). It completes an action (asking for deodorant). It is grammatically complete. It is treated as complete by Dawn, who takes the next turn. Finally, the end of the word 'stuff' is the first point that the turn is 'possibly' complete. This means that changing speaker is now apposite; normatively permitted and expected.

15 Dawn: Dave has. but you'll smell >like a ma:n,<

Dawn's turn is the second pair part to the adjacency pair set up by Marie. It shows us that Dawn has understood Marie's first pair part correctly, as both a question and a request for deodorant.

Dawn's response is built from two parts. The first part, 'Dave has', answers the question. It is a preferred turn – delivered without elaboration or delay. However, Dawn adds a second part to her turn, 'but you'll smell like a ma:n'. This qualifies her response and implicit offer of Dave's deodorant – which might not be what Marie is looking for. Each component of Dawn's turn, then, does a different, separate, action.

Let us see what happens next:

16 Kate: Eh [↑huh heh]

17 Marie: [Right has] anyone got any ↑fe:minine non sweaty stuff.

18   Kate: I've ↑got um:::, (0.6) roll on,

As Kate starts to laugh, Marie makes her request a second time, with some subtle changes. The word 'really' ('has anyone got any really non: sweaty stuff') is replaced with the word 'fe:minine' – with exaggerated intonation. Marie's *request* is responded to with an *offer* – which is the 'preferred' response.

This conversation gives us some technical insight and know-how into the organisation of turn-taking. We can identify points where it is possible for speakers to take turns, but also talk at the same time.

However, overlapping talk can also be treated as an interruption and thus a violation of one speaker's rights to take a turn. In the clip below, a police officer is interviewing a teenage suspect who has been arrested on suspicion of criminal damage. Our interest is that, although there are actually *no* moments of overlapping talk, the police officer treats the suspect as though she had interrupted her.

Example 10: Police interview

01   Police: Do you think that- (0.7) <u>yo</u>ur behaviour, (.) coupled

02   with the other: <u>twe</u>lve or so that came out,

03   (0.4)

04   Suspect: No, because everyone coming on the road so they

05   can- y'know-

06   (0.2)

07   Police: Are y'gonna let me finish what I'm s<u>a</u>yin'.

08   (0.5)

09   Suspect: °°I thought you had.°°[26]

---

26   The degree sign is used to indicate when a word is uttered very softly.

The transcription of the police officer's opening question is important. It ends with a comma. This represents 'continuing' intonation which, you may remember, sounds like reading a shopping list of items, or the chunks of a telephone number. Halfway through, our intonation is higher than when we come to the end. By the end of line 02, the police officer's turn is not complete in terms of grammar, intonation, or in terms of finishing an action that the suspect could respond to.

The four-tenths-of-a-second gap on line 03 is, coincidentally, the same length of time that Kate waited for Marie to come up with the word 'rapist'. However, in the friends' talk, Kate tried to help Marie out to complete her turn. Here, the suspect jumps in with an answer to an incomplete question. She does not help the officer out by completing her question. The suspect's next turn is also not complete, and the police officer comes back into the conversation when the suspect runs out of something to say.

Any notion you might have that power is attributed straightforwardly to police officers and not suspects is undermined by the suspect's response to the officer's 'yes/no' question, 'Are y'gonna let me finish what I'm sayin'.'. The suspect does not say 'yes' or 'no'. She challenges the very asking of the question – defending the fact that she started to talk. The little circles around her turn indicate that she is speaking quietly, suggesting that the suspect will not risk a more aggressive rebuttal.

This episode tells us that it doesn't take an overlap, or clash of voices, to constitute an interruption. The suspect interrupts the police officer's building of an action but does not talk over her.

Sometimes overlapping talk *is* the conversational problem. The next scene is again from *Friends*. The storyline focuses on Monica, who wants a baby but has no partner. She has decided to visit a sperm bank. Her brother, Ross, is trying to discourage her.

Example 11: *Friends*: 'The One with the Jam'[27]

01 Monica: So ↑this ↑isn't the <u>ideal</u> way t'[do something.=<bu-]=

02 Ross: [Oh it's <u>not</u>   the   ]=

03 Monica: =[.hh ↑<u>l</u>ips moving,] <u>still</u> talking,

04 Ross: =[ideal way (of it?)]

05 Audience: HEH HEH HEH HEH heh heh heh heh

Monica gestures
that her lips are
still moving

Monica has not finished her turn when Ross starts talking in overlap. This is treated as a violation of turn-taking by Monica, who stops what she is saying to chastise Ross: '↑lips moving, ↑still talking.' This is a sitcom, and so the audience laughs. In ordinary talk, the parties might laugh – or might start arguing.

To generate this scene, Ross must begin speaking at a point where Monica has obviously not finished her turn. What is the tacit knowledge needed to write and act the scene? The scriptwriters, and the actors, need to know several things about turn-taking and how to

---

27 Written by Wil Calhoun.

do an interruption. When Ross starts talking, Monica is in the midst of an incomplete turn – she is saying 'to do . . .' This is grammatically incomplete. It is incomplete in terms of its action. And it is incomplete in terms of its intonation. The first point of possible completion arrives on the word 'something', when the sentence is complete, Monica's pitch drops, and an action is accomplished.

Conversation analysts have found that speakers are generally entitled (by each other) to one unit in a turn. For Monica, one unit would end with the word 'something'. However, she tries to produce a multi-unit turn, which means keeping the floor. If you have ever wondered what not 'getting a word in edgeways' looks like, it is the moment in the transcript where Monica latches a second unit immediately on to the first ('=<bu-'). This is indicated by an equals sign. However, she stops the second unit to admonish Ross for talking when she has not finished her turn. Ross has breached the rules of turn-taking.

Breaches of conversational rules, like those we have seen through-out the chapter, and in Garfinkel's breaching experiments, are difficult to capture in real conversation. Examples of bald and direct 'dispreferred' responses have not been studied much by conversation analysts. They certainly exist; think about any argument you have ever had!

That said, conversation generally progresses more smoothly than we imagine. Think about the last time you wished you had said something, but did not. If only you had made that cutting remark or hung up the phone! In fact, it is easy to get trapped in a sequence, and be nicer than we want to be. People are more concerned with maintaining social harmony than we might guess.

So, our final example comes from a date between a heterosexual couple. It is the first time they have met. The woman is listing the qualities she finds attractive in a prospective partner.

Example 12: Speed date

01   Woman: Sense of humour::[::::   ] intelligence.=good fu::n,

02   Man: [Mm yeh,]

03   Woman: =(0.8) um:::: (1.1) an' loyal.

04   Man: An' loyal.

05   (0.3)

06   Woman   Yeh: an' whaddabout you.

07   (0.2)

08   Man: Yes.

09   Woman: £E(h)h?£ .hh ↑heh ↑heh ↑heh .hhh

10   (0.6)

11   Woman: Where d'you come from originally then.

The woman says the word 'humour::::' with a long stretch at the end, indicating that she is still searching for more qualities to list. She eventually finishes her list with 'loyal'. The man might be expected to start a reciprocal list, or agree with the woman. Instead, he just repeats her 'An' loyal'. He does not start to reciprocate at line 05, either. He is apparently resisting saying much about his own likes and dislikes.

The woman deals with the man's reticence to keep the conversation moving by asking directly for him to produce a list ('whaddabout you.'). What would fit the smooth progress of the sequence? A reciprocal list would address the woman's question. However, the man simply says 'Yes.' (line 08).

His is an ambiguous response, in terms of what it is doing. Perhaps it is agreeing with the woman's list (a gloss would be: 'Yes, all of those'). But the woman's question was not a 'yes/no' question. It was a 'wh-question'. This makes the man's one-word response a dispreferred one; it is not fitted to the format of the woman's question.

You do not need to take my word for the fact that this response is hard to deal with. The woman exposes its difficulty in her next turn. Her response combines two things: puzzlement and humour. She is wrong-footed by the man's response but treats it light-heartedly by laughing. Like our earlier example, in which friends responded to an offensive comment with laughter and horror, we can see that one way to deal with something delicate, offensive or confusing is to offset chastising, challenging or querying with laughter.

The man does not resolve the woman's confusion. Another gap develops at line 10. The woman launches a new sequence, by asking another question. She therefore interprets the silence as evidence that there is nothing more to come from her date.

The science of conversation

We know a lot about talking – implicitly. We now know more about the technology and machinery of talk. Talk is simultaneously simple and complex. It is messy – full of ums, uhs, false starts, pauses – but remarkably systematic. And its systematic nature is known to us. If it were not, we could not identify breaches, find scripted dialogue funny, or understand any of the examples presented in the book thus far. Talk is both unique and familiar. All fingerprints are unique, but we know a fingerprint when we see one.

Now that we know more about the science of talk, we will move on to examine how fundamental it is to who we are and how we live.

3

YOU ARE THE TURNS YOU TAKE

What kind of person are you? What kind of person do *others* think you are? What kinds of people are your friends, neighbours, family members or colleagues? Almost all of the answers to these questions involve listing traits, qualities, personality types and so on. But almost all of us are not psychologists. So when we describe people as 'so rude!', 'a bit neurotic', 'kind' or 'obnoxious', we are not using a psychological instrument to make such assessments. We do not halt an encounter to whip out a psychometric test. We are using what people *do*, what people *say*, and *how* people say things, to form part of our evidence base.

There are hundreds of books about the psychology of who we are. Psychologists often treat talk as a window on to the mind; as a route through to our underlying personalities, thoughts, motivations, memories, attitudes, emotions, intentions, prejudices and so on. For these kinds of psychologists, talk is the outward manifestation of who we are, and who we really are resides somewhere under the skull, in the grey matter, in our brains.

This book is not that kind of book. This book is about talk. Talk is a *public* phenomenon. While we might talk to ourselves, mutter under our breath, talk in our sleep, and so on, talk is . . . designed to be heard. We will see that, for most people, most of the time, our sense of *who we are*, and *who others are*, comes from the turns of talk we utter.

A decade or so ago, I was driving with my mother to visit *her* mother – my grandmother. My grandmother was very old and housebound. My mother started to tell me that, the previous week, she herself had 'had a fall'. 'No, Mum,' I said. 'Nana *has falls*; you *fell over*. You need to *own* that fall!' 'Old people' may have falls because of reduced strength in their bodies. 'Younger people,' I said, 'like you and me, Mum, still trip up, fall over, bash ourselves' and so on. 'There is no point in buying anti-ageing skin cream if you refer to yourself as "having falls". You need to anti-age your language!'

This was the moment that my mother started to understand a little of what I do, as an academic who studies talk. She suddenly understood that there are different ways to describe things and that those different ways have consequences for who we are and how we live. Our words build our sense of self. Some therapeutic approaches rely on this notion, focusing on getting clients to tell different stories about themselves, and talking a new self into being.

This chapter will pursue these ideas in different ways, by looking at *how*, and *when*, and in *doing what*, people describe themselves and others. People often refer to themselves and others as 'the kind of person who . . .' Speakers describe the actions of themselves and others ('. . . and he just walked off!') and provide an evaluative upshot ('how rude!'). We will examine the way *turns at talk* build people. That is, we will see how the types of *actions* a speaker does – or does not do – with their turns at talk can sometimes provide the *only* basis we have for deciding who the speaker is. We do not need the instruments of psychology to make these decisions. But we do have the CAPD: the 'Conversation Analytic Personality Diagnostic' . . .

First moves and *'first movers'*

In the telephone conversation below, Lesley is talking to her friend, Joyce. Lesley has said that she is 'boiling about something', and goes on to report an encounter she had while at a jumble sale with a man they both know. She refers to him at first as 'your friend and mine', a description Joyce does not appear to recognise. Just before we join their conversation, Lesley refers to him as 'Mr R', which Joyce *does* recognise.

Example 1: Sale at the Vicarage (simplified transcript)

01	Lesley:	<u>AND</u> uh <u>we</u> <u>were</u> looking round the stalls 'n <u>p</u>oking
02		about 'n h<u>e</u> came up t'me 'n he said '<u>Oh</u> h<u>e</u>llo Lesley,
03		↑<u>still</u> trying to buy something <u>f</u>or nothing'
04	Joyce:	((Tuts and takes a sharp intake of breath))
05	Lesley:	Oh! ((Takes a sharp intake of breath))
06	Joyce:	O<u>O</u>h [L<u>e</u>sley
07	Lesley:	[<u>Oo</u>:<u>hh</u> ((laughs))
08	Joyce:	Isn't-
09	Lesley:	What do <u>you</u> <u>say</u>!!
10	Joyce:	Oh isn't h<u>e</u> <u>drea</u>dful.
11	Lesley:	Yes.
12	Joyce:	((Tuts)) Wh<u>a</u>t an AWFUL MAN.

This kind of conversation – in which one person tells another something unpleasant that happened to them – is familiar between friends. Lesley has been insulted by Mr R for unjustified reasons.

Her friend, Joyce, makes all the right responses. She reacts with a mixture of shock, empathy, understanding and support for her friend.

First, note how Lesley recounts what happened at the sale. The man who insulted her did it *without occasion*. His attack was unprovoked. Lesley was just 'poking about'. Nothing *she* said prompted what *he* said. Lesley's encounter with Mr R, if transcribed, would look something like this:

Example 2: Insult at the Vicarage (invented)

01   Mr R: <u>Oh</u> he<u>llo</u> Lesley, ↑<u>still</u> trying to buy something <u>for</u> nothing.

02   Lesley: ((stunned silence))

Recall from Chapter 1 that conversations routinely start with three pairs of reciprocal actions: greetings, identifications and 'how-are-yous'. Instead, Mr R goes from greeting straight to an insult, skipping the so-called 'filler' talk.

Lesley's report provides further evidence that the absence of 'how-are-yous' helps us understand what kind of conversation we are in. The insult is partly an insult because it is embedded in a turn that is itself in the wrong place on the conversational racetrack.

Mr R's insult is based on the idea that Lesley is the kind of person who buys 'something for nothing'. According to the dictionary, this idiomatic phrase[28] means, 'If you say that someone is getting something for nothing, you disapprove of the fact that they are getting what they want without doing or giving anything in return.' Not only might Lesley be rather miserly at *this* charity sale; he suggests that she is tight-fisted on a regular basis – she is *still* trying to buy 'something for nothing'.

From Joyce's and Lesley's point of view, Mr R's words say nothing at all about the kind of person Lesley is. But they say *everything* about the kind of person *he* is. He is the kind of person who does not greet

---

28 www.collinsdictionary.com

people in the proper way, and he insults others in an uncalled-for manner when they were just minding their own business.

Mr R is, then, a first mover. First movers say something unwarranted, or out of place – or both. 'First moves' are non-sequiturs. Mr R's turn is unwarranted by anything that may have happened previously. First movers leave their interlocutors in a tricky interactional position. Imagine that the encounter unfolded like this.

01 Mr R: <u>Oh</u> hello Lesley, ↑<u>still</u> trying to buy something <u>for</u> nothing.

02 Lesley: How insulting!

03 Mr R: Oh don't be so sensitive, I was only teasing.

If Lesley called out Mr R's insult, he would end up being the victim of Lesley's overreaction, rather than being the one who insulted her in the first place. So, first movers can be detected across three turns at talk. In our 'Conversation Analytic Personality Diagnostic' tool, a first mover – Speaker A in the schematic below – can be diagnosed thus:

CAPD #1: The First Mover

Speaker A: Turn 1:   Unprovoked/unoccasioned/out-of-place turn

Speaker B: Turn 2:   Calls out the problem with Turn 1

Speaker A: Turn 3:   Treats Speaker B as the perpetrator, not victim, of trouble

We encountered 'first movers' in Chapter 1. Let us return for a moment to the start of a telephone call between boyfriend and girlfriend, in which Dana has called Gordon.

Example 3: Dana and Gordon

01		((ring))
02	Gordon:	Hello:,
03		(0.7)
04	Dana:	Hello where've you been all morning.
05	Gordon:	.hh HELLO!

We analysed this conversation to show how, even before Dana has spoken, we know that there is trouble ahead for Gordon. This is because of what happened at line 03; or rather, what did *not* happen. After Gordon does an answering 'Hello', Dana did not issue a reciprocal greeting. When she eventually does return the greeting, she does not go on to ask, 'How are you?' Instead, she immediately begins a new action: a question.

Dana's question is a first mover turn. It is exactly the same kind of turn, structurally, that Mr R took in his conversation with Lesley – skipping from 'Hello' to the 'first move'. Dana's question is not an innocent information-seeking question; it is a complaint. She is Gordon's girlfriend and so is entitled – from her point of view – to know where he is. She should not have had to try to get him 'all morning'.

We considered Gordon's options for responding to Dana's first move in Chapter 1. If he meets her turn head on, attacking or defending (e.g., 'What do you mean, where have I been all morning?', or 'We're not joined at the hip'), the couple might head straight into an argument. Dana may respond, in turn, by saying, 'Well, I was concerned about you.' Suddenly, Gordon is the perpetrator, not the victim. Another option is to resist the trajectory started by Dana's question, which is what Gordon does.

If you are on a first date, being a first mover could lead to difficulties. In Example 4, a woman and man are on a speed date.

We have already encountered this pair in Chapter 2 (the final example in the chapter), when we noted their somewhat sticky conversation about the qualities they like in potential partners. Here, the pair have been talking about the man's occupation – he is a physiotherapist, but also a part-time business coach and actor. The man has said that it is hard to make a living from acting, and that it is important to 'have the right face'. The gaps between their turns indicate that their conversation is still somewhat awkward. Line 08 is our target line of interest.

Example 4: Speed date

01	Man:	Y'<u>d</u>on't'ave to be anything else but the right face.
02		(0.7)
03	Woman:	<u>Sa</u>me as <u>da</u>ting really,=y'have t'ave the right
04		f<u>a</u>:ce.=d<u>o</u>:n't you.
05		(1.0)
06	Man:	Just 'ave to think y<u>e</u>:ah I quite like that person,
07		(0.5)
08	Woman:	So what's your: (0.2) history then.=relationship history.

The woman's question at line 08 comes out of nowhere. The pair have been talking about another topic. In fact, they have just disagreed about what 'having the right face' means. The man suggests 'having the right face' is important in the acting world. The woman suggests the same is true for dating. By ending her turn with 'don't you', the woman *presumes* that the man will agree with her comparison. He does not. The man switches 'having the right face' with 'I quite like that person'. Their lack of shared stance towards what is important in dating is subtle, but clear.

The woman's question about the man's 'relationship history' is a non-sequitur. It is a new, previously unaddressed, topic. And the end of the man's turn at line 06 has 'continuing' intonation (indicated by a comma). The woman does attend to the fact that it is disconnected from their previous talk, by designing her turn to start with 'so'. Conversation analysts[29] have found that the word 'so' is often used to introduce something that is incipient, but not from immediately prior talk. A gloss might be: 'Okay, enough small talk, let's get down to business and talk about what we're actually here for – dating.'

As a first move, then, the question is out of place. The man has myriad options for replying – including answering the question. This is what happens next.

```
09                    (0.4)

10    Man:     Well in what way.

11                    (0.5)

12    Man:     Have I ha:d them befo:re, yes [I have.

13    Woman:                              [>Oh yeh I kno:w< of

14              course you ha:ve, I'm £su:re,£ ((laughing))

15                    (0.6)

16    Woman:    Uh heh .hh ((still laughing))

17    Man:      How ma:ny [(   )

18    Woman:            [Well I'd ho:pe so: heh heh .hhh
```

The man's response is, first, delayed. And he does not just answer the question. Instead, he challenges the presupposition of the question.

_____

29 Bolden (2008).

He replaces her question with a new one – 'has he had relationships before?' The man implies that this is the woman's *real* question. The agenda behind her question is something like: 'Are you the kind of person who has *never* had a relationship?' He answers his version of her question – 'Have I had them? Yes I have.'

The man makes explicit the insinuation in the woman's first move. Her response to him is to claim that she 'knows, of course', she is 'sure' that he has had relationships, laughing as she responds. The woman's comeback pushes against the man's interpretation of what she was 'really' asking. He should not be so touchy – she did not mean what he thinks she meant.

Note the silence at line 15. The woman continues to laugh. The man starts to rephrase her question again – 'How ma:ny'. Whatever else he said is inaudible because the woman interrupts him, laughing, 'Well, I'd ho:pe so' If only the woman had not added this! She has confirmed, now, that the man's interpretation of her original question was correct all along: the woman is a first mover.

How turns build people

The fact that most of us are not psychologists does not stop us knowing – or *thinking we know* – who other people are. Another man and woman below are on a first date.

Example 5: Speed date (simplified transcript)

01   Man: I mean you're obviously very pretty.

02   Woman: Thank you (laughing)

03   Man: And you seem like you've got a nice personality as well.

Speed dates last five minutes, which is a short time to get to know someone. The man makes two assessments of the woman. The first, about her physical appearance, is something 'obvious' that the man can report about her – her attractiveness is there for anyone to see.

The man's second assessment is couched in different words: she *seems* like she has a 'nice personality'. The man is less entitled to know what kind of person the woman is. If the man said that she *obviously* has a nice personality, he would be going too far for what is only a five-minute encounter. One might think that he is *already* going too far! Perhaps the problem with speed dating is that people make such assessments far too quickly.

Despite the fact that assessing someone's physical appearance is a different thing from assessing someone's personality, saying that someone has a 'nice personality' is not outrageous. It is a sayable thing. The man on the date pays the woman a compliment, partly as an upshot of whatever she has said so far. Her turns have revealed who she is.

Our assessments of the kinds of people others are may be done face to face, like our dating example above. They are also done commonly in the way that Lesley and Joyce did, identifying a first mover through the kinds of turns Mr R took. And they are also done in the way that Emma and Lottie, two sisters, assess an absent third party, in the telephone call below.

Emma is talking about Bill, the husband of a friend, Gladys. Bill has been invited to become vice-president of their local angling club. But he is reluctant, because he is too busy with other things. Emma is reporting her conversation with Gladys.

Example 6: Emma and Lottie (simplified transcript)

01   Emma: And Gladys says 'MY BILL', she says 'I WANT HIM to

02   myself.=Everybody wants him y'know'. And I said 'Well he's just

03   that type of man.=He is just so- <u>wil</u>ling do things and he's'=

04   Lottie: =Mm::=

05   Emma: ='So charming!'

06   (0.2)

07   Emma: What a <u>charming</u> man.

Emma's assessment of Bill is that he is 'a charming man'. Her assessment is based on the kinds of things Bill *does* and is reported as doing. The things he does indicate what 'type of man' he is. Bill is 'willing' to do things, and is 'charming'. We make these assessments of a person's qualities through their turns at talk. What they *say* is what they *do*.

Our next example is scripted, again taking *Friends* as our source. The upshot of the scene we will examine is Monica's assessment of another character, Danny. She announces that he is 'so rude!' What does Danny *say* that permits this assessment?

Earlier in the episode, Rachel and Monica went to search for kitchen equipment in their building's storeroom. The lights go out and they see a hairy figure looming out of the darkness. Scared, they spray him with insect repellent. They later discover that the figure was Danny, who has recently moved into their building after a trek in the Andes, and who has a large shaggy beard. Rachel and Monica decide to apologise to Danny.

Example 7: *Friends*: 'The One with the Yeti'[30]

01   Rachel: ((knocks on door))

02   Danny: ((opens door))

03   Danny: >Yeh.<

04   Rachel: ↑Hi. ((clears throat)) <u>You</u> might not remember us.

---

30   Written by Alexa Junge.

Danny, with his   Monica and Rachel at
'Yeti' beard   Danny's door

05   Rachel: But <u>we</u> are the girls that fogged you. uh heh [heh heh heh]=

06   Monica: [heh heh heh]=

07   Monica: £We're- we're really sorry we fogged you. hh

08   Rachel: £Yeh.£ hhh

09   Monica: °Ye(h)h°

10   Danny: >>Okay.<< ((closes door))

11   Audience: HEH HEH HEH HEH heh heh heh heh heh heh

Remember, from Chapter 2, that turns at talk are organised into pairs. Rachel and Monica's apology ('we're really sorry we fogged you.') is a first pair part of an adjacency pair. The preferred response to an apology is an acceptance.

Furthermore, when one speaker accepts another's apology, their acceptance should also downplay or eliminate, rather than endorse, any offensive actions. For these reasons, common responses to an apology are 'That's all right' and 'That's okay', often accompanied with phrases such as 'no problem'.

Danny accepts Monica's apology, by saying 'okay', but there is no indexical term (e.g., 'that's'). His acceptance is brief and is accompanied by closing the door abruptly, thus ending the encounter. Danny gives a preferred response, but not in the way one might expect (e.g., 'oh, don't worry, it's fine'). As he closes the door, the audience laughs. The audience laughs because this is not the standard way to accept an apology.

As the scene unfolds, Rachel and Monica make further attempts to apologise. A few turns later, Rachel is now affronted by Danny's response to their apology.

12	Rachel:	↑Hi. ((clears throat))] <u>sor</u>ry to <u>bo</u>ther you.=but
13		↑I don't think <u>we</u> can ac<u>cept</u> your ac<u>cep</u>tance of our
14		apology.=it ↑just doesn't really seem like you <u>mean</u> it.
15	Monica:	°Myeh.°
16		(1.4)
17	Danny:	<Ohkay.> ((closes door))
18	Audience:	HEH HEH HEH HEH heh heh heh heh heh heh heh

Rachel complains about Danny's 'acceptance' of their apology on the basis that 'it just doesn't really seem like you mean it'. She makes explicit her interpretation of what kind of breach his actions comprise. To keep the laughter coming, Danny recycles his abrupt response once more to close his part in the sequence (line 17).

The scene concludes with Rachel and Monica giving up pursuing a proper acceptance from Danny. Instead, they begin to analyse the encounter they just had. Monica starts with an assessment of the kind of person Danny is.

19   Monica: Whow. ↑That ↑guy is so ↑ru:de.

20   Rachel: Rehally.↑What is ↑↑with that guy.

Rachel and Monica are united in their assessment of Danny: 'That guy is so rude', 'What is with that guy?' What did Danny do to warrant being called 'rude'? He took one kind of turn, and not another. Danny's character is produced through his turns – in a very explicit way. This is a scripted character. But this is what we do in real life, too.

The scene ends with Monica and Rachel showing the audience the correct way to respond to an apology.

21   Rachel: >I mean< ↑you'd ↑forgive me if I fogged yo:u,

22   Monica: Well you ↑di:d a little bit,

23   Rachel: ↑↑Ohh ↑↑my ↑↑Ghod.=↑↑Honey ↑I'm ↑so ↑so:rry.

24   Monica: .hh £↑I ↑totally ↑forgi:ve you [::.£

25   Rachel: [↑Really?

26   Audience: [HEH HEH HEH HEH HEH

27   Both: ((Rachel and Monica hug each other))

It turns out Rachel accidentally 'fogged' Monica. This provides an occasion for Rachel to apologise to Monica. Rachel then delivers an over-the-top apology, with a term of endearment ('Honey'), an intensifier ('I'm so sorry.') and markedly raised pitch. Rachel's apology is unambiguous. Monica's acceptance of Rachel's apology is equally over-the-top ('I *totally* forgive you!!'). The scene ends with Rachel and Monica hugging.

The humour in this scene relies on the audience 'getting' the contrast between 'appropriate' and 'inappropriate' ways to apologise and respond to apologies. But the scene also provides a neat example of the way people treat what others say as evidence for who they are.

Another fictional example shows how readily available people's words are for imputing their character. It does not matter whether or not people are really like that. The point is that we use what people say all the time to decide who they are.

Example 8 comes from the children's book series, the *Mr Men*, by Roger Hargreaves. The original series contained a host of characters, each called by some aspect of their characters – Mr Fussy, Mr Happy, Mr Messy and so on.

The extract below comes from *Mr Mean*. In this scene, Mr Mean is sitting in his house when a knock comes at the door. When he opens the door, a wizard is standing on Mr Mean's doorstep. What does the author have Mr Mean *say*, to warrant the moniker?

Example 8: Mr Mean

One day Mr Mean was sitting in his gloomy kitchen having a gloomy meal. Suddenly, he was interrupted by a knock at the door.

'Drat!' he said, because he didn't like people. 'Drat and bother!'

He opened the door, and there, on his doorstep, stood a wizard. A rather fat wizard.

'Hello,' said the wizard. 'I wonder if, by any chance, as it's such a warm day, you could possibly, if it's not too much trouble, be so kind as to, if it's not inconvenient, perhaps, as I'm very thirsty, provide me with, do you think, a glass, if that's not too much to ask, of water, please?'

He was a very wordy wizard.

'No!' replied Mr Mean rudely, and shut the door in his face.

The author constructs a scene not unlike that developed by the scriptwriters from *Friends*. Mr Mean is 'rude' because he does not respond in the correct way to a request. If the preferred response to an apology is acceptance, then the preferred response to a request is a granting, often in the form of an offer.

Not only does Mr Mean not make an offer, he turns down the request in a blunt matter, closing the door on the wizard – like Danny closes the door on Monica and Rachel. And – again like the *Friends* scene – the humour of *Mr Mean* is the contrast between the wizard's over-the-top request and Mr Mean's rude refusal to make an offer.

Being rude is a live concern for groups of real friends. In Example 9, Sophie is complaining to Chloe about someone she has previously had a relationship with – Rob. As they talk, music thumps in the background.

Example 9: Real friends talking

01	Sophie:	I COUld've gone spa::re when we was out that Saturday
02		though.=I could've gone spare. when he- (.) you reme:mber
03		when he jus' kinda like <u>wa:</u>lked pa:st. An' said <u>hi</u>: an:: jus'
04		walked off.
...		
15	Sophie:	An' y'know how sometimes y'see frie::nds,
16	Chloe:	Oh:[: ye::ah]
17	Sophie:	[Like people y'] not friends ↓with [but you jus' go up,
18	Chloe:	[You jus' go 'you all
19		right.'
20	Sophie:	Yeah an' walk off.
21		(0.2)
22	Sophie:	↑HE did ↑↑THAT to me! I thought that is so fuckin' ru:de,
23	Chloe:	That <u>is</u> ru:de.

Sophie's complaint about Rob hinges on the way he greeted her, when they bumped into each other at a nightclub. In some ways, Sophie's complaint about Rob is similar to Lesley's complaint about Mr R. Both men said 'hello' – and then broke a conversational rule.

Sophie knows that saying 'hello' without engaging in more talk is fine if the interlocutor is someone 'you're not friends with'. In those situations, it is okay to 'just go up and walk off'. As Sophie describes this scenario, Chloe shows that she is on the same page as her friend, by describing the same scenario at the same time – 'you just go "you all right"'. So, a two-turn sequence is appropriate when you do not know someone well – as in Example 9.

Example 10: Real friends talking (invented)

01   Sophie: Hiya

02   Acquaintance: Hiya

However, if the person you are talking to is an ex-partner, greeting someone but then not waiting for a response *is* rude.

Example 11: Real friends talking (invented)

01   Rob: Hi ((walks off))

02   Sophie: ((Stunned silence))

According to Sophie, her encounter with Rob looked like our invented Example 11. On this basis, Sophie reports that she 'thought that is so fuckin' ru:de'. And Chloe agrees. Rob is the turns he takes.

The consequences of deciding who people are on the basis of the turns they take can, of course, be significant. The next two examples come from initial enquiry calls to community mediation services. In each case, the caller has a problem with their neighbour.

Despite the fact that callers are phoning the service, they regularly resist mediation as a route to resolving their disputes. In fact, most callers start their enquiry call by saying that they 'have just been given this number', having called somewhere other than mediation first. Typically, callers have already tried the police, the council or a lawyer – they want their neighbour arrested, evicted or taken to court. And their neighbour is – *unambiguously* – to blame for the dispute. Indeed, throughout their initial conversation with the mediator, callers take *every* opportunity to negatively characterise their neighbour. With each negative characterisation of their neighbour, the caller is, by implication, the victim.

If callers take every opportunity to negatively characterise their neighbour, they will also take opportunities to say that their neighbour is the kind of person who will not engage in mediation. If mediators do not know how to overcome this hurdle, the call is over and the client is lost. The mediator has no business and so – ultimately – no employment.

Example 12: Calling mediation

01	Mediator:	I- if things did flare up d'you think that she's the sort of
02		person that would agree to mediation,
03		(1.4)
04	Caller:	No because she wouldn't see- she wou- she'd say it
05		wa- isn't her.=she hadn't done anything.=[she doesn't=
06	Mediator:	[Yeah.
07	Caller:	=understand this and- (0.4) an' all this, that an'
08		the other y'see.
09	Mediator:	Right. Rig[ht.
10	Caller:	[So she's manipulative.

We will examine more cases like this in Chapter 5, when we see what mediators can do to persuade callers to embrace, rather than resist, mediation.

The mediator in Example 12 has opened up the possibility for the caller to resist mediation. If mediators do not know that callers will take every opportunity to negatively characterise their neighbour, they are unlikely to have a strategy to avoid such opportunities arising.

By asking 'do you think that she's the sort of person that would agree to mediation', the mediator provides an exit strategy for the caller. He has asked a 'yes/no' question. The caller says much more than 'no' in response. But, between the caller and the mediator, the caller's neighbour is characterised. The caller spells out an answer to the mediator's question – the neighbour is the kind of person who would, if asked, say, 'I haven't done anything'; 'I don't understand', 'it wasn't me'. For the caller, these turns warrant the assessment that her neighbour is 'manipulative'.

Example 13 is slightly different in its structure, though the outcome is the same.

Example 13: Calling mediation

01   Mediator: If you want t'go down the route of um: .hh (0.2) trying

02   t'resolve things without resorting to um: solicitors or

03   anything like that .hh

04   [then mediation would be y'best starting po[int.

05   Caller: [Oh he's-   [He's not the

06   type of person love that's be able t- would be any

07   good for mediation.

The mediator is explaining the difference between mediation and other routes one might 'resort to' to resolve a dispute – including 'solicitors or anything like that'. The mediator does not explicitly provide an opportunity for a negative characterisation of the caller's neighbour. But the caller, demonstrating the fact that callers *do* take every opportunity, starts to resist mediation as a possible route to resolve the conflict. She does so *before* the mediator has finished speaking. The caller's neighbour is the 'type of person' who would not be 'any good for mediation'.

In both Examples 12 and 13, the caller does not become the client of the mediation service. Mediators can turn calls around, though, by saying a rather magic word in response to this kind of resistance. All will be revealed, in Chapter 5, when we see how one word can change the outcome of an encounter.

The next two examples show even more clearly that the consequences of deciding who people are on the basis of the turns they take is important. They are both about being racist. Example 14 is another call to community mediation. The caller is reporting racial insults from her neighbour. Until this point, the complaint has focused on problems over shared access to their properties. Now it begins to turn on something that might be upgraded to racially aggravated insults – something the caller's neighbour can be arrested for.

With that in mind, Example 15 comes from a police interview in which a suspect – probably someone quite like the caller's neighbour – has been arrested for racially aggravated harassment of her neighbours. In a legal context, the *precise words* that the suspect said are a key evidential feature of the alleged offence. Reports of the words people say are also the *only* evidence the police have.

Example 14: Calling mediation (simplified transcript)

01 Caller: She started in<u>sul</u>t me: .hh <u>ve</u>rbally and <u>eve</u>ry minute uh- 'go

02   <u>ho</u>me you bl- you go home you blah blah <bloody Pa<u>ki</u>>'

03 Mediator: ↑Ah:[hh.

04 Caller: [I'm not Pakistani.=[And she knows that ((laughs))]

05 Mediator: [Yeh yes ((laughs))   ]

06 Caller: And: <u>e</u>ven in the <u>co</u>urt she said 'I know that they are not

07   Pakistani but I'm <u>an</u>gry I'm sorry I said something like this.'

08 Caller: And I said- I told- her, 'look at YOU. you are living with a

09   <<u>bla</u>ck> <u>gu</u>y. And you are telling me "go home bloody

10   Paki?" What kind of person are you?!'

The configuration and grammar of racist insults are highly systematic.[31] So is the way people report racist abuse. It is common, therefore, for racist talk to be defined by its two-word composition – here, 'bloody Paki'. Racist talk often includes phrases like 'go home', or 'go back'. And those who report the racism often edit their reporting of it, constructing themselves – in contrast to whoever uttered the racist words – as the kind of person who does not use such language. The caller in Example 14 says 'blah blah' before completing the phrase, 'bloody Paki'. The caller attends to what her words say about *her*, even as she utters them.

The caller reports that not only is she 'not Pakistani', but her (white) neighbour 'knows that'. She says this with an ironic smile in her voice. The 'bloody Paki' insult illuminates the everyday workings of prejudice – it displays an indiscriminate lack of interest in

---

31 Stokoe and Edwards (2007).

the specifics of the caller's nationality, even when she apparently knows better. And, what is more, the caller cannot understand how a white woman living with a 'black guy' can be racist. The caller cannot understand 'what kind of person' her neighbour is. The caller's assessment is based on the inconsistencies of her neighbour's character, as displayed in the turns of talk taken by the neighbour.

In Example 15, a police officer asks the suspect if they 'use the word Pakis'.

Example 15: 'Racist suspect' (simplified transcript)

01   Police: D'you <u>u</u>se the word Pakis.

02   (1.3)

03   Suspect: I probably say- (0.6) bl<u>a</u>ck (0.2) ba-

04   (1.0)

05   Suspect: <u>Bee</u> if you wanna say it?

It is evident from the police officer's question that *some* words such as 'Paki' are pejorative – even when unaccompanied by other adjectives (e.g., 'Paki bastard'). After a long delay, the suspect replies that she probably says 'black (0.2) ba-'. The suspect halts her turn – stopping at the start of the word 'bastard'.[32]

After another delay, the suspect produces a euphemistic abbreviation of 'bastard' by uttering the letter that starts the word, '<u>bee</u>'. So, even when arrested for a racially aggravated crime, the suspect, like the caller in Example 14, carefully edits how she talks about racist talk. She is the kind of person who says 'black B', not 'black bastard'.

The final example in this section comes from perhaps an even more high-stakes setting – police negotiation with a suicidal person in crisis. The audio recording is made *in situ* by officers, as part of their standard practice – and the negotiation lasts several hours.

---

32 Stokoe and Edwards (2007).

The person in crisis, Mehdi, is standing on a roof. Among other things, Mehdi is anxious about the possibility of being deported by immigration authorities. The negotiators, in their attempts to persuade Mehdi to come down, and not to jump, have suggested that 'immigration will speak to you tonight, but they won't do that when you're standing on top of a roof'.

The conversation in Example 16 does not include Mehdi. From the standard unit of four negotiators that work these cases, Negotiator 1 has been talking to Medhi just before this extract starts. The negotiators are now discussing the latest attempts to talk to him, including asking if he needs anything. On the basis of their encounters thus far, the negotiators attempt to develop new strategies to engage Mehdi.

Example 16: Crisis negotiation

01	Negotiator 2:	Guys:: (0.4) I- I mean- I- I kno:w that I'm stereo-
02		typing but there is ā: (0.6) a characteristic.
03		amongst Arabic men.=also the: exaggeration
04		regarding-
05	Negotiator 1:	Yeah.
06	Negotiator 2:	You know- y'know taking things to an extreme.
07	Negotiator 1:	Yeah, yeh.
08	Negotiator 2:	Like being excitable.
09	Negotiator ?:	Yea:h.
10	Negotiator 2:	And so- so that- (0.5) that- that's how I: (0.6)
11		perceived him when I first spoke to him on the
12		phone.

13 Negotiator 1:   Yeah.

14 Negotiator 2:   That it was all or nothing.=you know.

15 Negotiator 1:   How do we give him an <u>out</u> of there.

N2 is building Medhi's character, on the basis of the turns Medhi has taken on the phone. N2 prefaces his description of 'how he perceived' Medhi by acknowledging that N2 is 'stereotyping'. He treats what Medhi does as characteristic of 'Arabic men' in general – 'exaggerating', 'taking things to an extreme', being 'excitable', and being 'all or nothing'.

Leaving aside the factual, prejudicial, or otherwise, status of N2's description of Medhi, the negotiators must decide how best to negotiate with someone who acts in this way – whether or not these characteristics are connected to a particular category. The negotiators try to figure out what kind of person Medhi is, based on the turns he takes, and proceed on the basis of their collective experience.

Speakers characterise other speakers pretty much all the time. The conversations we have seen so far all involve someone analysing the turns at talk made by another. On the basis of those turns, an interlocutor may assess what sort, or type, or kind of person they are talking to. As they describe what others say, people also monitor the words *they* use, attending to how *they* may be perceived by others. We focus in on the way people assess their own character in the next section.

You are the words you *say* you are

We are the turns we take. And there are many idiomatic expressions about the way we talk as their topic. Idioms characterise people. For instance, the idiom 'likes the sound of their own voice' refers to someone who talks 'too much'. Talking to some people can be like 'talking to a brick wall'. Others have 'the gift of the gab'.

As well as using idioms to characterise others, some idioms come alive across a sequence of turns at talk. We might describe someone as 'always fishing for compliments'. A related idiom is 'self-praise is no recommendation'. Paying someone a compliment, praising yourself, or being self-deprecating, all happen through turns at talk, and all are tricky to manage.

Conversation analysts[33] have shown that there is a 'system of constraints' against self-praise. And there is a range of idiomatic expressions to draw on if you *do* say something that sounds big-headed – 'without blowing my own trumpet', or 'even if I do say so myself'.

In Example 17, Lesley is talking to her friend Carrie, who has telephoned to say that she has become a grandmother.

Example 17: Lesley and Carrie (simplified transcript)

01   Carrie: So:: mum an' baby doing okay apparently [Steven says=

02   Lesley: [Oh: good.

03   Carrie: =she's beautiful 'but then WE would think so wouldn't we:'

04   he said.

To ensure that Lesley does not perceive Carrie's son as boasting about his new daughter, Carrie adds that he also admits their bias, as a way of managing the constraint against bragging.

Speakers also monitor each other for the unfettered use of self-praise. The next example is a recollected memory of a birthday party.[34]

---

33 Pomerantz (1978).

34 Speer (2012).

Example 18: Birthday party (simplified transcript)

01   Susan: How was the dinner party.

02   Mum: Oh Susan it was cooked to perfection.

03   Susan: ((Laughs)) even if you do say so yourself!!

Susan teases Mum for making an unmitigated compliment about her own cooking. Susan deploys the familiar idiom – 'even if you do say so yourself'.

The use of idioms like this, to avoid sounding immodest, is often associated not just with *one* person taking a turn at talk, but with the British national character! The text below is from a website and the writer is reporting her recent attendance at a conference.

Example 19: Lexical Lab[35]

A German friend of mine who was also talking at the conference asked me how my sessions had gone, to which I replied, 'I think they both went pretty well . . . even if I do say so myself.' On hearing this, he rolled his eyes, laughed and told me this was such a British way of saying things! 'Why can't you just do what normal people would do and say they went well? You know they went well. You know that I know that they went well. Why this false modesty? Why do you add, "even if I do say so myself"?'

While the writer correctly identifies the *function* of the idiom – to mitigate self-praise – it is stereotyped incorrectly. The earliest work on how compliments and self-praise work came from American conversations. At the very least, then, the constraint against self-praise is not limited to British English conversation. We will consider

---

35 www.lexicallab.com/2017/03/phrase-of-the-day-even-if-i-do-say-so-myself/

these and other stereotypes about talk in Chapter 4 – and why they are problematic, beyond just being wrong.

The flip side of self-praise is self-deprecation. While the 'preferred response' to most assessments (e.g., 'what a gorgeous painting!') is agreement, the 'preferred response' to someone's self-deprecating turn is to disagree with it.

Example 20: Ann and Claire[36] (edited)

```
01   Ann:      And I never was a great bridge player, Claire ((laughing))

02   Claire:   Well I think you've always been real good.
```

In Example 20, Claire disagrees that Ann is not a 'great bridge player'. Claire could also have said, 'Don't fish for compliments!'

In another scripted scene from *Friends*, the humour hinges on the audience knowing what the 'preferred response' to a negative self-assessment is. Chandler has fallen in love with his friend Joey's new girlfriend, and is feeling guilty. He is talking to the other characters about his feelings.

Example 21: *Friends:* 'The One With Joey's New Girlfriend'[37]

```
01   Chandler:   I mean- I'm a very bad person. I'm a very very ba:d

02               per- I'm a horrible (0.6) person.

03   Audience:   ((Laughter))

04   Chandler:   'No you're not Chandler, we still love you [Chandler,'

05   Audience:                                            [(((laughter))
```

---

36 Pomerantz (1984).

37 Written by Michael Curtis and Gregory S. Malins.

At line 03, after Chandler has made three strongly negative assessments of himself inside one turn, there is a space for his friends to provide the 'preferred response' – to disagree with Chandler. They do not. The audience laughs – recognising the scriptwriters' method for generating humour. Chandler then voices the response his friends should have provided – the disagreement he was seeking!

The final example in this section comes towards the end of a telephone call recorded at a double-glazing company. At the start of the call, the call-taker assumes the caller is a customer. However, the caller is making enquiries about a sales position that he has seen advertised.

The call is quite strange, from start to finish. The caller speaks very slowly and refuses to give his phone number so that the manager can call him back. The caller implies – but does not state outright – that he does not want a call-back in case his current employer overhears. The whole call is three minutes long – and we join it towards the end. Watch out for the caller interrupting the call-taker, and particularly the strange self-assessment at line 16.

Example 22: Calling double-glazing sales

01	Call-taker:	And are you- you're in work at the moment are you.
02		(1.0)
03	Caller:	Uh- (0.7) I'm working for a national company.=yeah.
04	Call-taker:	Right. In- in double glazing?
05		(0.6)
06	Caller:	((slowly, quietly)) Uh- £yes.£ Yeah. the dreaded
07		double-glazing. Yeh. hhh
08	Call-taker:	Okay dokey, [No problem at all-]
09	Caller:	[YES I AM] I am.

10		(0.2)
11	Caller:	I'm not sayin' any more at this second?
12	Call-taker:	No problem at all. =[I will give-
13	Caller:	[And I've had- I've got more
14		experience than I care to remember ((slowly))
15		(0.3)
16	Caller:	But [that doesn't mean to say I'm- (0.5) brilliant
17	Call-taker:	[Heh okay-
18		(0.4)
19	Call-taker:	No problem at all.
20	Caller:	I'm not being arrogant when I say that.
21		(0.5)
22	Call-taker:	No problem? I'll pass that on for you sir, no problem
23		at ↓all.

The call-taker tries on multiple occasions to end the call – he repeats 'no problem at all' at lines 08, 12, 19 and 22. The caller interrupts these pre-closing turns twice, at lines 09 and 13. What is strange is the caller's admission that, just because he has a lot of 'experience', this 'doesn't mean to say I'm- (0.5) brilliant'. This is *neither* self-praise *nor* self-deprecation – so the 'preferred response' is unclear. The fact that it is unclear is revealed in the delay in responding at line 18, before the call-taker says 'no problem at all' – making an attempt to close the call, rather than deal with the caller's strange turn.

The caller then supplies a turn that is designed to correct some careless self-praise – that he is 'not being arrogant when I say that.'. When he says *what*? That he might not be brilliant? The call-taker is confused again – repeating his strategy to attempt to end the call, rather than deal with the content of the caller's turn.

This episode contains instances in which one speaker takes turns that constitute self-praise and self-deprecation at the same time. His turns also attend to the impression he is giving to his interlocutor. Whatever else, the caller knows that turns build people. We would not be surprised to learn that this conversation – and the caller's turns – comprised a subsequent conversation between co-workers about the caller. The caller is the turns he took.

Conversation Analytic Personality Diagnostic

We end this chapter by returning to the 'Conversation Analytic Personality Diagnostic' tool. The 'CAPD #1' was a 'first mover'. A 'first mover' is a person who makes unprovoked or 'out of place' turns. We encountered several cases.

Mr R insulted Lesley at the charity sale. He was diagnosed as a 'first mover' because he went straight from 'hello' to an unprovoked 'insult'.

Similarly, in the conversation between Dana and Gordon, Dana went straight from 'hello' to a combative question. And, on a first speed date, the woman dater produced a non-sequitur by asking a discourteous question to her interlocutor. The man called her out on the question, and she then treated his 'calling out' as unwarranted.

I first introduced the notion of a 'first mover' while giving a TED talk in 2014. I mentioned that it is quite common – given that I study talk – for people to ask me, 'What is it that you actually *do*?' The question may come straight after 'hello', or replace a greeting entirely!

As well as being out of place, the question is not innocent. It has a challenge in it, like, 'you don't do something that *I* understand as a legitimate form of employment'.[38] If I call out the challenge, by saying something like, 'hang on, I wouldn't ask *you* that kind of question', then a likely third turn will be, 'I was just asking! Don't be

---

38 I recently appeared on a BBC Radio 4 programme called 'How to Disagree'. The *Radio Times*, a TV and scheduling guide, promoted the series. Simon O'Hagan, who wrote the programme blurb, described the list of people consulted as 'academics, philosophers, neuroscientists and a "conversation analyst"'.

so sensitive!' I would end up victimising the first mover, despite them being the one who asked the overbearing question in the first place.

After the TED talk, all of the speakers attended a wrap party. As I stood chatting to one of the other speakers, an audience member came up to both of us. He did not say 'hello', but directed a turn to the other speaker.

Example 23: TED wrap party (field note)

01	Man:	You seemed nervous.
02	Speaker:	((looking at Liz)) First mover!!
03	Liz:	Right!

The other speaker had immediately identified a 'first mover'! Here are some other easy-to-recognise CAPD types.

CAPD #2: The Mis-greeter

We encountered a mis-greeter in Example 9. Sophie complained about the way her ex-partner, Rob, 'jus' kinda like walked past. An' said hi an jus' walked off.'. Rob failed to do the standard greeting between friends which, in addition to 'hi', also requires reciprocal 'how-are-yous'.

Another type of mis-greeter will be familiar to anyone who has attended a party, a conference – just about any gathering.

Example 24: Mis-greeter (invented)

01	A:	Hello!
02	B:	Hello- ((looks over the shoulder of B to see if there is
03		someone more important to talk to))

Mis-greeters say 'hello', but their gaze, body position, head position, and so on, tells you that they would prefer that Speaker A was not you.

CAPD #3: The Recalibrator

Mis-greeters often turn out to be diagnosable with another CAPD category – the Recalibrator. Recalibrators are people who decide that the person they mis-greeted is actually quite important, and redo their original greeting.

Example 25: Recalibrator (invented)

01   A: Hello . . .

02   B: Hello!!! Sorry, I didn't realise it was YOU! How ARE you?

03   A: ((inwardly sighing))

It is through *taking turns* like these that we describe Speaker B, probably later to one of our friends, as 'superficial', 'insincere' or just plain 'bad-mannered'. We characterise people on the basis of what they say and do not say.

CAPD #4: The 'How-are-you' Subverter, or The Non-Questioner

We learned in Chapter 1 that there is a canonical way to greet people we are more or less familiar with – across pairs of turns that exchange reciprocal greetings, identifications and 'how-are-yous'. The correct way to greet someone is summarised in *Machell's Guide to Surviving Modern Life*.

When asked 'how're you doing', stick to the only two legitimate
answers: 'fine' or 'alright' before a throw-away 'You?' Be sure to
show your lack of interest in the enquiry: this really is not the time
to discuss the crushing reality of existence.[39]

Now, although Machell's guide provides an ironic take on what
'how're you doing' means in these quick encounters – people should
give pro-forma and not deep and meaningful answers – we also know
that missing out the 'how-are-you' can make you a 'first mover'.

Some people sabotage 'how-are-yous' to suit their own agenda.
Imagine you are Speaker A in the example below.

Example 26: 'How-are-you' Subverter (invented)

01   A: Hello!!

02   B: Hey. How're you?

03   A: Fine, how're you?

04   B: Yeah, okay, ((tells a very long story about themselves))

B has upended the implicit rule of opening 'how-are-yous', so that
they can talk about themselves. *Machell's Guide* has something to say
about this, too.

> Good conversation is made up of questions; if you haven't asked
> one within two minutes of speaking, stop yourself and get a grip.
> If you somehow reach the five-minute mark without a peep from
> your interlocutor(s), really, stop talking.[40]

---

39 https://reaction.life/machells-guide-surviving-modern-life-ii-make-conversation-bearable/
40 Ibid.

If you are Speaker B in Example 26, not only have you abused the 'how-are-you' turns, you have now talked about yourself without regard for your interlocutor.

And a corollary of the 'How-are-you' Subverter is also illustrated in Example 26. Are you the kind of person who asks other people questions, or not? Speaker B is likely to keep talking about themselves and never return the floor to Speaker A. People who never ask questions are the turns they take, likely to be regarded as egocentric and uninterested in others.

CAPD #5: The Non-Transitioner

To be a 'How-are-you Subverter', you need to be able to take extended turns at talk. More generally, if you have ever been trapped in a conversation with the feeling that you cannot get a word in edgeways, you are probably talking to someone who does not give cues for transition between speakers.

Example 27: Non-Transitioner (invented . . . sort of)

01	Alan:	Well, did you- I went to- no: (.) wait (0.2) heh heh what
02		happened with the- well .hh (.) was it in nineteen ninety nine
03		or so, I think I had just returned from- now, where was it,
04		um::::: I think- or was that two thousand and one- Jane was
05		already- Yes! It was ninety- or was it- anyway ((continues))

Of course, people *need* long turns to tell stories. Yet stories are still packaged into 'turn construction units', with 'transition relevance places'.

If someone is telling a story, their interlocutors generally pass up each 'transition relevance place' to allow the storyteller to keep telling. But these are the moments when interlocutors nod, smile, laugh, say 'oh yeah', 'ooh!', 'wow', or 'mm hmm'.

In Example 27, it is not clear when any such 'yeahs' or 'wows' might happen. Alan does not complete any 'turn construction units'. The people listening cannot know where any of his talk might be going. This way, Alan keeps the floor for a *long* time.

CAPD #6: The Recompleter

Another way that people hog the floor is to recomplete a turn that was just finished. This not only makes it difficult for people to jump in to the conversation, but also undermines any kind of response that another speaker might have had to the *first* completion. Recompleters finish turn construction units, but talk very quickly past the moment when their interlocutors could take a turn to say the same thing again.

Example 28: Recompleter (field note)

01	Mike:	I won't agree to this.
02	Sam:	I-[
03	Mike:	[I absolutely won't.
04	Sam:	Uh-[
05	Mike:	[I won't have it.
06	Sam:	Well[-
07	Mike:	[No. No. Let's move on.

Each time Sam attempts to say something, Mike jumps back in to recomplete line 01. Sam cannot take a turn; Sam cannot also say what he wants to say about 'this'.

CAPD # 7 The Passive-Aggressive

The term 'passive-aggressive' is used commonly to describe certain kinds of people based on certain kinds of turns of talk that they take. One nice example, is, 'Why are you getting so upset?'

> The passive aggressive person is a master at maintaining calm and feigning shock when others, worn down by his or her indirect hostility, blow up in anger. In fact, the person takes pleasure out of setting others up to lose their cool and then questioning their "overreactions".[41]

'First movers' are also a sub-type of passive-aggressive – they take an aggressive first turn, followed by a passive response when challenged about their initial aggression.

Example 29: Aggressive-passive (field note)

01   A: Why did you send that email?

02   B: Um, you asked me to send it . . .?

03   A: Okay okay! Don't be so defensive!

Understanding how these turns at talk work scientifically still may not help in defeating an 'Aggressive-Passive', or any of the other CAPD categories. Some people are just – well, people. We cannot always defeat first movers, but we can avoid them (and know *why* we are avoiding them). And we can stop ourselves from becoming one . . .

---

41 https://www.psychologytoday.com/blog/passive-aggressive-diaries/201011/10-things-pas-sive-aggressive-people-say

Talk builds people

For most people, most of the time, our sense of who people are comes from the turns of talk they utter. Most of us are not psychologists. But we are – whether we realise it or not – conversation analysts. We make decisions about who people are from what they do and say as our evidence base.

We will return to the CAPD in Chapter 6, when we consider how people get help, service and support from others. Some people are very good at getting others to do things for them. They are in CAPD #8 – 'The Recruiter'. If you are the kind of person who wonders, on a regular basis, 'Why am I doing *this* for him/her . . .?!', you are probably in CAPD #9 – 'The Recruited'.

The categories we have described in the CAPD are light-hearted, and not offered as a serious set of categories for classifying people and producing theory. But they are nevertheless based on evidence about how we talk. In the next chapter, we reflect on the many stereotypes we have about how we talk, how men and women talk, how our bodies talk, how different cultures talk – and discover whether or not any of these stereotypes are supported by evidence. If they are not – and given that stereotypes about talk can be very strongly held – we will also consider possible dangers in holding on to them.

4

STICKS, STONES, AND . . . TALK

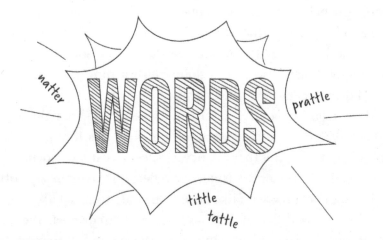

People often ask me, as a scientist of talk, about many aspects of human communication. Some questions draw upon commonly held myths about the way we speak. For example, if I am showing an audience how customer service works over the telephone, people ask about 'body language', and the limits of the voice-only mode. They ask about the relative status of talking versus what our bodies do to communicate. And their questions often reveal a presupposition about the answer. Body language, it is assumed, has primacy over words. Our words transmit one message, but our bodies leak another. Actions speak louder than words.

Myths about how we talk originate in language itself. The word 'talk' suffers from being something basic, ordinary and simple. It has hundreds of synonyms to characterise and evaluate its use: we 'banter' and 'chat'; we 'prattle', 'natter', and 'yap'. Conversation is also characterised in myriad ways: we engage in 'small talk', 'discussion', 'gossip' and 'tête-à-têtes'. 'Talk' is the subject of hundreds of idioms and proverbs: we 'talk the talk', 'talk is cheap', we 'talk a mile a minute', and until we are 'blue in the face'.

This chapter will examine myths about talk. I have chosen topics based on the most common questions audiences ask when I talk about talk – such as whether or not men and women talk differently, whether or not different cultures talk differently, or whether 'ums' and 'uhs' are superfluous errors made by bad speakers. Somewhere in the world of words and phrases we have learned to think we know all there is to know about talk. But does our knowledge have any scientific basis? And why are there so many myths about talk?

Do actions speak louder than words?

The notion that talk is secondary to something else – to action – forms the basis of many idioms, proverbs and phrases. The first recorded use of the proverb 'actions speak louder than words' was in 1628.[42] The proverb is shared across all major world languages, including Brazilian Portuguese, Finnish, Russian, Swedish, Persian, Chinese Mandarin and Irish. So the idea that people's actions are a better indicator of character than what they say is, perhaps surprisingly, universal.

Related phrases include the American colloquialism, 'to talk the talk', first used in 1906, and usually contrasted with 'to walk the walk'. The words of someone who 'talks the talk' are just rhetoric and without substance; someone who 'walks the walk' supports their rhetoric with action. Likewise, the American proverb, 'talk is cheap', is 'used for saying that you do not believe that someone will in fact do what they are saying they will do'.[43]

---

42 *Oxford English Dictionary*, 1628: J. Pym Deb. King's Message to hasten Supply 4 Apr. in Hansard Parl. Hist. Eng. (1807) II. 274/2 'A word spoken in season is like an Apple of Gold set in Pictures of Silver', and actions are more precious than words.

43 The phrase 'talk is cheap' is actually a shortened version of at least two other commonly used American idioms: 'talk is cheap but it takes money to buy whisky' and 'talk is cheap but it takes money to buy a farm'. The earliest date for publication of the phrase 'talk is cheap' is found in the Chicago Daily Tribune on 21 November 1891; https://idiomation.wordpress.com/.

For many years, implicitly if not explicitly, much of psychology maintained this separation between action and talk. Perhaps even more importantly, much of psychology – and the social sciences generally – treats language as a window on to the mind. Talk is the means by which we can access people's underlying real thoughts, emotions, personalities, attitudes and psyche. Of course, there is a massive branch of cognitive psychology dedicated to understanding the (typical and atypical) development of language and communication. There is also a great deal of work dedicated to understanding brain function, brain damage and language. But, overall, the mundane use of language is not of interest to psychologists.

However, in the late 1980s, a branch of psychology called 'discursive psychology' was invented by Derek Edwards and Jonathan Potter.[44] The aim of discursive psychology was to encourage psychologists to treat language seriously. They argued that language – in the form of real language in use – should be something of interest to psychologists. Discursive psychologists were influenced by the language philosophers Ludwig Wittgenstein, John Austin and John Searle. For these writers, words *do* things – they create 'speech acts'. Austin wrote that saying is doing – as one utters the words, 'I name this ship the *Queen Mary*', the ship *is named*. The action is done.

The science-fiction author, Ursula K. Le Guin,[45] wrote that 'utterance is magic. Words do have power. Names have power. Words are events, they do things, change things.' Like discursive psychologists – and other kinds of discourse analysts – conversation analysts share Le Guin's view that 'words are magic'. Discursive psychologists and conversation analysts can help correct our cultural idioms about talk. But we are probably some distance from creating new idioms about the action *talk* does – this book aims to kick-start their creation!

The idea that 'actions speak louder than words' drives our understanding of talk towards communicative practices other than

---

44   Edwards and Potter (1992).

45   Le Guin (2004).

talk as the place to find out what people are really doing. Somehow, then, talk is not action. Talk is disconnected from action. And the phrase figures repeatedly in advertising, art, culture and literature. Almost four hundred years after its first recorded use, it continues to capture the public imagination. A recent exhibition at London's Halcyon Gallery was promoted with the poster 'Actions Not Words'.[46] Aaron Reynold's 'Effin' Birds' shouts the question on Twitter, 'Can we stop talking and actually fucking do something?'[47] And Amazon advertises its web services with the strapline, 'While talkers talk, builders build'.

How do these ideas about talk and action get used in conversation? And how might they cause problems for successful communication? Let us start with a fictional – but very recognisable – example from Tom Sharpe's *The Wilt Alternative* (1979). Sharpe writes the following dialogue between two characters, Wilt and Eva.

> But on the domestic front suspicion still lurked. Eva had taken to waking him in the small hours to demand proof that he loved her.
>
> 'Of course I do, damn it,' grunted Wilt. 'How many times do I have to tell you?'
>
> 'Actions speak louder than words,' retorted Eva.

The next thing to happen is that Wilt and Eva have sex. The words, 'I love you', are not enough to convince Eva of Wilt's love. An embodied action is the proof she needs.

Note that everything in this example from Sharpe is words. It's all words, including the appeal to action, and including the explanatory scene-setting by Sharpe. We tend to look through language at the world it describes, ignoring how that world is itself given shape, nature and relevance by language. One thing that Eva's words do is get sex to happen, which is presumably Eva's project in saying them. 'Actions speak louder than words' is itself a sentence; a proposition;

46   Lorenzo Quinn, 'Actions Not Words', Halcyon Gallery, London, 2017.

47   'Effin' Birds', Aaron Reynolds, 2017.

a collection of words – and each time they are used, in some specific context, they are designed to make something happen.

The problem with 'talk', and just saying things, is that it is easy to challenge for not being action, as Eva does. Of course, the idea that words are powerful also regularly grips the popular imagination. We will see later in this chapter – and in Chapter 5 – that words matter to people. We know this. Hate speech does not exist without words. But I want to show you how cultural idioms about talk can actually hinder the progress of crucial conversations.

We first encountered police hostage and crisis negotiations in Chapter 1. When a person threatens to commit suicide, police negotiators attend the scene to dissuade the suicidal person in crisis. They try to persuade them to live, not die. But first, negotiators must get people to talk to them. Negotiators ask regularly if they can talk to the person in crisis. They also describe the negotiation process as 'talking'. Does this get them talking?

Example 1: Crisis negotiation

01	Negotiator:	Can we talk about how you are.
02		(0.5)
03	P in C:	No:, I don't want to ta:lk,

Persons in crisis frequently resist requests to talk to the negotiator. Not only do they say no to 'talk', they explain the reason why.

Example 2: Crisis negotiation

01	Negotiator:	You kept saying earlier about action:s rather
02		than wo:rds, .hh this i- this is genuine action that
03		we can [give you.]

```
04    P in C:                    [It's not ge]nuine action man, you're just

05                        talking.

06                            (0.4)

07    Negotiator:    Why don't [you think it-]

08    P in C:                    [It's talking.]=You ain't done

09                        anything.
```

In Example 2, the person in crisis resists talking. The negotiator summarises the position of the person in crisis, who has already invoked the now-familiar cultural idiom ('action:s rather than wo:rds') that talk is just talk and does not do anything.

The negotiator, in turn, is attempting to resist the idiom,[48] suggesting that the police *can* give 'genuine action'. The person in crisis resists the negotiator, who is 'just talking'.

We will see in Chapter 5 that another word for talk, a near synonym, works to get the person in crisis to communicate with the negotiator. But for now, note that by asking the person in crisis to talk, the negotiator opens up a slot for resistance. And the form of resistance is an idiom about action trumping words.

A second setting in which similar resistance occurs, for similar reasons, is in enquiry calls to mediation. This is another context that we will revisit throughout the book. People involved in a dispute may telephone mediation services – usually as a last resort, having tried other things first.

When people talk to services and organisations to get help with some aspect of their lives, one thing they often have to manage is why outside help is needed. Imagine you have a headache. After ignoring it for a bit, you might decide to take a painkiller. If the headache lingers for more than a few days, you might decide to visit the doctor. Most likely, when booking an appointment, and when talking to the

---

48 Kitzinger (2000).

doctor, you would describe your symptoms but also what you have done to try to resolve things yourself.

At the doctor's, then, patients often report their self-help. They establish the 'doctorability'[49] of their problem. Patients will report that they have had a headache for several days – it did not just arrive ten minutes before calling the surgery. And they will report what they tried to put things right on their own – various types of painkillers. Having presented with a 'doctorable' problem, patients hope that the doctor will do more than . . . offer painkillers. The latter's expertise in resolving a problem that patients cannot solve themselves is required.

Of course, there are cases in which self-help is less relevant, or even dangerous. If your partner appears to have stopped breathing, phoning the emergency services is the appropriate first port of call. But if you are calling a computer specialist about your PC, you are likely to report that you have 'tried turning it off and on again'. Calling for expert help, then, requires some attention to self-help, first.

For mediation services, the issue of self-help can be a hurdle to securing mediation clients. When people call mediation services, their problem is relational: it is conflict – at home, with neighbours, or in the workplace. One of the reasons that people call services other than mediators – such as lawyers, human resources, the council or police – is their concern to describe the problem as concrete and objective (e.g., about loud music, tall hedges or parking behaviour) and *not* about relationships.

However, if lawyers, human resources, the council or police cannot help, people may call – or be referred to – mediation services. People call services to get expert help with things they cannot solve for themselves. But they must have attempted to solve the problem. For mediation services, self-help is talking to the problematic other person. And herein lies the problem. [50]

---

49   Heritage and Robinson (2006).

50   Edwards and Stokoe (2007).

In Example 3, the mediator has just started talking to a caller involved in a noise dispute. Notice that the caller has tried calling elsewhere first, and has done some self-help, by calling 'security'.

Example 3: Calling mediation (simplified transcript)

01	Mediator:	Hi. How can I hel:p.
02	Caller:	Umm I've complained about- the girl downstairs
03		with her music.
04	Mediator:	Right.
05	Caller:	To the council and they've give me your number.
06	Mediator:	Right. Okay.
07		(0.3)
08	Mediator:	Uh is it loud noise that you're con[cerned about]
09	Caller:	[Yeah I've]
10		phoned security again last nigh[t. that=
11	Mediator:	[Yeh.
12	Caller:	=it's from morning t'night - it's on now!
13		(0.5)
14	Mediator:	Right.

The caller has been referred to mediation by the council. This tells us that the caller regarded the council as the place to get help – not mediation.

Now that she is telephoning mediation, the caller's goals are to say what she has already done. The mediator is concerned about the 'mediatability' of the problem – the caller has described 'music' but not its severity or duration – is this a serious enough problem? In response to the mediator asking if it is 'loud music', the caller replies by implying it was bad enough to call security. She also gives some details about its duration, and the fact that the music is 'on now' as she speaks to the mediator.

At line 13, a silence starts to open up. At line 14, the mediator says, 'Right' – confirming she has heard the caller but not immediately starting to do anything else. It is at this point that the caller decides to tell the mediator that she has tried the self-help for relationship problems – talking to the other person.

15   Caller: Ummm I <u>ha</u>ve talked to her <u>a</u>bout it but she's one of these

16   people you can't <u>ta</u>lk to.

By talking to the other person, the caller has tried to address the issue. She is asking for help because she cannot help herself. However, her neighbour is 'one of these people you can't talk to'. The caller's words are powerful. Not only is the caller a good and moral person; her neighbour is not. We can begin to anticipate the problems that lie ahead for the mediator when she tries to explain what mediation is.

17   Caller: She's twenty one year old with an attitude ((laughing))

18   you <u>know</u> what they're like at that age?

19   Mediator: Right. <u>I</u> see right.=And is that <u>m</u>usic being played uh- <u>a</u>ll

20   the time y'thin:k,=

21   Caller: <u>Yes</u> love it <u>is</u> yeh.

22   Mediator: Right. Okahy. .HHHh umm u- I'll °u-u-w-° I'll tell you a

23   little bit about <u>med</u>iation an' how <u>we</u> can help.

The caller continues to characterise her neighbour, while the mediator focuses on the 'mediatability' of the problem – is the music played enough to be a problem? Once the caller has confirmed that the music is 'played all the time', the mediator starts to explain what mediation is.

Think about the order in which things have happened in the call. Just after the caller says that her neighbour is the 'kind of person you can't talk to', the mediator begins to explain what mediation is – a *talk*-based solution to problems. The caller eventually says no to mediation.

The problem with talk-based solutions crops up in related ways across the calls to mediation services. In Example 4, the caller has a problem with the noisy children next door.

Example 4: Calling mediation (simplified transcript)

01	Mediator:	Have you spoken to their parents or . . .?
02	Caller:	Um well one of the parents she uh complained to
03		one of them and she ended up hitting me so there's
04		no point talking to them.

Unlike Example 3, in which the caller reported a failed attempt to talk to her neighbour, in Example 4 the mediator asks a self-help question. By asking the question, 'Have you spoken to their parents', the mediator opens up a slot for several potential responses. The first is a simple 'no'. But not trying to talk could make the caller appear recalcitrant. When callers say 'no', they always include an explanation for their answer (e.g., 'because I am scared of them') that further emphasises the problematic character of their neighbour.

A second possible response is to say 'yes, I have tried talking'. When callers say 'yes', they go on to report that attempts at talking have failed – as in Examples 3 and 4. Another (ironic) alternative response is to say 'Oh! I hadn't thought about talking – thank you very much for the suggestion!'

So by asking questions about 'talking', mediators leave wide open the opportunity to reject mediation. Callers have either tried talking and it has failed, or do not want to try talking because their neighbour is too difficult to talk to. The caller's self-help has failed. Mediators' talk-based solutions are not attractive.

Example 5 is particularly clear. The mediator is explaining how mediation works.

Example 5: Calling mediation (simplified transcript)

01	Mediator:	Mediation is really to help you both to sort it out
02		between yourselves through talking.
03	Caller:	Oh yeah, but I mean I've done all that. There's no
04		point in talking to them because it's like talking to
05		the wall.

The mediator highlights 'talking' as the route to sorting things out – something the caller rejects out of hand, using yet another idiom about the pointlessness of talking: 'it's like talking to the wall'.

In Examples 6–8, the same pattern occurs in three turns of talk:

Turn 1: Mediator:	Asks if the caller has tried talking to their neighbour
	Opens up a slot to reject talk as a solution
Turn 2: Caller:	Rejects talking as a solution
Turn 3: Mediator:	Explains talking as a solution

Example 6: Calling mediation (simplified transcript)

01	Mediator:	Have you spoken to your neighbour about it?
02	Caller:	I don't wanna talk to her.
03	Mediator:	Yeh. .hhh u:m .h alr- can I just really explain to
04		you briefly what mediation- (.) i- how mediation works

Example 7: Calling mediation (simplified transcript)

01	Mediator:	Have you spoken to her about that.
02	Caller:	Me no. cos we don't speak.
03	Mediator:	Right. Okay. .hh.hh (.) *u*:m .hhh what I'll do is I'll tell
04		you a little bit about mediation,

Example 8: Calling mediation (simplified transcript)

01	Mediator:	Have y- have you spoken to him: 'bout this: y'haven't
02		spoken to him.
03	Caller:	Uh shall I be honest with you. We've tried speaking to
04		him on other matters but there's no way getting through
05		to him.=he doesn't wanna know.
06	Mediator:	Right. Okay. .hh.hh *u- uh-* ri:ght. (0.2) u:mm right.=
07		s'shall I tell you a little bit about mediation an' how wh- how
08		we can help.

In each case, the mediator asks a question that begins the journey towards the caller rejecting mediation. The mediators probably realise this, once the caller has answered their question. The highlighted parts of each transcript show what happens after each caller's answer to the mediator's question about talk. The mediator acknowledges that they have heard the answer ('Yeh', 'Right' and 'Right', in Examples 6, 7, and 8 respectively), but then begins to stumble over what to do next. The detailed transcript exposes this in a way that a verbatim one would not. In each case, the mediator eventually starts to explain mediation. But not before they have littered the start of their turn with in-breaths, false starts, restarts and hesitations. These 'ums' and 'uhs' are not errors. They tell us that the mediator is having trouble formulating what to do next.

In each case, also, the caller goes on to reject mediation as a solution. When mediators do not ask self-help questions, about trying to talk to the other party, they reduce the opportunity for callers to use idiomatic phrases about the pointlessness of talk.

Just like police negotiators, then, mediators are more effective if they do not highlight talk as part of their business – even if talk is the *only* resource people have to resolve the situation they are in.

In fact, talk is often the only resource people have to make the world happen at all. It may be the only resource to establish the facts of the matter or mask the truth. George Orwell famously wrote about the power of language to control meaning. This power is played out in the following transcript from a rape trial.[51] The alleged perpetrator's attorney is questioning the alleged victim, as the witness.

Example 9: Rape trial (simplified transcript)

01	Attorney:	Well you had some fairly lengthy conversations with the
02		defendant didn't you?
03	Witness:	Well we were all talking.

---

51   Drew (1992).

04 Attorney: And during that evening didn't Mr Jones come over to sit

05   with you?

06 Witness: Sat at our table

((And, describing the location))

07 Attorney: And you went to a bar — is that correct?

08 Witness: It's a club.

09 Attorney: It's where girls and fellas meet, isn't it?

10 Witness: People go there.

Each pair of turns taken, between the attorney and the witness, shows how words build or resist versions of events. The attorney and witness use words to build alternative descriptions of what took place – and where it took place – on the night in question.

The attorney pushes for one version – in which the witness is a knowing party to an incipient relationship between herself and the defendant. She is out at a 'bar', in her capacity as a 'girl', to meet a 'fella'. The witness pushes towards another version – in which she is out with other friends and not looking for an intimate conversation with the defendant.

The attorney suggests that the witness and defendant *without mentioning other people* 'had some fairly lengthy conversations'. The attorney suggests that the defendant came to 'sit with you' *and not other people*. And the attorney describes the location as a 'bar . . . where girls and fellas meet'. In contrast, the witness suggests that the defendant talked to a group of people, *not her*; that he sat 'at our table', and *not with her*, and that the location is a 'club . . . where people go'.

The outcome of most rape cases – which involve acquainted parties, not strangers – will turn on the power of words to establish the facts of the matter. Forensic evidence can establish that sex took place. Words are the only resource to establish matters of intent and consent. The outcome of the trial in Example 9 depends on who the judge and jury believe.

Before we conclude this section, consider a final idiom about talk and words. The title of the chapter is 'Sticks, stones, and . . . talk' – adapted from the idiomatic phrase 'sticks and stones may break my bones but words will never hurt me'. The *Oxford English Dictionary* traces the use of this phrase to 1862, and describes its meaning 'to express or encourage an attitude of indifference to taunts, insults, or other verbal abuse'.

But, of course, words hurt. In *Harry Potter and the Deathly Hallows,* the author J.K. Rowling writes that 'Words are, in my not-so-humble opinion, our most inexhaustible source of magic. Capable of both inflicting injury, and remedying it.'[52]

Not only do words hurt, they can get you arrested. In the UK, under various iterations of the Public Order Act, it is an offence to use threatening, abusive or insulting words or behaviour within the hearing of someone likely to be caused harassment, alarm or distress by them. The offence is committed only if the words have that effect. Since 1986, iterations of the law have paid particular attention to language that is racist, or prejudiced on the grounds of religion and belief systems, or hateful about sexuality and gender.

What the law looks like in the real setting of a police interview is rather interesting. In the extracts below, police officers are putting witness testimony to suspects.

Example 10: Police interview (simplified transcript)

01	Police:	Carol then says that you said to her, 'Fuck off you
02		fucking white whore.'
03	Suspect:	No I didn't say anything racist.

---

52 *Harry Potter and the Deathly Hallows*: Copyright © J.K. Rowling 2007.

Example 11: Police interview (simplified transcript)

01   Police: You said <u>to</u> the lady 'why don't you go <u>b</u>ack to your own

02   country you bitch: Somali.'

03   Suspect: I never said <u>one</u> racist word.

In both examples, the suspects attend to the precise words they are accused of saying. They do not deny saying some of the words but do deny saying *all* of them. That is, the suspects deny saying 'white' and 'Somali' but do not deny saying 'fucking', 'bitch' or 'whore'. This is because 'white' and 'Somali' are the words that escalate the suspects' words as evidence of a 'racially aggravated' chargeable offence. The fact that words are powerful and do things is embedded in law. Although the Public Order Act separates out 'words and behaviour', they have equivalent status in terms of the harm they can do.

Actions do not speak louder than words. Words *are* actions. No talk is 'small'; talk does big things. In Chapter 5, we will see how words matter to people even as they produce them, and how words can change the outcome of encounters. But before that, the rest of this chapter will bust other common myths about talk.

Is communication 93 per cent body language?

If actions speak louder than words, then actions must be where the action is, when it comes to human communication. If actions speak louder than words, then it is what we do with our bodies – our faces, hands, gestures, eyes – that does most of the business of communicating. When I am giving lectures or delivering communication training, people often quote the 93 per cent statistic, about the proportion of communication that apparently happens via our bodies. The statistic varies. But the thrust of the comment remains the same.

Of course, we use our bodies all the time to talk to others. A great deal of conversation analysts' research focuses on people's embodied conduct working in aggregate with spoken talk. And we can get things done with just our bodies. Imagine you are chairing a meeting. The meeting room has a glass door. A colleague hovers outside the door trying to catch your eye. When they do catch your eye (and their body is the only resource they have to make that happen), they gesture at their watch. You gesture back, or nod, or smile. You do that discreetly or explicitly, depending on whatever else is happening inside the room.

The conversation between you and your colleague outside the door can happen in tandem with whatever other conversation is happening inside the meeting. The fact that we have multimodal resources for interacting with others means that we can carry on a conversation with words over dinner while acquiring the salt with our bodies. Imagine you are at home, talking on the telephone. Your partner uses their body – a nudge, with a gesture, or eye gaze – to get your attention to hurry you off the phone. Again, you can engage in two conversations at the same time, because of the multiple modalities we have as resources for interaction.

My father's namesake, William Stokoe, was, coincidentally, an academic and linguist. He researched American Sign Language and developed 'Stokoe notation'.[53] Sign language is a visual means of communicating using bodies – gestures, finger spelling and facial expressions – used mainly by people who are deaf or have hearing impairments. Researchers have found that people who are born blind use gestures as they talk. People do not stop gesticulating when talking on the phone. We also rely on our gaze and gestures to accomplish myriad daily actions, from getting other drivers to do things on the road to getting the bill in restaurants. We communicate silently with strangers on the street. I remember sharing a discreet, tiny, prolonged-just-enough moment of eye contact with another woman on the train while we were surrounded by a large group of drunken men passengers.

---

53 Stokoe (1960).

So, our bodies may speak as loudly as words. But there remain multiple senses in which we over-prioritise or think incorrectly about 'body language'. One problem is that if we think we already know something about communication – whether it is about body language, how women and men talk, or something else – we stop looking for more information. The incorrect assumptions solidify as facts.

In fact, the idea that communication is 93 per cent body language is very easy to upend. The sociologist and conversation analyst Maxwell Atkinson has written a great deal about this statistic and other communication myths. In *Lend Me Your Ears*, he complained that 'the most disturbing feature of claims like this is that they help to spread and consolidate the myth that non-verbal behaviour is so overwhelmingly dominant that the words we use to convey our messages are of little or no importance' (p. 343). Atkinson wrote that if the statistic were correct, then – quite simply – people across the planet would not need to learn any other languages. Their bodies would achieve 93 per cent of what they want to communicate. He notes[54] that those who support the 93 per cent statistic do not deal with obvious questions like, 'How come we can have perfectly good conversations in the dark? How come telephones and radio have been such spectacular successes?'

Much of Atkinson's own conversation analytic research focused on political speech-making. He points out that his early work used audio recordings. When technology moved on and he was able to collect video recordings, 'none of the audio-based findings had to be rejected or seriously revised, though the added visual dimension did help to extend our understanding and, in some cases, to explain apparently 'deviant' cases'. Irrespectively, conversation analysts and the Jefferson transcription system mop up a lot of what people typically class as 'non-verbal' features of talk anyway.

The 93 per cent statistic originates in a book about non-verbal com-munication by Albert Mehrabian.[55] However, Mehrabian's research is largely misquoted and misunderstood. Atkinson reproduces an email

---

54 http://maxatkinson.blogspot.de/2009/06/body-language-and-non-verbal.html
55 Mehrabian (1981).

exchange with Mehrabian on his blog, in which Mehrabian expresses his discomfort with the widespread misinterpretation of the original study. But the statistic is compelling, and quite hard to knock over – even when there is a 'Stop the Mehrabian Myth' campaign online![56] The founder of the campaign, Olivia Mitchell, argues that

> The main group of people who have propagated the Mehrabian myth are presentation trainers, public speaking coaches and other communications consultants. As a presentation trainer, I'm embarrassed that these figures are still being trotted out on a regular basis, when there is no substance to their real-world application. It's damaging to the credibility of the training industry.

A second myth about body language is that it is truer or more honest than our words. We say one thing, but our body language 'leaks' the opposite. Our words say 'yes', but our body says 'no'. Such observations are too simple. Recall the opening section of Chapter 2, in which we examined a series of brief, two-second silences. When a woman asked her lover, 'Do you think of me when we are not together?', he answered 'yes', but only after a two-second delay. The pace of interaction made the woman question her lover's answer. He did not shake his head to indicate 'no', while saying 'yes'.

In fact, we constantly monitor the words *and* the embodied conduct of the people we communicate with. We wonder, 'What did they really mean?' following a phone conversation. We ask, 'What did you mean by that remark?' during a face-to-face encounter. We speculate all the time about the conversations we have – in all their rich multimodality.

A related assumption is that gesture, body position, eye gaze and so on have clear and consistent meanings – the same gesture means the same thing. Atkinson writes about what 'arms folded' communicates. In his role as a communication trainer, he advises

---

56   https://speakingaboutpresenting.com/presentation-myths/mehrabian-nonverbal-communication-research

people not to fold their arms when speaking. This is not because he believes that 'folded arms' is a way of communicating defensiveness. Rather, it is 'because I know that there's a high probability that there will be someone in the audience who believes it is' (p. 341).

Depending on your source of evidence, body language signs can mean almost anything. Touching your neck can mean flirting or lying. But there is a more fundamental error here. Pursuing what people really mean behind their words or gestures misses something crucial about language. Think again about flirting. Whether we are using our words or bodies, or both, flirting is *designed to be ambiguous*. It is designed to be easily interpreted as something *other* than flirting. Then, if your recipient does not reciprocate, you are 'just being friendly'. If your partner catches you apparently flirting with someone else, again you are 'just being friendly'. Language – in all its forms – is not just for being clear. We do things all the time that are implicit, subtle, discreet, designed not to be seen or heard, and to be deniable.

The idea that a bodily gesture, like folded arms or touching your neck, carries a constant meaning is compelling. This very simplicity is one reason why communication myths proliferate. Research findings about communication are simplified and diluted at the same time as they become definitive. Complexity does not lend itself to sound-bites. The way to discover what people are doing when they fold their arms is to . . . study people in real settings, doing real things, including, perhaps, folding their arms.

Do women and men talk differently?

When I give lectures about talk, one of the most frequent questions from audiences is, 'Do men and women talk differently?' Indeed, it is often not asked, simply asserted – 'but, of course, men and women talk differently'. People who raise this topic generally assume I will confirm what they think they already know.

We think we already know that women and men talk differently for many reasons. We know it from the thousands of 'pop' psychology and communication books, from *Men Are from Mars, Women Are from Venus* to *He's Just Not That into You*. There are thousands of scientific articles that report sex differences in behaviour of all kinds. We think we know about gender difference because research that does *not* show difference is often not published. Indeed, using gender as a research category is often not interrogated at all. That women and men talk differently has long since passed beyond the realm of academic enquiry and is just *what we know*.

Researchers have addressed questions about gender and language for several decades. In the 1970s, the linguist Robin Lakoff identified a so-called 'women's register'. It is through language, Lakoff argued, that women's inferior place in society is maintained. Women's talk is more polite than men's; women use more tag questions (e.g., 'isn't it?'), use weaker directives, avoid swearing, and use more empty adjectives (e.g., 'cute') than men.

Lots of research followed Lakoff's original ideas, testing out gender differences in who talks most, who interrupts more, who uses more 'minimal responses' (e.g., 'mm', 'yeah'), and who controls the topic of a conversation. But many apparent findings about gender difference are built on shaky foundations.

For example, the idea that men grab power by interrupting women (more than women interrupt men) is based on a mistaken understanding of interruption. Consider Example 12 (and contrast it with Example 11 in Chapter 2, when Ross interrupts Monica). The square brackets on lines 02 and 03 indicate when the speakers talk at the same time.

Example 12: From Beattie (1983)

```
01    A:      ... so he (.) he gives the impression that he

02            wasn't able to train them up.  [Now

03    B:                                     [He didn't try hard

04            enough heh heh heh
```

The original analyst of this example claimed that 'Speaker B clearly interrupts Speaker A'. Another analyst, Celia Kitzinger, points out that, in fact, Speaker B starts talking at the precise point when Speaker A reaches the end of their sentence – in technical terms, the end of a 'turn constructional unit'. Speakers frequently – and unproblematically – start to speak at the end of another speaker's sentence. B does not interrupt A.

In Example 13, Tony and Marsha are talking about their son's vandalised car. Kitzinger points out that Tony – a man – starts his turn before Marsha – a woman – completes hers.

Example 13: Tony and Marsha[57]

01	Tony:	That really makes me mad.
02		(0.2)
03	Marsha:	.hhh Oh it's disgusti[ng as a matter of] fact.
04	Tony:	[P o o r J o e y.]

Some researchers would use these three lines of talk as clear-cut evidence of men's dominance over women. However, a closer look reveals that when Marsha describes the vandalism as 'disgusting', her turn has already delivered something that could be complete. Adding 'as a matter of fact' is not necessary. So Tony is not interrupting when he says, in overlap, 'Poor Joey'. The parents talk in tandem to share the same feelings about what has happened to their son.

A little later in the same call, Tony and Marsha are discussing a problem for their son, who is travelling on a standby flight from Marsha's home back to Tony's. On lines 05 and 06, both speakers talk at the same time.

57 Kitzinger (2008).

Example 14: Tony and Marsha

01	Marsha:	What time did he get on the plane.
02	Tony:	Uh::: (0.2) I: don't know exactly I think it was
03		arou:nd three o'clock uh something of that sort.
04		(0.2)
05	Marsha:	Oh: maybe he g[ot s'm-
06	Tony:	[He took it at four. Gerda says.

This time, Tony starts talking at a point in Marsha's turn where she is clearly not finished – she has not completed her turn in terms of its grammar, intonation (there is no full stop) or action (she has not finished her speculation about her son's circumstances). Tony interrupts Marsha. But, as Kitzinger points out, Tony's interruption is cooperative.

> In response to Marsha's enquiry about when their son boarded a plane, Tony reports not being sure and then gives an approximate answer ('around three o'clock or something of that sort'). At line 05 Marsha is apparently using this report as the basis for some speculation about what may have happened and it is this speculation, based on his (as it turns out erroneous) report, that Tony interrupts. Tony's new partner, Gerda, who has overheard his report of Joey's departure time, has apparently corrected him and he is relaying this correction ('four o'clock') to Marsha before she can develop a theory about Joey's flight based on incorrect information. The interruption is here used to implement a correction that has consequences for the turn Marsha is in the course of producing, and it is thus clearly a cooperative action, and from Marsha's point of view, a helpful interruption.

All of this shows us that simply counting instances of overlapping talk says very little about interruption.

Other claims about gender differences in talk have also later been revealed to be flawed. A common assertion is that women talk more than men. The words that characterise the way women talk perpetuate this myth – women chatter, gossip, prattle, natter – about trivial matters. At the same time, feminist researchers have claimed to find that men talk more than women, hogging the floor in public and workplace settings.[58] Yet more scientists have found that no gender difference exists in who talks more. [59]

Throughout this book, there are hundreds of examples of men, women, salespersons, mediators, police officers, clients, customers . . . using tag questions (e.g., 'don't you'), 'minimal responses' (e.g., 'mm', 'yeah'), initiating topics, and overlapping each other. If we categorise all of our examples in terms of gender alone, we will make erroneous claims about women and men at the same time as we miss what is going on in each case. We will stop looking for other explanations for the way people talk.

Consider two examples from the start of a telephone call to a double-glazing company (Example 15) and the vet's (Example 16).

Example 15: Calling double-glazing sales

```
01    Sales:      G'd afternoon, Fine Bar Wi:ndows,

02                        (0.6)

03    Customer:   .shih (.) .hh >hi< w'd it be po:ssible f'somebody

04                t'come an' give me a quote on uh: a window an:

05                some doors please.
```

58 Karpowitz and Mendelberg (2014).

59 Mehl et al. (2007).

Example 16: Calling the vet

01	Vet:	Dunnetts Vets.=Highuptown, Maggie speaking, how
02		can I ↑he:lp.
03		(0.4)
04	Pet owner:	Hello there:.=um: I need t'make an appointment
05		t'bring the cat in t'get its um: updated ↓vaccina:tions.

In both cases, the callers are making a request. They design their requests differently. For some gender difference researchers, the customer calling about windows uses stereotypically female language, with hedges and modal verbs ('Would it be possible'), hesitations ('.shih (.) .hh'), and in a polite manner ('please'). The pet owner is stereotypically male, with a direct request ('I need . . .') which is less polite.

The caller in Example 15 is a man; in Example 16 a woman. Perhaps these are just atypical cases – obviously not *all* men and women speak like their stereotype! But if we start and stop with gender as the only lens through which to interpret the data, we identify only exceptions that prove the rule.

Instead, conversation analysts start with action – what are the speakers doing? Are they entitled to do it? Do they know about the service and what it provides? What is at stake? People begin requests with 'I need' when, say, calling for an ambulance, or a doctor, or for something relatively important and urgent – like vaccinations. People also say 'I need' when they know what the service offers, and that they are entitled to use it. However, when people are less familiar with the service and what it offers, or they are less entitled to ask for it, or if their problem is not urgent, they often ask 'would it be possible'.[60] These kinds of contingencies better explain the differences in the way people talk.

---

60 Curl and Drew (2008).

Plenty of myth-busting science about gender difference exists.[61] Yet our ideas about differences between women and men persist. Gender difference studies start with the assumption that all women and all men can be classified, even with caveats, into two homogeneous groups. Often, then, researchers do not really study gender difference. They simply create and maintain it. They make selective observations to confirm what we already know about how women and men behave.

As a PhD student in the early 1990s, I struggled with all these ideas. I wanted to say something about gender and language. But I didn't want to make assumptions about what I would find when I analysed interaction. I didn't want to reproduce stereotypes. At the same time, I felt that gender imbalance and stereotypes *were* all around me. How could I capture them? The conversation analyst Curtis LeBaron[62] had the answer.

> we should not . . . say 'oh, look, here's a man and a woman talking; . . . oh, we can make these conclusions about gendered communication'. But rather we should say, 'gender only becomes an issue when the participants themselves make it one and we can point to different things about that'.

And, it turns out, people invoke gender a lot. Gender matters to people. Making it relevant does things. Here is just one example, from the PhD I eventually wrote. My research was on gender and conversation in university tutorials. My initial interest was in whether or not male students dominated the floor, leaving female students less verbal space to participate.

My data were thirty hours of tutorials. I quickly realised that coding and counting and correlating with gender would tell me little about what was going on in the encounters. I was also increasingly unhappy with the *Men Are from Mars . . .* view of gender. So I

---

61 Fine (2011); Saini (2017).

62 LeBaron (1998), quoted in Tracy (1998).

asked LeBaron's[63] question: how does gender become an issue for participants themselves?

In Example 17, four psychology students are analysing an image in a magazine. They have been instructed to produce a collaborative written report about the materials they are discussing. Bob reminds them of this task.

Example 17: University tutorial

01   Bob: Is somebody scribing. who's writin' it.=

02   Ned: =Oh yhe:ah.

03   (0.8)

04   Matt: Well you can't [read my   ] writin' once I've

05   Ned: [She wants to do it.]

06   Matt: [wri:tten it.]

07   Klara: [.hehhhh   ]

08   Ned: We:ll secretary an' female.

Ned points at
Klara at line 05

---

63 With the help of Professor Derek Edwards, who was my PhD co-supervisor, and who introduced me to using conversation analysis in this way.

As the person asking the question 'Is somebody scribing. who's writin' it' – taking the 'first pair part' – Bob relieves himself of the obligation of answering the question and becoming the scribe. Ned is first to respond, saying, 'Oh yhe:ah.'. He remembers that they must do this, but does not volunteer. After a gap, Matt provides a reason why he cannot be the scribe (his writing is indecipherable). At the same time, Ned nominates Klara. He says, 'She wants to do it.' as he points to her. Ned's words and embodied conduct are fitted together.

Klara has also not volunteered to scribe. Her small laughter particle ('.hehhhh') could be responding to Matt's comment about his own handwriting, or Ned's suggestion that she wants to scribe. Ned then provides an account for his nomination of Klara: 'We:ll secretary an' female.'. At this point, gender becomes relevant to the encounter. It is invoked by Ned to do something. The stereotype that women are secretaries is used at a particular point to make something happen. And Klara becomes the secretary. Her participation in the discussion is reduced to note taker.

You might agree that this is a powerful moment in which gender and language come together. You might also think that this is a one-off. So what? It is much easier to divide the world into two genders from the start and count the things people do. How do we capture sufficient numbers of moments like this to say something meaningful and generalisable?

There are several answers to this question. First, Example 17 is a demonstration of a method of investigating gender and language – one that does not start with any assumptions about women and men. We can capture moments of gender relevance without using gender as a scientists' category, at all. We can investigate gender as a speaker's category.

Second, conversation analysis is neither a quantitative nor a qualitative method. It is sometimes both. One conversation is not a useful unit of analysis. One conversation contains many questions, many answers, many overlaps, many pauses, many 'ums' and 'uhs'. An apparently single conversation delivers lots of instances of particular phenomena. In the conversation analyst

Emanuel Schegloff's words, 'one is also a number, the single case is also a quantity, and statistical significance is but one form of significance'. Claims about gender and interruption may be based on large datasets, but if there is a basic error in identifying interruption in the first place, Schegloff is correct to point out that 'quantification is no substitute for analysis'.

Third, conversation analysis is a form of logical analysis. An example from linguistics makes the point:[64] the sentence 'Peter forwarded the letter to his aunt Mary' is grammatical (if you don't agree with me, you don't understand what 'grammatical' means, or you don't speak English), and its grammar can be sensibly analysed. On the other hand, 'To aunt the forwarded Peter letter Mary his' contains the same words but is not grammatical, and has no structure. It is not a matter of counting *how many times* people say these things, or asking how many people agree about their grammaticality. It's a matter of knowing how to speak English, and you can make definitive analyses of these things from just one example.

What makes a turn in conversation *analysable* is that it is recognisable and understandable by people, including analysts, who are members of a culture and a linguistic community that talk in those ways. We don't need huge samples and probabilistic statistics to do an analysis, even though we do need collections of instances of a phenomenon to analyse and figure out how they work. But even then, the analysis of each and every 'instance' is done on the same basis, including recognising something *as* an instance, which is the tacit ability that people have, and that anthropologists need, to understand the uses of their own natural language, or one in which they have acquired some competence.

Fourth, when people ask me a 'how many' question, I respond with an illustration to challenge the presuppositions built into it. I ask how many black holes (or big bangs) does a physicist need to say something meaningful about the science of black holes? Most people laugh, and then say 'one'. I recently asked a physicist this question.

---

64 I am grateful to Derek Edwards for providing this illustration.

He looked thoughtful for a moment, and then replied 'five'. So how many negotiations with persons in crisis do we need to study before saying something meaningful about effective practice? How many times would you need to see that asking people to talk does not get people to talk? I do have more than one example. And it is helpful to show that asking people to talk does not work in other settings too. But the logic and explanation remain the same.

Fifth, quite simply, it would be strange to discount an analysis of a conversation because there is only one instance. Sometimes there may only be one instance to study. If you are at a party, and a guest collapses, hopefully you or someone else will call for an ambulance. If the ambulance takes a long time to arrive, and the guest dies, the telephone call will be a source of evidence in any subsequent investigation. Compared to the numbers of patients calling their GP receptionist, there are very few police negotiations with suicidal persons in crisis. But it is important to know how they work.

Finally, I have spent a good chunk of my career showing that, actually, one can identify and analyse moments like 'Well secretary an' female' systematically. With large datasets of lots of interaction, it turns out that people often invoke gender (or other categories such as age or ethnicity) in the same kinds of settings, in the same kinds of turns, doing the same kinds of actions. We just need to study real talk – the answers are often right in front of us.

Do different 'cultures' talk differently?

Much of what is true for gendered assumptions about talk is equally true for presumed cultural difference. And, as with gender stereotypes, the basis for asking if 'different cultures talk differently' is that all members of a culture are the same (like women), and that all members of one culture (like men) differ from all members of another culture, in the same way. I imagine that you know lots of very different men and women. You might also be thinking about what the throwaway word 'culture' actually means.

When people ask about cultures talking differently, they often follow up their question with anecdotes about how the French talk, or how the Japanese interact, or what Americans are like. Like gender, it is easy to think of people who fit and do not fit stereotypes. The problem is that, as we saw in the previous section, many of our stereotypes are simply wrong. They are groundless and compelling, at the same time.

One way of addressing the gender and the culture question is to think again about action. Think about the actions that people want to get done, in all human cultures (and some animal ones, too!). People request, offer, question, answer, invite, complain, greet, compliment, challenge, assess, apologise . . . and so on. We have myriad resources for doing any of these actions. We can make requests with words, gestures, sign language. We make them differently depending on our entitlement to ask, who we are asking, and what is at stake. If we speak English, we have English words at our disposal. If we speak German, then the building blocks of action are different. Sometimes there are equivalent words in many languages; sometimes there are not. First and foremost, however, people do *actions* with talk. The actions are pretty universal.

In recent years, these analysts have begun to provide evidence for conversational universals. For example, when testing anthropological claims that there are big cultural differences in the timing and pace of turn-taking, they found that, in fact, there are remarkable similarities across the numerous languages tested. Across indigenous and major world languages, the researchers found 'clear evidence for a general avoidance of overlapping talk and a minimization of silence between conversational turns'.[65]

Evidence that features of talk are universal is emerging all the time. The linguist Mark Dingemanse has shown that speakers around the world use a word like 'huh?' to indicate that they have not heard or understood what the previous speaker said.[66] Dingemanse makes the point that 'huh' is not universal because it is innate. Rather, it is

---

65   Stivers et al. (2009).

66   Dingemanse et al. (2013).

universal because it accomplishes another universal feature of talk called 'repair'.

Our communication system has built-in mechanisms for detecting and correcting problems of speaking, hearing and understanding. Sometimes, we repair our own errors (see Chapter 5, 'Every word matters'). For instance, the person talking below is a Member of the European Parliament. He is discussing gender discrimination in the workplace on a radio programme.

Example 18: BBC Radio 4 *Woman's Hour*, 12 November 2007 (simplified transcript)

```
01   MEP:     I think it's terrible that young ladies are- or young

02             women are discriminated against in this way.
```

The MEP switches the way he refers to the group in question, halfway through his turn. He swaps the word 'ladies' for the word 'women'. Even though 'ladies' is adequate – it makes sense, and its replacement is a synonym – it is, nevertheless, replaced. This is another way that gender gets made relevant to conversation.

Speakers also get each other do repairs; 'huh?' is a common method to do so.

Example 19: From Kendrick (2015)

```
01   Wil:     Got football later.

02             (0.7)

03   Jam:     .fhh Yeah. ((looks down at watch))

04             (0.8)

05   Max:     Are [you playing?
```

06　Wil:　　　　　[Better go soo(h)n actually.

07　Jam:　　Huh?

08　Max:　　Are you playing footy?

09　Jam:　　Y:eah I think so.

When Max asks Jam if he is 'playing', Jam apparently does not hear or understand Max (who speaks at the same time as Wil announces his intention to leave). At line 07, Jam says 'Huh?' Max asks Jam again, but not with exactly the same question (which would treat Jam's problem as one of hearing). He adds the word 'footy' (which includes the possibility that Jam has not completely understood the question).

Dingemanse and his colleagues show that 'huh?' is used frequently (on average, once per 1.4 minutes) in the numerous languages (and language families) they studied. So, in contrast to what people often assume about cultural difference, he finds a universal system for resolving, in real time, 'breakdowns' in conversation. These 'breakdowns' are so frequent as to be entirely normal. They are not errors, or actual communication breakdowns. And what this shows is that talk has a common infrastructure; a 'universal bedrock upon which linguistic diversity rests'.[67]

When we start to examine what people do with talk, we reveal the mechanics of social interaction. At this point, the differences we assume must be there fall away. This does not mean that there are no differences. We have different linguistic and multimodal resources for communicating. It is the context, the contingencies, our obligations, and our entitlements, that make the difference.

Are 'ums' errors?

By now, you have read many transcripts of real talk. This book shows how systematic and organised talk really is. But it looks messy. It is

---

67　Dingemanse et al. (2015).

full of complexity and detail. It is full of hesitations, pauses, restarts and corrections. Many of these little linguistic features of real talk, like 'I mean', 'you know', 'uh', and 'um', are treated by some scholars as 'filler words'. Their use is correlated with the 'obvious' variables (e.g., gender, age) – but without considering their context of use. 'Filler words' are sometimes regarded as markers of personality.[68] Or they are thought to indicate a speech production problem, or a cognitive processing problem.[69] They are treated by professional communicators as superfluous, as disfluencies, and as errors produced by careless speakers.

When conversation analysts study small words like 'um' and 'uh', we transcribe them carefully and we examine where and how they are placed in turns they occupy. Let us look again at Gordon and Dana's telephone call, from Chapter 1. We compared the start of their call to others in which the greetings, identification and 'how-are-yous' happened rapidly, and reciprocally. These things did not happen in Gordon and Dana's call. We know there is trouble ahead from the silence at line 03. But this time, focus particularly on line 05.

Example 20: Gordon and Dana

01   ((ring))

02 Gordon: Hello:,

03   (0.7)

04 Dana: Hello where've you been all morning.

05 Gordon: .hh HELLO! Uhm (0.6) .pt I've been at a music workshop

In Chapter 1, we noted the details that a conversation analyst's transcript can reveal, including Gordon's 'Uhm'. This 'uhm' is not an

---

68 Laserna et al. (2014).

69 Fox Tree (2007).

error. It is not an instance of superfluous disfluency, or carelessness. One place that 'uh' and 'uhm' frequently occur is when speakers are confronted with an inapposite or unexpected prior turn – which Dana's is. And this analysis is supported by the fact that what Gordon did first *was* what Dana could expect – a 'hello' of recognition. So Gordon's 'Uhm' is a kind of symptom or reflection of Dana's prior turn. It also signals to Dana that Gordon is treating her turn as problematic.

Here is another example in which 'uh' has the same function. It comes from the call that we encountered earlier in this chapter, Example 15, in which a potential customer calls a double-glazing company. He has asked the salesperson if it is possible to get a quote for new windows. The salesperson asks if he wants to both buy windows and have the company install them.

Example 21: Calling double-glazing sales

01	Sales:	Is it t- t'obviously sup<u>ply</u> and install the windows.
02	Caller:	<u>Ye</u>h supply an' install yeh.h
03	Sales:	O:kay, and ↑how did you hear about Fine ↑Bɑ:r?
04		(1.9)
05	Caller:	<u>Uh</u>: I've just- looked it up on the internet.

At this point in the conversation, the salesperson has not asked anything about what kind of windows the caller wants, how many, or for what kind of property. So there are many aspects of any future sales transaction that, from the caller's point of view, have not been discussed at all.

At line 03, the salesperson asks the caller how he heard about the company. We might think that it is too early in the call to ask this. We might also think that it would be better to ask at the end of the call, once the customer's business has been completed. And we might think it would be better to ask, 'Just before you go, would you be able to tell me where you heard about Fine Bar Windows?' The salesperson is not particularly entitled to ask customers for this information; nor are customers obliged to supply it. The salesperson's question not only comes too soon, it is also overly entitled in its design. It is a stereotypically 'male' question, according to the stereotype, uttered by a woman . . .

At line 04, there is a long gap of almost two seconds. As we saw in Chapter 2, these silences are not 'doing nothing'. They are not leaving time for cognitive processing, even if some kind of cognitive processing is going on. Such delays predict something about the speaker's upcoming responses. Just like Gordon does not expect a question about his whereabouts in place of the 'how-are-yous', the caller does not expect a survey question about the company when he has not said anything about the windows he needs. Again, like Gordon, he answers the question, but not until after a delay and an 'Uh:'.

Like 'how-are-yous', 'uhs', 'ums' and other so-called 'filler' words are not pointless. They tell us a lot about how speakers – turn by turn – analyse each other's turns and make those analyses hearable to the other person in the interaction, just as they also monitor their own talk as they produce it. To treat 'uhs' and 'ums' as signs of bad speakership – especially without examining them in real talk – keeps this particular myth alive.

Example 22 comes from a radio interview between the British businessman and pro-Brexit politician, Jonathan Marland, and the interviewer, Nick Robinson, on the BBC's morning radio news programme, *Today*.[70] Robinson has been pushing Marland to be precise about new trading relationships between Britain and the EU, when (and if) Brexit happens. The commentator David Schneider[71] tweeted a transcript of their encounter.

---

70 www.bbc.co.uk/programmes/b09k0ng1

71 https://twitter.com/davidschneider/status/948481912724709376

Example 22: Political interview

Classic Brexit just now on #r4Today:

'Which trade rules would you like to see changed?'

Lord Marland, a Brexiter: 'How long have you got?'

'OK. Give me just one rule.'

Lord M: [hesitates] 'Er . . . well . . . that's too simplistic.'

Schneider's transcript includes the information that Marland 'hesitates' and also says 'Er', with ellipses representing further hesitations. While Schneider's transcript is not 'wrong', it provides an opportunity to contrast a layperson's transcript with one produced by a conversation analyst. Here is my transcript of the same sequence.

Example 23: Political interview (retranscribed)

01 Lord Marland: [an' as you-   ↑well-   ]

02 Nick Robinson: [C'n you give (some) examples of] things you'd like to

03   see the <u>ba</u>:ck of.=in order t'do more trade.

04   (0.3)

05 Lord Marland: .hhh £W(h)e(h)ll(h)£ I (h)mean- how long have you

06   go̲:t. hhh uh heh heh heh [I don't ( ) uh heh heh .hhh]

07 Nick Robinson: [£W'll ↑one'll do. T'start£]

08   with.

09 Lord Marland: One.=W'll, .hhh (.) uh- u- uh- u- m- it- it's- it's- it's-

10   <u>too</u> (.) that's <u>too</u>: uh- simplistic a- u- >if y'don't me

11   saying so.<

In fact, there is no hesitation at line 08 before Marland starts to speak. There are many details missing in the tweeted transcript. Note its basic inaccuracy too, in terms of just the words that were said ('see the back of', 'Well, I mean' etc.). This is surprisingly common in typists' transcripts, even those of experienced, paid transcribers employed on research projects, when they are not producing technical transcripts. Much of the detail of talk, including the actual words said, is vulnerable to loss, omission and alteration. But notice, in particular, all the apparent 'errors' and 'disfluencies' in Marland's talk. These are much easier to understand as indicating trouble in answering Robinson's question, than indicating that Marland is a careless speaker. Quite the opposite is true!

Why are there so many myths about talk?

We think that 'ums' are errors for the same reason that we assert other unfounded facts about talk. It is because, in general, psychologists and communication scholars do not study talk. The research base for popular science books about communication does not, quite simply, include studies of live, unfolding, often mundane, talk. Instead, to find out about talk, we run experiments about it, ask people to report on it, or simulate it. (It's often an analysis of written text rather than talk, and even then, of invented sentences and texts rather than examples recorded from everyday life.)

Plenty of commentators have noticed this gap in our knowledge. For example, over a decade ago, the American psychologist Roy Baumeister[72] wrote in a high-ranking journal, *Perspectives on Psychological Science*, that while psychology calls itself the 'science of behaviour', much of psychology never studies behaviour directly. Instead, psychologists rely on questionnaires and other proxies for studying actual social life. For Baumeister, 'psychology pays remarkably little attention to the important things that people do'.

---

72 Baumeister et al. (2007).

Ten years later, another psychologist working in America, Matthias Mehl,[73] made the following assessment of psychology.

> Laypersons often think of psychologists as professional people watchers. It is ironic, then, that naturalistic observation, as a methodology, has a remarkably thin history in our field. In contrast to ethologists (and researchers working with infants), psychologists are in the privileged position to be able to obtain valuable data by simply questioning their subjects. At the same time, there are clear limitations to what self-reports can assess . . . the psychological scientist's tool kit also needs a method to directly observe human behavior in daily life . . . naturalistic observation can bring behavioral data collection to where moment-to-moment behavior naturally happens.

It is probably evidence of the lack of interdisciplinarity in academia – despite all sorts of interventions and efforts – that Baumeister's and Mehl's evaluations of psychology remain correct. It is also because psychologists lack imagination when they conceive their research. And I speak as a psychologist. Yet conversation analysis (rooted in sociology, not psychology) has been producing knowledge about what people do for over half a century. Some of this research is among the most cited in academia, including 'hard science' disciplines. A lot of people need to start talking!

The idiomatic split between talk and action is false. Our spoken words and our bodies work together to do things. Talk is not cheap. Talk walks the walk. Sticks, stones and words hurt. Words are deeds. Talk is not small. Talk is not 'just talking'.

Words are actions. Let's look at some more of them.

---

73 Mehl (2017).

5

EVERY WORD MATTERS

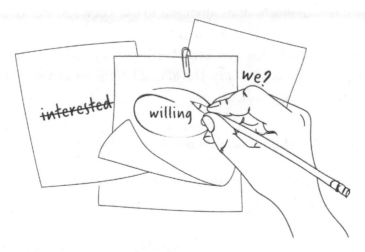

Words matter. People care about the words they use when they communicate. Evidence for the fact that words matter to speakers can be found everywhere. Indeed, people often draw attention to the selection of the words they utter, even as they utter them.

Towards the end of Chapter 4, we encountered the following conversation. The person speaking is a Member of the European Parliament. He is discussing gender discrimination in the workplace on a radio programme.

Example 1: BBC Radio 4 *Woman's Hour*, 12 November 2007 (simplified transcript)

01   MEP: I think it's terrible that young ladies are- or young

02   women are discriminated against in this way.

As we observed previously, the MEP changes the way he refers to the people he is talking about, halfway through his turn. He notices his own use of the word 'ladies'; halts abruptly mid-sentence, and swaps 'ladies' for 'women'. Even though 'ladies' makes sense, and its replacement is almost a synonym, it is, nevertheless, replaced. We will think about when, how and why people make these kinds of replacements in the first part of this chapter.

Our choice of words can also find its way into our idioms. In turn, we use idioms to draw attention to our choice of words. Mary and her husband, David, are in a dispute with their apparently noisy neighbour, Jennifer. They are complaining to a mediator, whose job it is to get – eventually – Mary, David and Jennifer into mediation, to try and resolve the conflict.

Example 2: Neighbour dispute mediation

01   Mary: On <u>three</u> occasions we've had to come in from the gar:den

02   because: (0.4) how shall we s- <u>we</u>:ll. there's no delicate way

03   of say- (0.3) um the young lady's love n- <u>love</u>making next

04   door with all the <u>wi:n</u>dows <u>op</u>en.

Mary's complaint about hearing Jennifer having sex is full of moral judgement. But our interest is in the difficulty she shows in reporting this particularly problematic noise. Between the word 'because' and 'lovemaking' are pauses, hesitations, and restarts – all drawing attention to finding, and saying, the word 'lovemaking'.

Mary deploys an idiom about words – 'there's no delicate way of saying this'. She also refers to Jennifer as a 'young lady', rather than using a more derogatory word (several are readily available!). Together, her way of describing this episode suggests Mary is someone of high virtue who has trouble saying words like 'sex', can just about say 'lovemaking', and would certainly not disrespect her neighbours by allowing coital noise to float out of an open window. Jennifer, on the other hand, *is* that sort of person. Immoral Jennifer, then, is the one at fault, and the cause of the conflict.

Words also have the power to change the outcome of encounters. People often assume that their actions and behaviour are determined by their personalities, their gender, their status, their nationality . . . the go-to variables for psychologists and social scientists. But we are pushed and pulled around by language far more than we realise. This chapter will show you how.

Every conversation we have provides the basis for a natural laboratory experiment. Something happens after every turn we take – one way or another. We can say one thing and it can be misunderstood or get no response. We say another and it makes sense or gets an answer. In Chapter 1, we saw how different starts to a conversation between a person in crisis and a police negotiator altered the trajectory of the negotiation. The friendlier, caring phrases did not work to get the person in crisis talking. Shorter and more direct questioning did.

In the second part of this chapter, we dig further into the difference that language makes to the upshot of encounters. We will see that changing *one word* can make a difference. It is people's words that change outcomes – their tacit experience and expertise. But speakers are not generally aware of their word selections. People cannot report later the words they used that made the difference. We need to locate our investigations in the natural laboratory of real, recorded, conversation.

Word selection matters

When we talk, we make mistakes. Correcting wrong words makes sense.

Example 3: Carol's brother[74]

01   Larry: Hi. I'm Carol's sister- uh brother.

---

74 Jefferson (1996).

Larry is a man. This makes him Carol's brother, not Carol's sister. Conversation analysts have found that this kind of correction – in which the speaker corrects himself – is very common. Gail Jefferson[75] calls errors like Larry's categorial errors. Speakers select the wrong category from a collection which is strongly associated with the correct category that the speaker was presumably heading for. In Example 3, Larry says 'sister', stops himself, and then provides the solution to his error ('brother').

In cases like Larry's, if he did not correct himself it is likely that another speaker would expose his mistake. They would say something like, 'huh?', 'do you mean brother?', or just 'brother!' Here is Larry again.

Example 4: Larry and Norm[76] (simplified transcript)

01   Larry: They're going to drive back Wednesday.

02   Norm: Tomorrow.

03   Larry: Tomorrow. Righ[t.

04   Norm: [M-hm,

Larry's error is exposed and corrected by Norm, then accepted by Larry. Larry's talk about 'driving back on Wednesday' is temporarily suspended. Correcting is, for two turns, the business of the conversation.

People also swap words in and out of conversation, using an alternative pronunciation, say, or a near synonym. In Example 1, the MEP made the swap from 'ladies' to 'women' himself. In Example 5, Ken and Roger use *different* words to refer to the *same* group of people.

---

75 Jefferson (1996).

76 Jefferson (1987).

Example 5: Police–cops (Jefferson, 1987)

01   Ken: Well- if you're gonna <u>race</u>, the police have said this to us.

02   Roger: <u>That</u> makes it even <u>bet</u>ter. The <u>chal</u>lenge of running from

03   the <u>cops</u>!

04   Ken: The cops say if you wanna race, uh go out at four or five in

05   the morning on the freeway . . .

In his second turn, Ken adopts Roger's word, 'cops'. 'Cops' has replaced Ken's original word, 'police'. No one notices, overtly. Ken could resist Roger's alternative word by continuing to use his own word, 'police'. One could imagine Roger noticing *that* – it would be marked – even though Roger changed Ken's word in the first place! Perhaps Roger is a 'first mover' . . .

Ken could also use the pronoun, 'they'. Speakers use a pronoun regularly to replace the noun they first referred to. But Ken adopts Roger's word. We do not know why – maybe Roger is 'cool', and Ken wants to be 'cool'. The conversation just continues.

On any given occasion, there are indefinitely extendible ways to refer to a person. Each of the following references – 'this man', 'Roger', 'that bastard', 'my neighbour', 'Dr Smith' – may be correct. So it is immediately interesting to see which words people use when referring to someone.

One explanation for selecting between different words is what conversation analysts call 'recipient design'. So we use – and fix – reference terms so that our recipients understand our referents. Consider the following four examples.

a) 'I spoke to the girl – uh, I spoke to Jane . . . '

b) 'I spoke to Jane – uh, I spoke to the girl in the admin office . . . '

c) 'I spoke to the girl – uh, I spoke to the man . . . '

d) 'I spoke to the girl – uh, I spoke to the woman . . . '

Setting aside the politics of language choices, it is routine in both British and American English to use 'girl' to refer to adult 'women', although etymologically 'girl' implies youth.

In each example, the speaker swaps one word for another. However, each replacement is quite different. In (a), let's assume that 'the girl' is not a mistake – *both* are correct ways of referring. However, just saying 'the girl' might not make sense to whoever is listening. In (b), the speaker swaps their way of referring when realising their interlocutor will not recognise 'Jane'. The replacement gives some context – 'in the admin office' – to the description to help with recognition. In (c), let's assume that the speaker *has* made an error.

This leaves us with (d) – in which the speaker swaps 'girl' for 'woman'. Both are adequate. The swap does not fix an error. It does not help with recognition. It is doing something else. Like the MEP in Example 1, this swap from one word to another attends to a wide range of interactional contingencies. One of these is something like being a 'gender aware' speaker. Word selection matters. It says something about the kind of person the speaker is, not just the person being referred to.

The trouble with 'women'

In Chapter 4, we explored the problem with the idea (and the evidence) that men and women talk differently. Conversation analysts examine topics like 'gender' without starting with the idea that women and men speak differently. Instead, they might ask how people themselves – in their daily conversation – make this idea relevant. One way that people make gender relevant is through word choices.

People swap, fix and change the words they use for referring to people and things, in conversations of all kinds. The mechanics of these repairs – pausing, cutting off a word, recycling some parts and deleting others – is one of many systematic things about talk.

In Example 2, Mary, in a dispute with her neighbour, drew explicit attention to the fact that words matter. Example 6 is a recording from a dispute of another kind – the kind that leads to marriage guidance counselling. Connie and Jimmy have separated following Jimmy's affair with another woman. Jimmy has said his affair had nothing to do with their separation; Connie disagrees.

Example 6: Marriage guidance[77]

```
01   Jimmy:     I didn't leave Connie for another woman.

02                  (0.6)

03   Jimmy:     But- (0.6) I was liv- livin' away for: (1.0) about three- three

04              weeks, four weeks three weeks, whatever, when I moved

05              in: (.) with a wo- (0.2) girl. which I did have (1.2) a bit of

06              a fling with.
```

We should immediately put 'scare quotes' around the word 'affair', because Jimmy uses other words to describe things – 'a bit of a fling'. The advantages of saying 'a bit of a fling' over 'an affair' are pretty obvious – the latter is perhaps more serious and more threatening to a marriage. Similarly, 'living away for about three weeks' is less permanent and less serious than 'being separated'.

Jimmy denies leaving 'Connie for another woman'. Imagine if he had referred to this 'woman' by her name (e.g., 'Rose'). It would bring 'Rose' into the room in a rather immediate way that 'woman' does not. Avoiding referring to 'Rose' is probably a good idea in marriage guidance counselling, in the presence of his wife, with whom he wants to remain!

But notice Jimmy's tiny switch of words on line 05, from 'woman' to 'girl'. At line 01, he says 'woman'. But at line 05 he abandons the word 'woman', stopping in his tracks after the first syllable. He pauses, then swaps 'woman' for 'girl'. Why?

---

77 Edwards (1998).

We cannot answer this definitively. If that sounds like a cop-out, it is not. No one in the room asks why, either. As analysts, it is not our job to pin things down more explicitly or precisely than people themselves do. If we do, we are ignoring a fundamental feature of talk. We sometimes make great efforts to be clear, explicit and precise. People also make efforts to be vague and implicit. Or they are clear, or vague, by accident. It does not matter. The point is that language is a resource for speakers to imply and hearers to infer. If it was not, we would never need to ponder, 'I wonder what she meant by *that*?' And there would be no need for analysis, of any kind . . .

Jimmy swaps 'wo-' for 'girl' because, at the very least, they carry different meanings. They can have the same referent (that is, they can be used to denote the same person), but they are not the same word. 'Woman' is a 'default' way to refer to an 'adult female'; 'lady' connotes older age, status, and grace; 'girl' connotes female child, youth, unmarried, and so on.

This means that speakers can imply things about the person being referred to, depending upon their word selection. Category words and phrases, such as 'woman', 'lady', 'girl', or 'you know what men are like', package meaning. While people can say, 'no, I don't know what men are like', shortcuts mean speakers do not have to spell things out.

Jimmy's switch from 'woman' to 'girl' works in tandem with admitting he had 'a bit of a fling'. He did not have 'an affair' with 'a woman'. From Jimmy's point of view, 'girl' seems to fit better with his overall project of downplaying the seriousness of any extra-marital relationship he has had. For Jimmy, 'woman' is a more substantial category, which would upgrade the seriousness of his 'fling' just when he is trying to make things work with Connie.

You might be thinking that Jimmy's switch is a one-off instance. It is not. Once we begin to investigate the natural laboratory, we find similar kinds of repairs everywhere. And they do similar kinds of rhetorical work.

In the police interview below, the suspect has been arrested on suspicion of robbery. The police officer has pursued a line of questioning about the involvement of the suspect's partner in the crime. The suspect has denied her involvement, stating that she has never been in trouble. Indeed, he just wants a quiet, crime-free life with her.

Example 7: Police interview (simplified transcript)[78]

```
01   Suspect:    She's a fuckin' fantastic woman!

02                (0.2)

03   Suspect:    She's a woman.

04                (0.2)

05   Suspect:    A lady.

06                (0.2)

07   Suspect:    Not a- (0.2) some girl on the street.

08                (0.5)

09   Suspect:    What I'm sayin' is wha- yeah, .hh she

10               keeps me out of trouble.
```

The suspect takes five turns in quick succession. None of them are really necessary; they are not 'second pair parts'. So why does he go to all of this conversational effort?

Each turn specifies, intensifies, or builds cumulatively on the prior. And they all work together to produce a contrast with the idea that the suspect's partner is 'some girl on the street'. She is not the type to be involved in criminal activities.

---

78 Stokoe (2011a).

In the suspect's first turn, he makes an assessment of his partner. She is 'a fuckin' fantastic woman!' In the next, he uses intonation to emphasise and isolate the word 'woman'. This signals that the suspect's partner represents the *essence* of the category 'woman'.

In his third turn, the suspect produces another word to describe his partner – 'a lady'. This pins down the precise qualities of the category 'woman' that are, in his view, particularly relevant (e.g., she is refined, genteel, polite).

The suspect's consecutive turns combine to characterise his partner as someone – by virtue of being a woman and a lady – unlikely to be involved in criminal activity. Indeed, she is 'not a- (0.2) some girl on the street'. The details of this turn are important. The suspect starts by saying she is 'not a-'. What is she not? There are many possible derogatory words – 'hooker', 'tart', 'scrubber', 'slag'. Instead, he says that she is not 'some girl on the street'; that is, any girl; any anonymous girl, as distinct from this actual person, the actual woman in question.

At this point – or earlier in the book – you may be wondering whether these ordinary speakers can really be in control of every word, at this level of detail. Do people think this fast? Harvey Sacks suggested that we need not bother with questioning how people do it, how their brains do it, and so on (neuroscientists have answers to some of these questions), but rather, should just examine the detail of conversation and see that they *do* do it, regularly, meaningfully and systematically. Remember – in day-to-day conversation we can't whip out a psychometric test, or an MRI – those are not the resources we use to interact. We just use what the police officer and suspect use – words, built into turns.

By using different words with different emphasis – and by not producing a likely offensive word at all – the suspect presents his partner in the best possible light. His goal, of course, is to ensure that she is not arrested too. The tools he has to achieve this goal are . . . words.

Whether or not the suspect is making errors – and so making replacements and corrections in his interview with the police – is unclear. In our examples from marriage guidance counselling, and in the MEP's radio interview, it seems clearer that Jimmy and the MEP are keen to swap 'girl' for 'woman' and 'woman' for 'lady'. Because they are talking, Jimmy and the MEP cannot hide these replacements.

In online written communication, however, one can hide these kinds of errors before posting one's words to the world. But consider this sample of writing for a moment.

Example 8: www.anothermonkey.blogspot.com

'There's definitely a girlish quality about it, in the way that the Lifetime channel or a Lisa Loeb video have a girlish feel to them. Which is not surprising, given that Jen is, in fact, a girl. Woman. Sorry. Woman.'

The writer could have edited their text and used the word 'woman' to describe 'Jen' in the first place, before posting. So they are doing something *ironic* – exposing an error when it is not really an error. A gloss might be, 'Hey, I know the correct word to use; I am "politically correct"' – something like that. But the fact that the writer writes this at all is further evidence that people know words matter. Indeed, they are not just showing that they are the 'right' word to use, but are also displaying the very practice of replacing one word with the other.

For our final example, we return to a scripted scene from *Friends*. Ross and Phoebe are discussing recent events in which Ross, already twice-married and divorced, married Rachel while drunk in Las Vegas. Rachel wants to get the marriage annulled. Ross has told her that he has done so. However, he admits to Phoebe that he has *not* organised the annulment. Phoebe is astounded.

Example 9: *Friends*: 'The one where Ross hugs Rachel[79]' **(simplified transcript)**

01   Phoebe: So you're gonna be <u>married</u> to a <u>girl</u> who doesn't even

02   <u>know</u> about it?!

03   (0.2)

04   Phoebe: Oh. <u>Woman</u>! <u>Sorry</u>.

05   Audience: HEH HEH HEH HEH HEH hehh heh heh heh

Phoebe says girl

Phoebe says woman

Remember that this is a television script. It does not need to expose 'errors'. Much like the blogspot author in the previous example, when word replacements are included in written talk, the swaps do something self-presentational. They say something about who the speaker is. In *Friends*, Phoebe is arguably the most 'feminist' character – if any characters are.[80] So this bit of scripting gets its humour from her initial use of a 'sexist' word, and how she hurries to correct it. The details are interesting too, as always: the sudden

---

79   Written by Shana Goldberg-Meehan

80   www.bustle.com/articles/101596-8-reasons-phoebe-buffay-is-a-feminist-hero-on-friends

recognition marked by 'Oh', and the 'sorry', marking the error as a transgression, rather than just a mistake.

We have spent some time in the first half of this chapter discovering that, and how, words matter to the speakers who utter them. In the second half, we shift our focus to the way people respond differently to different words. We dive even deeper into the natural laboratory.

How words change outcomes

Readers of this book are probably familiar with behaviour change research in psychology. Richard Thaler and Cass Sunstein's classic book, *Nudge*, shows how people's behaviour can be changed in predictable ways by subtly guiding their 'choice architecture'.

Some of the best-known demonstrations of nudge theory are language-based. For example, which words are more likely to get hotel guests to reuse their bathroom towels? Bathroom signs that appealed to environmental concerns were less effective than signs that appealed to social norms. When bathroom signs read, 'the majority of guests in this room reuse their towels', reuse rates increased substantially.

Despite their origins in different academic disciplines – and with somewhat antithetical premises – conversation analysts and behavioural scientists (explicitly or implicitly) assume that language alters outcomes. In conversation analysis, this becomes the study of differences in, say, the way actions are designed (e.g., alternative formats for requests, offers or questions) and the impact of those differences on the next turn.

The impact of language changes can often be identified endogenously. For example, the effectiveness or otherwise of a telephone sales pitch can be assessed by the caller saying 'yes' or 'no' *inside* the conversation itself.

The conversation analytic equivalent of *Nudge* is a groundbreaking study of medical encounters in the USA. John Heritage[81] and his colleagues conducted a randomised control study of the

---

81 Heritage et al. (2007).

impact of differently worded questions in primary care. Their aim was to address the issue that, while patients frequently have several concerns to raise with their doctor, they often fail to articulate more than one. This is both unsatisfactory and inefficient.

One explanation for why patients report just one concern, when they actually have at least two, is that the doctor's opening question – 'What can I do for you today?' – regularly elicits a single answer. Recognising this as an issue, medical school training recommends that, immediately after discussing the initial problem, doctors 'survey additional concerns' by asking 'is there anything else we need to take care of today?'

Example 10 comes from the training intervention video supplied by the researchers to doctors in the trial.

Example 10: Doctor–patient training

```
01   Doctor:    A'right, uh- I understand about th↑: sore throat an' swollen

02              glands.

03                   (0.4)

04   Doctor:    Before we deal with that, (0.4) are there ↑any other

05              things: y'd like us to address during this visit,

06   Patient:   No, that's it,
```

When patients are *asked* if there is 'anything else' – that is, they are given an opportunity to say more – why might they not? The obvious explanations are the traditional ones. Perhaps men say 'no' more than women. Or women are more likely to say 'yes' more than men. Or the other way around. Or older people report all their concerns. Or do not. And so on.

The researchers found that when doctors asked this question, the most common response was 'no' – even though they had established that patients did have further concerns. The question 'Is there anything else . . .' is a 'yes/no' question. Either option is possible, but the word 'any' is negatively polarised. Put simply, when the word 'any' is used in a question, it takes more conversational effort to reply with a 'yes' than a 'no'.

Think about the last meeting you attended. At the end of the meeting, one of two things can happen when the Chair asks, 'Any other business?'

Example 11a and 11b: Committee meeting

01	Chair:	Any other business? ((gazes from person to person))
02	Colleague:	No.
03	Colleague:	No.
04	Colleague:	No.
05	Colleague:	No. (etc.)

Or:

01	Chair:	Any other business? ((gazes from person to person))
02		(2.0)
03	Colleague:	Well, actually, I just wanted to ask about ...
04	Colleagues:	((collective sigh, eye rolls around the room)).

Like asking 'any questions' halfway through a lecture, asking such questions – intentionally or not – is unlikely to generate responses. It is a token question. It may tick boxes, such as 'engage the audience' or 'consult colleagues', but it is not the most effective way to generate participation if you actually want some.

Knowing that the word 'any' has a closing-down function has implications for training people – Chairs of meetings, lecturers and many others – to know what, instead, to ask. The examples below show a university tutor making two attempts to get the students talking in a tutorial.

Example 12a and 12b: University tutorial

01   Tutor: Has anybody had a go at the questions.

02   (3.7)

03   Tutor: Ye:s?

Or:

01   Tutor: Cassie, what did you find out?

02   Cassie: Well, at first I thought that . . .

When tutors ask the first type of question, with the word 'any', not only do we know that it is tilted towards a negative outcome, it also requires a student to *volunteer* an answer in front of all the other students. Research has shown that this can be challenging, once students are past primary-school age! However, in their second attempt, not only does the tutor replace the original 'yes/no' format and word 'any' with a 'wh-' question, she *nominates* a student to respond. This makes participation much easier.

Armed with their knowledge about the word 'any', the researchers in the doctor–patient study designed an intervention to reduce patients' unmet concerns. In the trial, one group of doctors asked the standard 'any' question. However, another group substituted the word 'any' with the word 'some'. Although both are 'yes/no' questions, 'some' is positively polarised. Here is a doctor modelling the intervention wording.

Example 13: Doctor and patient training

01   Doctor: A'ri:ght.

02   (0.3)

03   Doctor: I understand about the cough: an' runny nose.=.hh

04   before we deal with that, (.) is there some other issue

05   you'd like us to address, (0.3) during this visit?

06   Patient: Yes w'll I also have this skin thing on my arm,

Heritage and colleagues found that this one-word change produced a statistically significant uplift in patients reporting their concerns. In the 'any' condition, 50 per cent of the patients reported more than one concern, meaning that 50 per cent left their consultation with unmet issues. In the 'some' condition, 90 per cent of patients reported all their concerns, meaning that only 10 per cent did not.

'Some' or 'any'?

The 'some or any' study tells us that words change outcomes. The research also tells us something crucial about what drives behaviour. Given the way randomised controlled trials work, the difference in outcome cannot be attributed solely to personality, age, gender, culture, and so on. The difference is generated by language. We are constrained by words more than we realise. We can discover which words make the difference by exploring our natural laboratory.

Heritage et al's study also shows us that it would be a mistake to assume that conversation analysts are behaviourists. People do not just automatically give the same answers to the same questions – stimulus-response. There are three important things to know. First, an initiating action – a question with the word 'any' – will not be composed or spoken identically by all of the speakers, all of the time.

Like fingerprints, each turn at talk is unique, when we get down to the physiology of talking, tiny nuances in emphasis, amplitude, intonation, and so on.

Second, even in the 'some or any' study, lots of patients said 'yes' in the 'any' condition. It may require more effort, like saying 'yes' to 'any other business'. It is just that more people said 'yes' in the 'some' condition. Just because someone says 'hello' to you does not mean you have to say 'hello' back. It's likely. And it is noticeable – and accountable – if you do not. In conversation, the orderliness is normative, not causal.[82]

Third, then, conversation is much more interesting that the culmination of a series of stimulus-response turns. The design of a turn, and individual words, tilts the likelihood of a particular response. So when that response does not happen – someone does not return your 'hello' – we discover something about human beings and their actions.

This book is based on the premise that although we talk, we do not know *how* we talk, scientifically. Conversation analysts discover how talk works by examining real talk, in the natural laboratory. We do not invent talk, simulate talk or ask people to remember their talk, to study it. Our job is to identify people's tacit understandings of their social interaction and identify the systematic way real talk works.

In Example 14, two mediators are trying to help two neighbours, Terry and Diane, resolve a dispute about noise. Mediator 1 is summarising the dispute, from each party's point of view.

Example 14: Neighbour dispute mediation (simplified transcript)

01	Mediator 1:	So you both feel uncomfortable living in your own
02		houses at the moment, Terry because you can't get

---

82 Edwards (2012).

03		a good night's sleep and it's late and Diane
04		because you're walking on eggshells.
05	Diane:	Yeah.
06	Mediator 1:	Is there anything that might change that?
07		(1.8)
08	Mediator 2:	There must be something that needs to change.
09	Terry:	Well . . .

After summing up Diane and Terry's problems living next door to each other, the first mediator gets down to the business of mediation – getting the clients to come up with their own solution to the problem. But her question – containing the word 'anything' – fails to engage the parties. It is not because it is a 'yes/no' question. It is because it is designed for a 'no'.

There is a delay following the first mediator's question. It signals trouble. Perhaps the clients do not want to say 'no', actually – it would make either one of them look uncooperative. But the second mediator has noticed the trouble, and so takes a turn himself. Not only is the grammar of his turn different (it is a statement, not a question) – he has replaced 'anything' with 'something'. And . . . the clients start talking.

The second mediator's turn reveals his analysis of the first mediator's. The second mediator reveals his tacit knowledge that 'any' is unlikely to get clients talking. His turn reveals further tacit knowledge of what might work, or what is worth a try. But the second mediator is unlikely to be able to articulate what worked, after a one-hour mediation, if asked later by a researcher.

Doctors know that patients routinely report just one concern at the start of a consultation. They are therefore trained to probe for more concerns. It is in their communication 'manual'. So our conversation analytic evidence suggests that communication training is flawed from the start. The guidance to ask 'is there anything else?' is based on supposition rather than evidence. It assumes that if people have more to say, and they are invited to say more, they will just say more. Well – they might. It will depend on how they are asked.

Consider a final example. In Example 15, a student has called a university to enquire about his application to a degree course. The student has failed to get the grades required to secure the place and has just heard the bad news.[83]

Example 15: 'Student calling university' (simplified transcript)

01	University:	Unfortunately, the minimum requirement for our
02		computer science courses through clearing,
03		is A A A?
03	Student:	Okay,
04		(1.4)
05	University:	Can I help you with anything else?

The question 'Can I help you with anything else?' closes the slot for further requests. And, given that the student has not been 'helped' in this call, offering to help with other things just adds insult to injury. This question is commonly used at the end of service encounters – and often in calls where service has not happened. It leaves the caller feeling irritated with the call-taker and with a bad impression of the organisation.

In another example, the call-taker still uses 'any' to end the call, but with a different overall function for their turn.

---

83 Hoey and Stokoe (2018).

Example 16: 'Student calling university'
(simplified transcript)

01	University:	Um: our A level requirements are A A B.
02		(0.4)
03	Student:	Okay.
04		(4.4)
05	University:	Is there anything else I could (0.7) look up for you?

Again, the student has received – in this case, by implication – bad news about his degree course application. The call-taker starts to end the call, asking, 'Is there anything else I could . . .' But rather than complete the question with the standard 'help you with', she pauses, and ends with a different offer – '. . . look up for you?' Her question still closes the slot for responding, but, as she offers something useful, rather than 'help', it is probably a better way to finish the call.

Getting people to donate to charity

Imagine that you are asked to train staff to maximise charitable donations in their encounters with members of the public. This was *not* the purpose of another conversation analytic study but it was an implication of its findings, once completed.

Conversation analysts are interested in any and all talk – and embodied conduct – in any and all settings. Like other scientists, our aim is to describe the world and identify its patterns, constituent features, anomalies, and so on. This means that, across the history of studies of real conversation, analysts have unpicked interaction in myriad domestic and professional or workplace settings. At the outset of a conversation analytic project, the data supply answers to an almost infinite number of interactional questions. Indeed, conversation analysis has been caricatured as a method in search of a problem. But sometimes it unearths amazing things.

One such study[84] video-recorded people walking into an art gallery, approaching the desk to pay, making the financial transaction, and then walking into the exhibition. This gallery, like many in the UK, offered a choice of entry tariffs to its customers, listed on the wall behind the cashiers. In addition to the familiar price differences for adults, children, students, seniors, and unwaged persons, each of these prices was further subdivided into two. That is, each price category came in either 'standard' or 'gift aid'. 'Standard' prices were on the left-hand side, with 'gift aid' on the right. 'Gift aid' prices included an additional 10 per cent.

'Gift aid' refers to a British government scheme through which, if people pay 'gift aid', organisations can reclaim income tax. In effect, the customers who paid a slightly higher price made a donation to the gallery, as a charitable institution.

However, customers rarely expressed a preference for standard or gift aid ticket type when approaching the sales desk. Indeed, they appeared not to notice the right-hand column of prices at all. They focused on identifying which *category* of payment they should make, from the left-hand column. A typical encounter therefore started with the customer asking for 'two adults, please'.

The fact that customers did not ask for 'a standard adult, please' or 'a gift aid adult, please' meant that cashiers almost always had to elicit the information.

The cashiers were not trained to ask about 'gift aid'. The gallery was not focused on this communicative task. Cashiers need to know how to process payment using the computerised tills and general facts about the gallery. This setting was, therefore, a perfect natural laboratory in which to see how people go about a particular task with no research or other interest in it whatsoever.

So it was an accident that an analyst *happened* to have chosen this site to study, without knowing what about the encounters might be interesting. The cashiers approached the task of asking about ticket

---

84   Llewellyn (2015).

sub-type in two main ways. One way almost always led to customers paying for a 'gift aid' ticket. The other did not.

Example 17a: Paying at an art gallery

01	Desk:	On the ticket you're paying for would you like to gift
02		aid that today?
03	Customer:	Yes I will.

Or:

Example 17b: Paying at an art gallery

01	Desk:	Would you like to gift aid that today or just pay the
02		standard.
03	Customer:	Uh- standard please.

To ascertain which type of ticket the customer wanted, cashiers asked either yes/no questions (e.g., 'Would you like to gift aid that today?') or questions containing alternatives (e.g., 'Did you want to pay the standard or the gift aid?'). Analysis revealed that customers were more likely to say yes to pay gift aid than opt for gift aid. That is, they were less likely to select gift aid as an option than agree to pay it.

So, if you were now given the task to train cashiers to nudge customers to pay a slightly higher price and donate to charity (whatever you may think of the ethics of doing that), you have evidence to base the training on. Whether or not people paid gift aid was endogenous to the interaction – the decision happened in the next turn.

Communication training – like getting doctors to elicit *all* of their patients' concerns – is rarely based on evidence. Most people simply do not consider underpinning training with this kind of solid foundation. Or they assume that small tweaks to, say, the wording of a question will not make a difference – people are the *type* to pay gift aid or they are not. This assumption is incorrect.

These findings all push us towards a proposition that communication training is best when built bottom-up – from direct observation and analysis of people doing their jobs. This is what I do with organisations of numerous kinds. The final part of the chapter will describe two case studies in which communication training was developed from conversation analytic research.

'Talk' or 'speak'?

If you have read Chapter 4 of this book, you may remember that we spent some time discussing problems with the word 'talk'. 'Talk' suffers from being the target of multiple idiomatic expressions (e.g., 'talk the talk') that imply that words do not do anything. Hopefully, by now, you are convinced that words can often be the only tool for getting things done.

In the penultimate part of this chapter, we will see the potentially disastrous consequences of using the word 'talk' in conversation. Although one may hope that conversation analysts will eventually overturn wildly held beliefs about talk being *just talk*, we are probably some distance from new idioms about the action talk does.

Some years ago, I was approached by the police about a research project. They had heard about my work and wanted to know if conversation analysis could be applied to hostage and crisis negotiations. When a person threatens their own life or someone else's, police negotiators attend the scene to try to talk the person in crisis off the roof. They try to persuade them to live, not die.

The negotiations are recorded routinely. Rein Sikveland and I started to analyse the harrowing recordings. The aim of our research was to identify words and phrases that made it more likely that the person in crisis would keep talking. We wanted to see what worked to make it more likely that the person in crisis would keep taking turns. Every time the person took a turn, they chose life – they did not jump.

Crisis negotiations are often very long encounters – hours or even days. We immediately adopted a spiral metaphor to understand them. At the top of the spiral is the negotiator, the person in crisis, and life. At the bottom of the spiral is the negotiator, the person in crisis, and death. Across the entire negotiation, with each turn at talk, the person in crisis moves up or down the spiral.

Every word matters. Another useful analogy when thinking about crisis negotiations is a football match. Whatever the outcome of a match – win, draw or lose – the players, manager, coach and fans will scrutinise every pass of the ball. They will determine every successful and failed pass. A team can only win, and keep winning, if players land each pass with the *next* player. Every *pass* matters.

As we saw in Chapter 4, negotiators regularly used the word 'talk' in their attempts to engage the persons in crisis. They asked if they 'could talk' and described the negotiation process as 'just talking'. In the natural laboratory provided by the police recordings, the effectiveness or otherwise of these turns revealed itself in the next turn.

Example 18: Crisis negotiation

01	Negotiator:	Can we talk about how you are.
02		(0.5)
03	P in C:	No:, I don't want to ta:lk,

Persons in crisis frequently resisted requests to *talk* to the negotiator. In Example 18, the person in crisis hangs up the phone connection shortly after this exchange.

In the next case, another person in crisis similarly resists a request to 'talk'.

Example 19: Crisis negotiation

01	Negotiator:	Moona,=↑Talk- talk to me about these
02		immigrɑtion [p r o b l e m s.]
03	P in C:	[(I don't) want to] talk
04		to you guys now,
-		
05	P in C:	That's my LAST word man.
06		That's my lɑst word.

Not only does the person in crisis resist talking, he recruits a near-idiomatic phrase about talking – 'that's my last word' – to emphasise his commitment to not talking.

In Example 20, the person in crisis also resists talking. He draws explicitly on the familiar cultural idiom that talk is just talk and does not *do* anything. The negotiator, in turn, is attempting to resist the idiom.

Example 20: Crisis negotiation

01	Negotiator:	You kept saying earlier about ɑction:s rather than
02		wo:rds, .hh this i- this is ǧenuine ɑction that we can
03		[ǧive you.]
04	P in C:	[It's not ge]nuine action man, you're just tɑlking.
05		(0.4)
06	Negotiator:	Why don't [you think it-]
07	P in C:	[It's talking.]=You ain't done anything.

This example, and others like it, shows us that when negotiators ask or suggest that the person in crisis should talk, they open up a slot for resistance. They provide a space in the interaction for the person in crisis to use the idiom. Even though in the act of taking this turn the person in crisis is choosing life – not jumping – the lines of communication are temporarily fraught. The very thing that negotiators need persons in crisis to do – *keep talking* – is now framed as something useless.

Words matter. Words change outcomes. People select from myriad words to build their turns. Speakers make corrections to their selection of words, even as they utter them, and replace them. Replacements are often near-synonyms, because words have their own subtly different connotations.

What word – if not 'talk' – *will* engage persons in crisis to talk? What kind of football pass will land with the next player? Which words will result in the person in crisis and negotiator moving up the spiral, towards life? Example 21 contains the answer.

Example 21: Crisis negotiation

01   Negotiator: I wanna come down and I wanna speak to you, .hhh

02   [and see if we can sort this out.]

03   P in C: [Miss.   I'm   so   scared.   ]= I stabbed myself in the

04   neck. And . . .

In the natural laboratory of real talk, we can identify what works. When negotiators frame the proposed activity as speak – *not* talk – the person in crisis starts to . . . talk. At line 03, the person in crisis starts to talk before the negotiator has even completed their first turn.

Perhaps even more importantly, when persons in crisis make requests to 'communicate', they also use the verb 'speak'.

Example 22: Crisis negotiation

01	Negotiator:	You said for the sake of your children.=Why don't you
02		come down for them.
03	P in C:	I've already spoke. I'm spea- I wanna speak to her.
04		Not you.
05	Negotiator:	You want to speak to who:?
06		(0.9)
07	P in C:	THAT police officer.

We would never know that the verb 'speak' is more engaging of persons in crisis than the verb 'talk', unless we analysed real interaction. The words are near-synonyms. We tend to believe that persons in crisis will either talk or not because of some other psychological motivation – their personality, the strength of their suicidal intent, and so on. It is assumed that persons in crisis will talk or not depending on factors that precede this particular moment in interaction.

But think about it. There are no equivalent idioms about 'speak' – we do not say, for instance, 'he can speak the speak but can he walk the walk?' Persons in crisis do not say, 'I don't want to speak', or 'it's just speak' or, more grammatically, 'it's just speaking'. 'Talk' is a noun and a verb – 'speak' is not. When negotiators suggest that they 'speak', they do not open up a slot for resistance. We are pushed and pulled around by language more than we realise, and we can discover how when we look.

'Are you willing?'

This chapter started with some examples of the way people focus on every word they utter, even as they produce each word. The recordings we examined came from mediation services – one providing conflict resolution services for workplace colleagues and another for neighbours in dispute.

I want to show you how my work on the power of words started. In the late 1990s, I began working with community mediation services. My initial interest, as a social psychologist, was in neighbour relationships – it was a type of relationship that surprisingly few psychologists had paid attention to.

As a conversation analyst, I wanted to study people being neighbours in real settings, and how their relationships – and disputes – unfolded. I did not want to interview people about being neighbours, ask them to complete a survey, or run a simulation. Capturing people enacting and living their neighbour relationships seemed like a challenge, until some mediation services offered to record their meetings with clients. I would be studying neighbour relationships gone wrong.

Gradually, I became less interested in what the reported causes of neighbour disputes were, or how people built their cases about their noisy neighbours. In addition to recordings of mediators meeting their clients – individually and together – mediation services provided recordings of their initial telephone calls with potential clients. This was partly because mediators were reluctant to record full mediations. But they were more open to initial enquiry telephone calls being opened up to analytic scrutiny. For mediators, these calls are *not* part of the mediation process. They are encounters in which appointments are arranged.

Callers regularly resist mediation as a route to resolving their disputes. So I started to notice that there were multiple points across the telephone calls in which callers lost any interest they might have in mediation, and said 'no' when offered mediation by the mediator.

There are fairly obvious reasons why people resist mediation. First, people are not as familiar with mediators as they are with, say, lawyers, the police, or the council, as agencies that can help resolve a neighbour dispute. In fact, most callers started their enquiry call by saying that they 'have just been given this number', having called somewhere other than mediation first.

Second, the fact that people call lawyers, the police, or the council to get help with their neighbour tells us the kind of help they want and who they think can provide it. A person with a neighbour dispute wants the police to arrest their tiresome neighbour, the council to evict them, or a lawyer to initiate court proceedings. This is because their neighbour is – from the caller's point of view – unambiguously to blame for the dispute. Indeed, throughout their initial conversation with the mediator, callers take every opportunity to negatively characterise the other party. With each negative characterisation of their neighbour, the caller is, by implication, the victim.

Mediators offer mediation to these callers. They have to explain what mediation is, because most callers do not know what is involved. Mediation involves talking to the other party. It involves identifying solutions together. Mediators are impartial – they do not take sides.

Mediation is, unsurprisingly, unappealing to someone who wants action, not talk – just like persons in crisis, as we have just seen. It is unappealing to someone who knows that their neighbour is the 'kind of person you can't talk to'. And for someone who has already telephoned the police, the council or a lawyer, it offers a 'less-than' service. Mediation is especially unappealing to someone who thinks they are in the right, because they are offered a service that is impartial.

When people call mediation services, they agree – or do not agree – to a first meeting with the mediator at the end of the call. When callers say 'no' to mediation, they say 'no' at particular points. They say 'no' when mediators explain mediation in terms of its guiding ethos – as an 'impartial service that doesn't take sides'. But callers are more likely to say 'yes' when mediators explain mediation as a process and avoid references to 'impartiality'.

Even when explained as a process, callers may still resist saying 'yes' to mediation. If insufficient numbers of callers say 'yes' to mediation, the service will not secure sufficient clients to run successfully. The service ceases to exist. Initial enquiries turn out to be the *most important* step in the overall mediation journey.

If callers take every opportunity to negatively characterise their neighbour, they will also take opportunities to say that their neighbour is the kind of person who will not engage in mediation.

If mediators do not know how to overcome this hurdle, the call is over and the client is lost.

In Example 23, the mediator has explained mediation and is now asking the caller directly if she wants to use the service.

Example 23: Calling mediation

```
01   Mediator:    Does that sound .hhh like it might be helpful to you?

02                (0.7)
```

We know from line 02 – a gap of 0.7 seconds – that it is likely that the caller is about to say something other than 'yes'. If the caller was enthusiastic about what she heard about mediation, this would reveal itself at line 02. The caller could say something like, 'That sounds great!'; 'Yes it does', or a more tentative 'Um, okay . . .'

The caller says 'no'. At least, she produces a 'dispreferred response', done with all the classic features of such a response that we were introduced to in Chapter 2.

```
03   Caller:      I- uh- (0.2) it might be but um:: (0.3) I'm not too sure at

04                this stage about (0.6) you know, how long- y- seein' this:

05                gi:rl, at all,
```

The caller's response is delayed; it includes an appreciation – 'it might be' – and an account which starts to invoke the other party – 'this girl'. It is a 'no'.

When I train mediators to make their initial enquiry calls more effective, I ask them to consider what they might do to nevertheless encourage the caller to become their client. Ninety-five per cent of mediators do not come up with what works, even though mediators do change callers' minds quite regularly. This suggests that we are not good at recalling our experience sufficiently to know what works in these crucial moments, even if we actually do effective things! What works?

```
06   Mediator:   W'yeah.=↓yeh, but you'd be willin' t'see two of our

07               media[tors jus' t'talk about it all. .hhhh]

08   Caller:      [Oh of course.   Yeah.  Yeah   ] definitely.
```

When mediators ask if callers are *willing* to mediate, or propose that they are – as in this case – callers are more likely to say 'yes' to mediation. But this tiny fragment of recorded talk is packed with important details.

First, notice the precise moment that the caller starts to reply – where the two square brackets line up. She begins to say 'yes' long before the mediator has finished her own turn (and before the mediator has used the word 'talk' . . .!). Indeed, the caller begins her turn before knowing what the mediator is proposing she is willing to do.

Second, the mediator is *not* asking a question. She is making a statement about the kind of person the caller is – the kind who would be willing to see the mediators. Now, we know that callers take every opportunity to negatively characterise their neighbour. They often say that their neighbour is the kind of person who will not mediate. By implication, the caller must be the kind of person who will – they are, after all, the good and reasonable party.

Third, the mediator is impartial. They *cannot* say that they think the caller is the aggrieved party and their neighbour is to blame for the dispute. But they *can* imply that the caller is the kind of person who is willing to mediate. This mediator appears to have empathy for callers in dispute and what kinds of things they like to hear.

Fourth, the mediator opens up a slot for the caller to say 'I'm nice.' By confirming that they are 'willing', the caller says, 'I'm the good one'. The mediator's proposal about the caller is a moral one: the caller, unlike her neighbour, *is* the kind of person who will mediate. Indeed, being willing motivates callers to say yes, sometimes explicitly. For example, in another call to a family mediator, the caller refers to his wife as unwilling, while he is willing to mediate ('I'm not sure if she's willing to do that, but I'm making a step to say "well yeah I'm willing to do mediation"').

Fifth, the caller's response is immediate. It is also a strongly positive response – she does not just say yes. She starts by saying, 'Oh of course . . .' A gloss might be – 'I was *always* willing – you did not need to ask.' Indeed, callers sometimes say exactly this. Example 24 is from a family mediation service call.

Example 24: Calling mediation

```
01   Mediator:    So:- (0.6) uh:m- (0.6) from what I've told you. does

02                that sound something that you- you want to find out

03                more about, and you- you're willing to try?

04                     (1.6)

05   Caller:      I was never not willing to try,
```

So – 'willing' works.[85] Having discovered one case, the other examples leapt out of the data. And they were everywhere – including across other types of mediation services.

```
01   Mediator:    I'm sure he would be will:ing t'come in and see our

02                mediat[or:?

03   Caller:           [Oh yeah:
```

And:

```
01   Mediator:    I just- wanted to see if you would be willing to attend

02                a: a session as well.

03   Caller:      I'm more than happy to go down that route.
```

85 Stokoe (2013a); Sikveland and Stokoe (2016).

And:

01 Mediator: Okay then, so would you be <u>wi</u>llin' f'two of our

02 mediators to call round and talk to you about it all?

03 Caller: Yeh I'm more than willing.

And:

01 Mediator: Is <u>th</u>at something that you would be <u>wi</u>lling

02 to [<u>do</u>:.   ]=

03 Caller [I would-] I ↑<u>wo</u>uld be willing to ↓<u>do</u> it.

04 =ye[s:.   ]

05 Mediator: [.ptk (th)<u>a</u>t's grea:t.

06 Caller: [Just- (<u>do</u> <u>a</u>nything just to try and get to see my <u>so</u>n.

Many of the callers' responses are not just agreements to mediate, but are immediate, upgraded responses, which are classic features of 'preferred' responses.[86] So callers are 'more than' willing, not just willing. Upgrades provide an additional sense of sincerity and independence rather than merely going along with somebody else's suggestion.

Other words do get callers to agree to attend an initial mediation appointment – for example, 'would you *like* to mediate?', or 'are you *interested* in mediation?' However, callers' agreements are less strong when these verbs are used. And only 'willing' gets a complete turnaround from resistance to 'yes'.

Eagle-eyed readers may also have spotted earlier, in Example 17a, that the gallery staff asked their customer 'would you like to gift aid that today?' The customer replied, 'Yes I will'. 'Would' is the past

---

86 Pomerantz (1984).

tense of 'will' – the same verb is used; the customer is the kind of person who is willing to pay gift aid. Even though 'would you like' is an auxiliary verb, it shares the same sense of being willing to do something, rather than just referring to the future.

Our final example brings mediation and crisis negotiation together again. In Example 25, the person in crisis is resisting the negotiator's request to come down.

Example 25: Crisis negotiation

```
01   P in C:        Bloody- (0.2) you can just fucking go back to your

02                  station.=

03   Negotiator 1:  =No I CA:N't. How can I do that. You know how it

04                  works, I can't do that. Can I. I have to sta:nd he:re,

05                  (0.4) With you.

06                       (3.1)

07   N1:            But you're telling me you're not trying to piss me

08                  o:ff.

09                       (7.1)

10   N1:            It feels like you are₎ It feels like you just want to

11                  upset me.

12                       (3.2)
```

The negotiator says something that is almost antithetical to the training manual for negotiators. Rather than saying how much she cares for the person in crisis, she says that she has to stay with him.

And she expands on this, pushing the person in crisis by saying he is 'pissing her off' and 'wanting to upset her'.

The negotiator has clearly built enough of a relationship with the person in crisis to judge that this will not damage the negotiation. When I showed this clip to negotiators, there was a collective sharp intake of breath. But the negotiator is building a sequence with a successful outcome. And then comes the final evidence that 'willing' works – that words matter.

13 Negotiator 1:   Will you come do:wn.

14   (1.5)

15 Negotiator 2:   Watch your step mate,

16   (0.3)

17 Negotiator 2:   Watch your step.

In the space at line 14, the person in crisis starts to move. The negotiator has asked him to come down – if he 'will' come down. And, it turns out, he 'will'.

Talk matters

Many of the findings about effective and ineffective *words* underpin my training approach – the Conversation Analytic Role-play Method. I will explain more about CARM in Chapter 7. CARM presents professionals – hostage negotiators, mediators, doctors, salespeople, police officers – with a line-by-line transcript of real encounters like the ones presented in this chapter.

CARM allows people to see real talk. They see people like them doing their job in real life, with real stakes, rather than staged, hypothetical conversations. They get to see what happens next when one type of turn is taken rather than another. CARM provides a training environment for participants to assess what really happens in their communicative world. They can practise what they might say next, and see what works.

Crucially, CARM uses conversation analytic research to ensure that people learn about real talk. Sometimes, CARM overturns what people already think they know about talk. It challenges the training they might previously have had, including role-plays they might have experienced. But if *words* can make the difference between life and death, these are challenges worth accepting.

6

ARE YOU BEING SERVED?

This book is about talk. Talk *does* things. Talk builds action. And one of the most recognisable actions that we use talk to do is to get help. We use talk to get service from organisations. We need help to remember a word or lift a heavy object or borrow a pen or see a doctor. We use talk to offer help to others and to resist offers of help.

Why is it worth dedicating a chapter to investigate help, support, assistance and service? One answer is that we generally do not 'just ask' for help. Indeed, the fact that people say things like, 'I hate to ask, but . . .', 'you only need to ask', 'don't hesitate to ask', or 'just ask!' tells us that asking for help may be more complex than we think. Another answer is that anyone who has telephoned an organisation for service – from the bank, the council, the doctor's, the police – has probably had more than one frustrating experience. And yet another answer is that you have probably experienced excellent service, great support, and subtle offers of help that are discreet and expert – in both personal and professional life.

This chapter starts by examining some basic features of getting and giving help in ordinary domestic settings, before examining service situations. We will see from the opening few seconds of calls to the council, to shops, to emergency services, to the vet's or doctor's, that getting help is both simple and intricate. What are the features of service failure, or dissatisfaction? And what are the quick wins for improving service?

We conclude the chapter by reflecting on moments when we wonder, 'why am I doing this?' while making an offer to do something for someone. Are you the kind of person who gets people to do things for you? Or are you the person who ends up offering help – even when you don't want to? This chapter will help you decide.

How to get help

In Chapter 2, we spent some time analysing a conversation between friends getting ready for a night out. One of the friends, Marie, has announced that she is sweating profusely before they have even left the house. Let us focus on some additional aspects of this encounter, as we consider what Marie does in the pursuit of assistance, and what her friends do in response to help – even though Marie does not ask for help at all, in the first instance. Line numbers are reproduced from the first presentation of this data, in Chapter 2.

Example 1: Real friends talking

04 Marie: <Oh ↑↑ma::n >I 'aven't e'en< gone <u>OU</u>t and I'm sweating

05   like a, (0.4) [rapist,]

06 Kate: [Man.]

Marie is sweating like ... something. She pauses while she searches for a good way to complete the metaphor she is building. At line 06, Kate supplies a possible category to complete it. Marie has not asked for help, but in pausing, her friend has identified a moment to help out with Marie's search for a word.

Speakers often help each other out with something very basic – the very conversation they are currently having. Sometimes others jump in too soon, or come up with the wrong word, or are not helpful at all. But, for now, just notice that this is a very basic kind of help – supporting and collaborating with other speakers to find words. And we might do this more, less, or differently with, say, children, non-native speakers, or adults with language impairments.

Marie's announcement about herself, and description of her sweatiness, might also generate another response from her friends. It is easy to imagine an *offer* happening next (e.g., of a fan), or some advice (e.g., how to cool down). When people announce things, they may end up with offers that remedy some problem – without asking for anything at all.

You may remember from Chapter 2 that her friends collectively laugh and show some ironic disgust at Marie's eventual metaphor – she is 'sweating like a rapist'. As the laughter subsides, Marie makes another announcement.

11   Marie: I'm rea:lly ho:t!.

What does 'I'm really hot!' mean? Is it an explanation, a simple description, a request for help, or something else?

Marie's second announcement provides an explanation for why she is sweating. Again, it is easy to imagine possible responses to 'I'm really hot!' – a deodorant, a fan, or something else that might help Marie to cool down and be less sweaty. But none of her friends treat 'I'm really hot!' as seeking help – or, at least, they do not make an offer in response. It is interesting, then, that Marie's next turn is an explicit request for help.

13	Marie:	↑Has ↑anyone- (0.2) ↑has ↑anyone got any re̲ally non:
14		sweaty stuff.
15	Dawn:	Dave has. but you'll smell >like a ma̲ːn,<
16	Kate:	Eh [↑huh heh]
17	Marie:	[Right has] anyone got any ↑fe̲ːminine non sweaty stuff.
18	Kate:	I've ↑got umːːː, (0.6) roll on,

We analysed this sequence in Chapter 2. Dawn offers Dave's 'non sweaty stuff' but suggests that it might not be right for Marie – a gendered moment in their conversation. As Kate starts to laugh, Marie redoes her request, swapping the word 'really' ('has anyone got any really non: sweaty stuff') with the word 'fe:minine' – with exaggerated intonation. Finally, Kate offers Marie her 'roll on [deodorant]'.

We also encountered Donny and Marsha in Chapter 2. We examined the start of their telephone call in which, after the preliminaries, Donny delivers some bad news about his car.

Example 2: Stalled

01		((phone rings))
02	Marsha:	Hello?
03	Donny:	H'lo M̲arsha,
04	Marsha:	Ye̲ːa[h.]
05	Donny:	[It's D]onny.
06	Marsha:	H̲i Doːnny.
07	Donny:	Guess what. hh
08	Marsha:	What.
09	Donny:	.hh my ca̲ːr is sta̲ːːlled.

What might you expect to happen next? It is Marsha's turn to talk. It is probably obvious already that Donny is not calling Marsha just to give her some information. So, we might expect an exclamation, perhaps sounding sympathetic ('Oh no!') and possibly the start of something that indicates Marsha could help. Instead, this is how the conversation unfolds.

10   (0.2)

11   Donny: An' I'm up here in the Gle:n,

12   (0.2)

Donny has added a further detail to his problem. But we can see from the small gaps at lines 10 and 12 that Marsha is not jumping in to show understanding of his situation or express sympathy, never mind to make an offer of help.

At line 13 she makes her first response.

13   Marsha: Oh::.

The conversation analyst John Heritage refers to 'Oh' as a 'change-of-state' token[87] – we say it to mark a shift from 'not knowing something' to 'knowing something'. Intonation can inflect our 'ohs' to show our stance towards the new thing we know – interest, excitement, surprise, shock, disappointment, and so on. It is hard to describe quite how Marsha sounds – but the upshot is that she does not do anything more than say 'Oh'.

As Donny keeps describing his problem, note the gaps between each chunk of talk that he adds.

14   (0.4)

15   Donny: A:nd. hh

---

87 Heritage (1984).

16		(0.5)
17	Donny:	I don' know if it's po:ssible but, .hhh see
18		↑I have t'open up the ba:nk. hh
19		(0.5)
20	Donny:	A:t uh: (0.2) in Brentwood? hh=

Each gap creates a slot for Marsha to offer help. We could see that, from line 09, help is probably sought. The closest Donny gets to making a request is at line 17, 'I don' know if it's po:ssible but' – but still he does not ask for help.

Eventually, Marsha responds to the action Donny is implicitly doing.

21	Marsha:	=Ye::ah:- an' I know you want- (0.2) an' I wou:- (0.3)
22		an' I wo:uld, but- except I've gotta le:ave in about five
23		min(h)utes.[(hheh)
24	Donny:	[>Okay then< I gotta call somebody else
25		right away.

Marsha understands what Donny was after, but reveals that she is not in a position to help. So Marsha turns down Donny's request for help, without a request ever actually happening. In fact, conversation analysts have shown that explicit requests are often avoided. Instead, one speaker lays the groundwork for an offer of help from another.

Here is the end of Donny and Marsha's conversation.

26   (0.2)

27   Donny: Oka:y?=

28   Marsha: =Okay *Don[.*

29   Donny: [>Thanks a lot.=bye-<

30   (.)

31   Marsha: Bye.

Despite the fact that Marsha has *not* helped Donny, he closes the conversation (rapidly, note the signs which indicate speeded-up talk) saying '>Thanks a lot.=bye-<'. He does not sound sarcastic; he does not say, with irony, 'thanks a *lot*!' (translation: thanks for nothing!). But we will see later in the chapter that 'thank you' does not always mean what we might assume. It can, in fact, indicate immense displeasure.

Of course, when it comes to calling service providers – shops, the doctor, the vet – we often make direct requests. But, equally often, we do not 'just ask'. What would 'just asking' even look like? We might think that we design our requests differently because of politeness, because we are a woman (or a man), or because we come from a particular 'culture'. But conversation analysis shows that we design our requests according to other tacit rules – depending on what is at stake, and how much we are entitled to ask. And these issues and eventualities may be revealed in the first few seconds of a conversation.

Service in seconds

The first few seconds of a conversation are powerful. In Chapter 1, we saw numerous examples of conversation openings, and began to see that we can learn a lot about the likely trajectory of encounter before one party even speaks. In this section, we will examine the opening moments from a host of service encounters, in which the caller makes a request . . . or doesn't.

Example 3 is the start of a call to a double-glazing company, which we first encountered on page 123.

Example 3: Calling double-glazing sales

01 Sales: G'd afternoon, ↑Fine Bar ↑Wi̱:ndows,

02   (0.6)

03 Customer: .shih (.) .hh >hi< w'd it be ↑po̱:ssible f'somebody t'come

04   an' give me a quote on uh: a window an: some doors

05   please.

What can we say about the way this request is made? The caller wants a quote for a window and some doors – he is probably in the right place. But he seems not to know, definitively, what kind of service he can get from the company. Does someone 'come' to the caller's house? Who is 'someone'? The call-taker? Who, then, gives quotes?

The caller asks, 'would it be possible . . .' It is easy to imagine an alternative wording, such as 'Can I get a quote . . . These alternatives are not arbitrary or interchangeable. Words *matter*. When speakers make requests with modal verbs (could, would, 'can I . . .', 'can you . . .'), it implies an entitlement to ask.[88] But if they ask, 'I wonder if . . .', 'is it possible . . .', and so on, the speaker tacitly reduces their entitlement to ask, or their knowledge about what the service actually provides.

These observations make more sense as we consider further examples. Here are the opening moments of calls to a holiday company and a veterinary practice. For each case, try swapping the request designs around ('I'd like to', 'I need', 'I want', 'can I', 'I wonder if'); the feel of the request will change.

---

88 Curl and Drew (2008).

Example 4: Booking a holiday (simplified transcript)

01   Sales: Good evening Rindley Leisure Hotels, you're speakin' to

02   Diane.=how c'n I help.

03   Caller: Uh: I want t'book a holiday at Rindley's plea:se?

Example 5: Calling the vet (simplified transcript)

01   Reception: Dunnetts Vets.=Highuptown, Maggie speaking, how can

02   I help.

03   Client: Hello there.=um: I need t'make an appointment t'bring

04   the cat in t'get its um: updated vaccina:tions.

In both cases, the callers appear to know what the companies offer, and what services they are entitled to ask for. In the holiday call, the caller makes a request using a declarative grammatical format – a statement of her 'wants'. It turns out that the caller is a regular customer and knows what she can ask for.

Similarly, in the vet call, the caller uses the grammar of a declarative (the standard grammatical form for making a statement rather than, say, asking a question) to express a 'need'. But 'need' is different to 'want'. 'Need' raises the stakes of the outcome – declining *this* request might have negative consequences for the cat's health. Consider the following example, in which a mother and her young daughter are at the counter in a cupcake shop.

Example 6: Cake shop (field note)

01   Mum: Which one do you want?

02   Daughter: I need two!

The fact that the daughter replaces the verb 'want' with 'need' (as well as altering 'one' to 'two', of course . . .) tells us that children learn not only to produce words, but how to build actions. They learn that a 'need' is a different type of action to a 'want'. In this instance, the daughter's choice of verb raised smiles between me, her mother and the shopkeeper – but she still only got one cupcake!

Consider the difference between the callers in the next two cases involving requests for medical help. Example 7 is a transcript of an emergency phone call made from Michael Jackson's home when he died, released by the Los Angeles Fire Department.[89] Example 8 is from a call from a patient to her doctor's receptionist.

Example 7[90]: Michael Jackson (simplified transcript)

01	EMD:	Fire and paramedics thirty three what is the address
02		of your emergency:
03	Caller:	Yes sir. I need to I- I- I need an ambulance as soon as
04		po:ssible sir.

Example 8: Calling the doctor's (simplified transcript)

01	Reception:	Good morning, surgery: Cath speaking,
02	Patient:	Hello have you got an appointment for Frida:y
03		afternoon or teatime please.

Imagine if the caller from Michael Jackson's house to the emergency services asked, 'I was just wondering if it would be possible to get

---

89 http://news.bbc.co.uk/1/hi/8121884.stm

90 Berger, Kitzinger and Ellis (2016).

an ambulance.' Instead, the verb 'need' communicates something specific about the caller's assessment of the situation. The importance of the need is upgraded by the inclusion of time frame in the request – 'as soon as possible'. In contrast, the patient calling her doctor asks for an appointment several days after she calls.

The way patients make requests at the doctor's is consequential for the way receptionists progress the call. Receptionists often ask patients if their request is urgent or 'just routine'. This leaves patients in a difficult position. If patients say 'just routine', then they undermine their reason for calling – and admit to using a scarce resource needlessly. If their problem is not life-threatening, saying their request is 'urgent' is also difficult. And, of course, patients may not know what kind of medical problem they have; serious illnesses do not always start with dramatic symptoms.

When patients ask for an appointment a few days later than the time of their call, as the caller does in Example 8, there is no need to ask about urgency.[91] By asking for an appointment later rather than for 'today', the patient tacitly categorises their request as 'routine'. However, patients sometimes insert a time frame into their request right from the start.

Example 9: Calling the doctor's (simplified transcript)

01	Patient:	Hello.=Can you tell me if there's any available
02		appointments for this afternoon please.
03		(0.5)
04	Reception:	tk uh the first free slot I've got >coming up< is (0.2)
05		<tomorrow> at nine fifteen, Is that any good to you?=
06	Patient:	=I need one this uh tonight,

91 Sikveland and Stokoe (in press).

Notice that when the receptionist suggests that the next free appointment is 'tomorrow', the patient switches the format of her request from 'can you tell me' to 'I need' – and gets an appointment.

In Example 10, the receptionist creates a problem by asking the patient if they 'just' want a 'routine appointment'.

Example 10: Calling the doctor's (simplified transcript)

01	Reception:	Good morning reception.=Melanie speaking,
02	Patient:	Good morning.=I'd like to make an appointment to
03		see a doctor please.
04	Reception:	Is it just a routine appointment,
05		(0.7)
06	Patient:	Uh:: (0.8) ↓how do you mean.
07		(0.8)
08	Reception:	Well I've either got ↑urgent for today bu:t::- uh: I'll
09		have to get the doctor to give you a ring back with
10		telephone advice, or we are booking Monday.
11	Patient:	Uh that will be fine for Monday,

The patient is 'fine for Monday'. She did not ask for an appointment 'today', or say that she 'needed' an appointment. The receptionist could, therefore, simply offer the next available appointment, rather than open up a moment of misunderstanding, or tension – deleting lines 03–08. This would also reduce the call length.

In all of the conversations we have regarded so far, callers show that they *know* what kind of organisation they are calling, and what kind of service they can ask for. From there, people calibrate the design of their request depending on their entitlement to ask; how easy it is to grant it; and how important it is.

Sometimes, however, the opening turns reveal that callers are less clear about these factors. For instance, if you have a noisy neighbour, who do you ask for help? There are several possibilities – here are two.

Example 11: Calling environmental health (simplified transcript)

01	Env Health:	Good afternoon environmental health, Deirdre
02		speaking,
03	Caller:	.hH Hi I don't know whether you can help me, um I
04		need to speak to someone .hh about uh: disturbance
05		an' some loud music,

Example 12: Calling mediation (simplified transcript)

01	Mediation:	Mediation in Southtown, g'd mo:rning,
02	Caller:	.hh Hhello.=see I've bin given y'number by Citizens
03		Advice Bureau. Um: that you do: mediation service or
04		something,

In Example 11, a caller tries to get help from the environmental health services of the local council. But she does not ask 'would it be possible' (like buying windows), or use formats that we have seen earlier, such as 'can you', or 'I'd like'. Instead, she starts by saying that she does not 'know whether you can help me'. The caller does, however, 'need' to speak to 'someone' – the problem is important. It will turn out that the current call-taker is the person that the caller 'needs' to speak to, but she does not know that yet.

In Example 12, the caller appears to know even less about the service he is calling. In fact, he has not called the mediation service in the first instance. He has been referred from another service – the Citizens Advice Bureau, which gives free legal advice. This caller does not know what mediation is ('you do: mediation service or something') – which will create problems later for the mediator when they start to offer help.

Our final cases all start differently. Example 13 comes from a member of the public calling his local Member of Parliament's constituency office. The call is taken by a caseworker who works for the MP.

Example 13: Calling a Member of Parliament Consituency[92] office (simplified transcript)

01 MP office: How can I help you.

02   (0.4)

03 Caller: Well, (.) I live on a boa:t,

04 MP office: Yeah.

05   (0.6)

06 Caller: And I've just been diagnosed with kidney failure,=

07 MP office: =Oh: dear,

08   (0.5)

09 Caller: And I am having (0.3) dialysis regular three times a wee:k,

10 MP office: Yeah.

11   (0.7)

---

92 Hofstetter (2016).

12 Caller: Um,

13   (0.7)

14 Caller: Then I had a <heart attac[k,>

15 MP office: [Oh:: dear,

In this case, the caller describes a list of problems, building up to the reason for calling – he wants help to move from his boat into a council house. Like Donny, earlier, he does not make a direct request, but describes his circumstances in such a way that the request is clear, if implicit – a very common way to make requests. Describing circumstances is not just giving the caseworker information, of course – and, once the description of the problem is finished, the caseworker offers help.

Indirect requests can be done by 'describing the circumstances' because 'describing the circumstances' functions as a kind of 'pre' for an upcoming request. But an upcoming request may never have to be made explicit because it is enough to elicit an offer. This is how people avoid making direct requests and thereby avoid direct rejections.

In Example 14, we return to the suicide negotiation conversations introduced earlier in the book. These conversations are particularly interesting when thinking about service, offers and requests. By locating themselves (in the first instance) in a public or accessible place, persons in crisis are available for conversation. Their visibility sets up the conditions for an offer of help to happen. And negotiators offer help to persons in crisis, without being asked.

Example 14: Crisis negotiation (simplified transcript)

01 Negotiator: Hi darling. My n- my name is D̲avid.

02 P in C: Who are yo̲u,

03 Negotiator: I'm just here to try and h̲elp.

04   (0.7)

05 P in C: Yeah. Wh̲o are you.=You know fr̲om wh̲ere.

06   (0.3)

07 Negotiator: Oh- I- I'm from the po̲lice. But m̲y job is to sit here and

08   talk to you and try and h̲elp.

09   (0.4)

10 Negotiator: See what we can do to h̲elp ya.

11   (0.5)

12 P in C: You ca̲:n't. I'm dy̲ing tonight.

Right from the start, and unsurprisingly, the negotiator and person in crisis have different conversational goals. It will take hours before the two come together, to share the goal of keeping the person in crisis alive. The negotiator offers help and the person in crisis resists their offer.

Example 15 is a call to the 999 British emergency services. There are many cases like this, in which people call the police for apparently 'non-emergency' reasons. They are assessed beneath the recordings, with comments like, 'Unbelievable what people would phone the 999 number for in the UK!', 'time-wasters', and so on. Here is an example, which you can listen to on YouTube.[93]

---

93 https://www.youtube.com/watch?v=DC3uaeJVGcA – first call.

Example 15: Emergency call

01	Dispatch:	Police how can I help.
02	Caller:	Hello:: Um I know this isn't an emergency,
03		(0.8)
04	Dispatch:	Yeh-
05	Caller:	.hh Um- but- (0.2) uh- what's today's date.
06		(0.8)
07	Dispatch:	Right: is that why you're callin' a >nine nine nine.<
08		(0.5)
09	Caller:	~Ye(h)ah~
10		(0.8)
11	Dispatch:	Okay it's not- y- you're right it's not an emergency an'
12		its not something you dial nine nine nine for okay.
13		(0.2)
14	Dispatch:	Right. Goodnight.

This seems like a straightforward case of 'time-wasting', and the dispatcher ends the call swiftly. It probably is a case of 'time-wasting', especially as the caller frames her request for information with, 'I know this isn't an emergency'. Listen to the call online, if you can, to see what you make of line 09. The caller confirms her reason for calling 999, and the way she says 'yeah' sounds like there is a laughter particle embedded in it. But it might be a different kind of tremble. We do not know.

For contrast, watch out for the moment in Example 16 when the dispatcher suddenly realises that the caller is not a 'time-waster'. Nine one one is, of course, the emergency number in the USA.

Example 16: Emergency call

01	Dispatch:	>Nine one one¿< operator.=Nine (an') one.
02		(.)
03	Dispatch:	Where's the emergency.
04		(0.4)
05	Caller:	One twenny seven Denir?h
06		(0.3)
07		((phone beep))
08		(.)
09	Dispatch:	Okay: what's goin' on there.
10	Caller:	I'd like t'order: a pizza for delivery?h
11		(0.7)
12		((phone beep))
13	Dispatch:	Mam you've reached >nine one one,< this is an
14		emergency [line.
15	Caller:	[Yeh.h uh: large with half pepperoni half
16		mushroom?
17		(0.2)
18		((phone beep))

19	Dispatch:	Um:: you <u>k</u>now you've called nine one one,
20		(.)
21	Dispatch:	This is an emer[gency line.
22	Caller:	[(D'y'kno:w how lo:ng it'll be?
23		(.)
24		((phone beep))
25	Dispatch:	'kay mam.=is everything okay: over there_
26		(0.3)
27	Dispatch:	D'y'<u>h</u>ave an emer[gency or not.
28	Caller:	[°hhhh°
29		(0.6)
30	Caller:	<u>Y</u>es.
31		(1.0)
32		((phone beep))
33	Dispatch:	An' you're unable t'<u>t</u>alk because[:
34	Caller:	[<u>R</u>ight.
35		(0.2)
36	Caller:	Right.
37		(1.0)
38	Dispatch:	I:s there someone in the <u>r</u>oom with you,

If the dispatcher had ended the call at a similar place to our previous case, around line 13 in Example 16, then he would not have been able to help the caller. How does the caller communicate her real reason for calling? The answer starts with her responses to the dispatcher's statement that 'this is an emergency line'. He says this twice – at lines 13–14 and 19. In both cases, the caller responds before he has completed his turn, and as though talking to another recipient entirely.

At line 15, the caller says she wants 'large with half pepperoni half mushroom?' which is a sheer *non sequitur*. She does this again at line 22. So the dispatcher can see, based on these gross breaches of conversational sequences and order, that the caller may have a problem she cannot express. Given that it is the emergency services, the dispatcher infers what kind of problem it is likely to be.

If the caller in Example 15 had, say, started to respond to the dispatcher's question, 'is that why you're callin' a >nine nine nine.<' midway through, perhaps the dispatcher would interpret her call another way. So there are implications for police and for callers in distress or danger. The first is for police dispatchers to remind the caller that this is an emergency line more than once, to allow space for the kind of interaction we see in Example 16 to develop. The second is for callers to interrupt dispatchers as though involved in an entirely different conversation.

Example 16 shows dramatically the power of language and our tacit skills to understand the *actions* people do with talk. Using just words, on the telephone, with no access to gesture or any other visible information, the caller communicates that she is in danger, and the dispatcher understands that this is not a time-wasting hoax call. The dispatcher understands that a request for pizza is a vehicle for a request for urgent help from the police.

Service burden

Sometimes our requests for help and service can lead to frustration and dissatisfaction. One common feature of bad service is burden – the effort required by service users, customers, clients, and so on, to

achieve service. Here is a lovely example, from a café. The customer
has been sitting with friends, drinking tea.

Example 17: Wifi (field note)

01	Customer:	((Approaches counter)) Do you have wifi?
02	Café staff:	Yes we do.
03	Customer:	Can customers use it?
04	Café staff:	Yes they can.
05	Customer:	Is there a code or . . .
06	Café staff:	((Points at code written high up on the café wall))
07	Customer:	((Walks back to her friends with eyes rolled))

The burden is on the customer to push for service; the staff member
does not offer it. Rather than responding to the function of the
customer's questions, the staff member responds to their form, as
grammatical yes/no questions. Imagine how odd it would be if you
asked someone, 'do you have the time?' and they responded only
with 'yes'. Bad service, then, can include responding to the form and
not the function of talk.

A better way to respond to the customer's initial request would be
to skip turns 02 to 05 and jump straight to 06:

Example 18: Wifi (invented)

01	Customer:	((Approaches counter)) Do you have wifi?
02	Café staff:	Sure ((points at code written high up on the café
03		wall))

Here is another example, from a hotel bar.

Example 19: Hotel bar (field note)

01	Customers:	((Walk into the bar; bar staff member greets them))
02	Bar staff:	Just sit down and we'll take your order.
03	Customers:	((Turn towards nearest table))
04	Bar staff:	Sorry those tables are all reserved.
05	Customers:	((Turn to look at bar staff member))
06	Bar staff:	((Starts moving/walking away))
07	Customer:	Um . . . sorry, where can we sit . . .?

Again, the burden is on the customers, not the bar staff, to achieve service – and find somewhere to sit. They have to push for information about where to sit, whereas we might expect that this information is supplied proactively by the bar staff – especially as he has told them where *not* to sit.

There is something quintessentially British about the next example. Four customers arrive at a bakery café at 3.30 p.m.

Example 20: Bakery café (field note)

01	Customer:	Hi! Are you still open?
02	Bakery:	Yes – open til four.
03	Customer:	Great! Could we order coffee?
04	Bakery:	I'd have to put the machine on.

05		(2.0)
06	Customer:	Um . . . is that a yes or . . .?
07	Bakery:	Yes.
08	Customer:	Great!

Although there is plenty of evidence to indicate that the café is open (lights on, goods for sale, staff milling around – no 'Closed' sign on the door!) the customer checks. This opens up the possibility that, while the bakery part of the shop may be open, the café may be finished for the day. However, the staff member confirms that they are open. She does not qualify her response, and the customer proceeds with an order. At line 04, the staff member does qualify how 'open' the café is: 'I'd have to put the machine on.' Her response defines customer service as a chore, to 'have to' put the machine on. Now the customer is in the position of placing a burden on the staff member to provide service, despite the fact that they are a café . . .

Pushing for service, in which the burden is on customers, patients and service users to get help, is very common. It is so common that it can be a surprise when the burden is lifted by great service. I recently left a pair of expensive gloves at a famous Yorkshire tearoom while visiting friends. When I called the shop, the call-taker said she would look for the gloves and call me back. She did. And not only that, she offered – without me having to ask – to post them back. Free of charge!

Here is another example of service burden from a recording of a customer calling the double-glazing company we encountered earlier in the chapter. Like Example 13, in which the caller does not make a request when phoning their MP's office, but describes their problems, this caller has also told a story about a faulty pane of double glazing.

Example 21: Calling double-glazing sales (simplified transcript)

01	Customer:	I did speak to one of your colleagues actually,=And:
02		uh (.) .thhh I was expecting a call-back from someone
03		today:,=but- (.) perhaps it didn't get passed through.
04		(.)
05	Customer:	.hhhh uh: m: (0.2) But*- (0.2) *above one of the
06		window:s, hhh==where they fitted a uh:m: (0.3)
07		.ptkhh (0.6) a p- >a- a-< a piece of: uh light oak:
08		uh (1.0) .hhh I don't know how to describe it.=I do- I
09		s'pose it's about six seven foot long:,=it goes to a
10		point:,=(y-) like a semi circle effect.=d'you know?
11		(0.3)
12	Sales:	Yes,
13	Customer:	Above the one window. That's just come o:ff:.
14		(0.2)
15	Sales:	Oh right.=Okay,

The customer reports something that is doubtless familiar to us all – waiting for a promised call-back. So the first burden on the caller is that he has to call back himself. He is not disposed to make too much of this – he suggests a reason that someone has not called: 'perhaps it didn't get passed through'. But the salesperson does not say anything at line 04 – we might expect an apology, and some reassurance that his issue will be dealt with now.

Next, the customer continues to describe his problem, with some difficulty in articulating the technical aspects of the broken window. At line 13, he delivers the core message, that something has 'come off'. Again, nothing happens in response at line 14, before the salesperson responds with a 'change-of-state' token – 'Oh'; she now knows what the problem is. The 'oh' could sound sympathetic; she could say 'Oh dear' – but it sounds like routine news for her. The call continues as the customer does more and more work describing his problem, hoping that the salesperson will make an offer without him having to make a request!

Example 21 (a few seconds later)

21		(0.6)
22	Customer:	uhm (0.3) <u>W</u>hether the <u>wi</u>nd's <u>c</u>aught under<u>n</u>eath it, I
23		i- I- I just don't <u>k</u>now.
24		(0.2)
25	Customer:	<u>B</u>ut uh i- it's <u>c</u>ome o:ff,=and it's: uhm-
26		(0.8)
27	Customer:	If you actually look how it was se<u>c</u>ured <u>ori</u>ginally I
28		<u>don</u>'t think it was: <u>th:</u>at suc<u>c</u>essful in the way it was
29		se<u>cu:</u>red.
30		(0.7)
31	Customer:	Uh:::: uh:: so I don't know whether- could <u>you</u> hhh
32		(0.2) <u>s</u>end someone out to have a <u>l</u>ook at <u>th</u>at.
33		=for me?
34	Sales:	<u>Y</u>es,=of <u>c</u>ourse we <u>c</u>an:.=uh::m:: °I'm just trying to
35		have a look at the <u>d</u>iary°.

The salesperson does not offer to do what the caller has to eventually request directly – 'send someone out to have a look at that.=for me?' The burden is on the customer to achieve service, and also make an explicit request when an offer was relevant much earlier in the call. This is what poor service looks like.

I want to look in more detail at some of the calls we encountered earlier, in which patients rang their general practice surgeries. The GP Reception Project started a few years ago, when I was approached by a GP who had heard me speak about conversation analysis on the radio. He wondered if I might be able to analyse recordings of patients calling the surgery, to identify what was effective – and what was not. Our aim was to improve patients' experience when calling the doctor's – within the constraints of the UK National Health Service and its limited resources.

Working with colleagues,[94] analysing calls from three different surgeries, we immediately encountered the problem of service burden. Here is a particularly clear example from the hundreds of calls we analysed.

Example 22: Calling the doctor's

01	Reception:	Good morning, surgery Cath speaking,
02		(1.6)
03	Patient:	Hello have you got an appointment for Friday afternoon
04		or teatime please.
05		(0.4)
06	Reception:	This Friday.
07		(1.1)
08	Patient:	Yeah,
09	Reception:	Uh I'm sorry we're fully booked on Friday.
10		(1.6)

Rather like the first example of burden – the customer asking about wifi – the receptionist treats the patient's question as requiring information and nothing more. It is like answering just 'yes' to the question, 'have you got the time?' From the receptionist's point of

---

94 Sikveland et al. (2016); Stokoe et al. (2016).

view, the caller's enquiry has been dealt with. At line 10, a long gap develops. There is plenty of time for the receptionist to do what other receptionists do at this point – offer the next available appointment. The patient has not indicated that the problem is urgent – she does not 'need' an appointment and she does not ask for one 'today'.

As the call[95] unfolds, the receptionist reconfirms that they are 'fully booked', and it looks like the call will end soon. Watch out as the patient and receptionist talk at the same time, on lines 19 and 20.

Example 22 (continued)

11	Patient:	Right.
12		(0.3)
13	Reception:	We're fully booked.
14	Patient:	Okay,
15		(0.3)
16	Reception:	Okay.
17		(0.4)
18	Patient:	Yeah, uh okay, [uhm,]
19	Reception:	[Than]k yo[u]
20	Patient:	[Is] it worth me ringing
21		Flaxton.

---

95 Listen to the call (and other examples from the book) at www.carmtraining.org/talk/extras.

It is clear that, from the receptionist's point of view, the business of the call is over. The patient has asked a question, and she has given an answer. At line 19, she says, 'Thank you'. Saying 'thank you' at the end of a call does not indicate gratitude – especially when uttered by the service provider first! It is very common for people to end service encounters with reciprocal 'thank yous' – even when service has not been achieved. This is because 'thank you' has another function – to close the call.

So, as the patient says 'uh okay, uhm' (line 18), trying to keep the conversation going, the receptionist starts to close it. The only thing that the patient can do is push for service. So, also in overlap, the patient asks the receptionist if it is worth calling their sister surgery in the next village. The receptionist makes no offers of help at all. Here is another example.

Example 23: Calling the doctor's (simplified transcript)

01	Reception:	Hello:,
02	Patient:	Hello there, >just wondering if I can get an
03		appointment with Doctor<Warrington please.=
04	Reception:	=He's on holiday at the momen:t,

The receptionist responds to the patient's request with an implicit no – and stops. The patient keeps the conversation going.

Example 23 (continued)

05	Patient:	Oh:, wh- uh when 'til,
06	Reception:	Ooh not while we're (uh) end of October.
07		(0.3)
08	Patient	Oh right,=>okay that's a good holiday< isn't it.
09		.Hhh u:hm,
10	Reception:	Hm hm hm hm.

At line 07, after answering the patient's question about when her doctor might be available, a lapse in the conversation occurs. Again, the burden is on the patient to keep things going, in the face of the receptionist failing to drive service forward. After an ironic assessment of her doctor's lengthy holiday, the patient is still no further forward. She suggests another doctor.

Example 23 (continued)

11	Patient:	.ptkhh anything with de Doctor de Courcy at all?
12	Reception:	Mmm, °Just a moment°.
13		(10.9)
14	Reception:	No̲:,=I've not got anything with him at the momen:t,
15		(2.5)
16	Patient:	Right,
17		(1.1)
18	Patient:	U:h:m
19		(0.5)
20	Patient:	Doctor Grantham?
21	Reception:	Sixteenth of October,=Doctor de Courcy.
22		(0.7)
23	Patient:	Wi- sorry- sorry?
24	Reception:	Sixteenth of Octob[er,]
25	Patient:	[Tha]t suits me perfect.

So, it is the patient, and not the receptionist, who suggests an alternative doctor. Note the long gaps that develop as the patient remains in conversational limbo. Eventually, the patient makes yet another suggestion at line 20. However, it appears that the receptionist has been searching for an appointment with the patient's second choice of doctor, Dr de Courcy. But she has not informed the patient of this – causing confusion at the end of the conversation (lines 22–23). Imagine if the call had unfolded like this:

Example 24 (23 reimagined)

01	Reception:	Hello:,
02	Patient:	Hello there, >just wondering if I can get an
03		appointment with Doctor<Warrington please.=
04	Reception:	=He's on holiday at the momen:t, but I could
05		do Doctor de Courcy on the sixteenth?
06	Patient:	That suits me perfect.

The receptionist was unable to meet her patient's initial request. And an offer of an appointment with another doctor never happened; the patient had to push for it. Even if the receptionist did not know at that point, as seems the case, that Dr de Courcy was available on the sixteenth, she could still have said, 'I'll see if another doctor is available, if that's okay?' while checking to see.

Some receptionists do make offers following an initial inability to grant patients' requests. Example 25 is one such case.

Example 25: Calling the doctor's

```
01   Reception:   Good morning,=Limetown Surgery,=

02   Patient:     =Good morning,=Could I have an appointment to see

03                Doctor <Wilkinson plea:se>¿=

04   Reception:   =.ptkhhh hh°uh:m° >#let me#< see when the next

05                available one is.=I don't think I've got anything pre

06                bookable this wee:k¿ D'you want me to look for the

07                week after:¿
```

While patients regularly have their first request turned down, in this case the receptionist simply offers to search for the next available appointment. The receptionist removes any burden from the patient, who does not have to push for service – it is offered.

The burden on patients to push for service was one of two main problems we identified in calls to the doctor's. The second problem generally arose at the end of the call, when the main business was complete. In Example 26, we return to the conversation in which the patient, after initially asking for an appointment with Dr Warrington, is eventually offered an appointment on 'the sixteenth' with Dr de Courcy. So, the patient has made her appointment, and the receptionist now checks the patient's address.

Example 26: Calling the doctor's

```
01   Reception:   What's your address please.

02                (0.6)

03   Patient:     Eighty four Tern Way.
```

04	Reception:	Okay then,
05		(0.5)
06	Reception:	[Thank you,]
07	Patient:	[So it's th-]
08		(0.5)
09	Patient:	That's the sixteenth?
10	Reception:	=The sixteenth, [at ten pa]st eleven.
11	Patient:	[Okay then.]
12		(0.3)
13	Patient:	Ten past eleven, thank you.
14	Reception:	Thank you,
15		(0.2)
16	Patient:	T[hank you,]
17	Reception:	[B y e .]=
18	Patient:	=Bye.

The receptionist starts to end the call at line 04, saying 'Okay then', and then, after a gap, says 'thank you'. We saw earlier that one function of 'thank yous' is to indicate that a conversation is at an end. However, in Example 26, like Example 22, it is the receptionist, not the patient, who says 'thank you' first. Also like Example 22, as the receptionist says 'thank you', the patient attempts to keep the call open (lines 06–07). Here is a reminder of the end of Example 22.

13	Reception:	We're fully booked.
14	Patient:	Okay,
15		(0.3)
16	Reception:	Okay.
17		(0.4)
18	Patient:	Yeah, uh okay, [uhm,]
19	Reception:	[Than]k you

In both cases, the patient and the receptionist are misaligned. In Example 26, the patient keeps the conversation open to secure a confirmation of her appointment from the receptionist. Given the earlier confusion about which doctor the appointment was with, a confirmation would bring the conversation to an effective end. But the patient has to push for it.

Other receptionists summarise the main business that has been transacted in the call without the patient asking. They confirm appointments, when to call back, when results will be ready – the thing that may happen next in the patient's life. Here is an example. The patient has made an appointment and the receptionist, like in the previous case, checks a piece of information about the patient.

Example 27: Calling the doctor's

01	Reception:	And date of bi:rth.
02	Patient:	.hh fourth of the fifth ninety one.
03		(0.5)
04	Reception:	↑Okay, Ten past six:. Tuesday the twenty eighth

05		of October.=
06	Patient:	=That's lovely.=↑Thank you very much
07		[for tha:t, [>Right<
08	Reception:	[Thank y o u[:.
09	Reception:	By[e:.]
10	Patient:	[Bye by]e:ȥ

This time, the receptionist (re)confirms the patient's appointment. And this time, the patient says 'thank you' first. What's more, the patient expresses her satisfaction with the service – 'That's lovely', and upgrades her 'thank you' to 'Thank you very much for tha:t,'. By evaluating the call, and saying 'thank you' first, the patient initiates the end of the call, now that all her business is done.

What have we learned from these calls? People often suggest that receptionists do not offer appointments unless 'really pushed', to spread out resources and to 'gatekeep' for doctors. We found little evidence of this reasoning. Patients almost always got an appointment, eventually. Resource was there. In fact, resource was wasted when receptionists were not proactive in helping patients – calls took far longer.

We coded the two types of burden identified – pushing for an appointment and pushing for confirmations. We correlated the amount of burden with the surgeries' national patient satisfaction scores, on items asking about experience of reception and appointment-making. Unsurprisingly, the higher the burden to achieve service in calls, the lower the patient satisfaction scores. And now we had something to train receptionists to do. After we trained receptionists to offer alternative appointments and confirm whatever has happened in the call, satisfaction scores rose. These communication tweaks were easy – and cost nothing.

We have also learned something about what words actually do, which might be counter-intuitive. Saying 'thank you' at the end of a call does not indicate gratitude. This is most clearly seen when receptionists say 'thank you' before patients, to end the call. Another indicator of (dis)satisfaction, then, is the order in which 'thank yous' occur. When patients go first, they indicate that they are done – whether or not they got service. If they also got good service, they add an evaluation, like we saw in Example 27 ('that's lovely') and upgrade 'thank you' to 'thank you very much'. Only then should the receptionist align with the patient to end the call, with their own 'thank you'.

This tells us that, say, counting examples of 'thank you' at the end of a service encounter tells us nothing about customer satisfaction. And here's an experiment for you. The next time you have an irritating customer service call, try to withhold saying 'thank you' at all – even to close the call. Your heart will race and you will feel very rude. But that is all it takes to indicate strong displeasure with a call. We do not typically say, 'I am very dissatisfied', or get angry. Even when we hang up a call, we show that we are done with a 'thank you' before putting the phone down! Try it . . .

Recruiters and the recruited

Have you ever wondered 'why am I doing this?' at the same time *exactly* as you make an offer to do something for someone? In the final section of this chapter, we examine how it is that we come to help others – including when we don't want to.

Consider the following case.

Example 28: Restaurant (field note)

01	Waiter:	((Brings the bill))
02	Diner 1:	I'll get it.
03	Diner 2:	Okay!

When people offer things like paying for dinner or giving a lift – when some prior arrangement is not already in place – there are different ways to respond. Accepting an offer too rapidly can make the person giving the offer feel taken for granted. Or, as Sarah Cooper puts it, a 'people pleaser'.[96] These are people who always seem happy with everything, never end a phone call, never say what they want, and offer to do things they don't want to do.

A better way to accept an offer is to check over a short series of turns, allowing the offerer a way out.

Example 29: Lift (field note)

01	A:	Can I give you a lift?
02	B:	Oh no, it's really out of your way.
03	A:	No, honestly, it's fine!
04	B:	Oh . . . okay . . . if you're sure?
05	A:	Absolutely.

The conversation analysts Kobin Kendrick and Paul Drew[97] discuss the way we get and offer help in terms of 'recruitment'.

> The concept of recruitment is developed to encompass the linguistic and embodied ways in which assistance may be sought—requested or solicited—or in which we come to perceive another's need and offer or volunteer assistance. We argue that these methods are organized as a continuum, from explicit requests, to practices that elicit offers, to anticipations of need. We further identify a class of subsidiary actions that can precede recruitment and that publicly expose troubles and thereby create opportunities for others to assist.

---

96 https://thecooperreview.com/people-pleasers-guide-pleasing-people/
97 Kendrick and Drew (2016).

People can anticipate each other's needs, and fulfil them before a request is made. Imagine being at a restaurant with an empty water glass. You may glance at it and your co-diner may notice, and fill up the glass. You may not notice your empty glass at all, but your co-diner may, and offer to fill it. Or you might ask your co-diner to fill it up – if the jug is nearer to them. Asking them to fill it up if the jug is nearest to you might cause an interesting ripple in the conversation!

If you are the person who looks round for help when you could help yourself, you are a 'recruiter'. And if you respond to a 'recruiter', you are 'the recruited'. We can add these two categories to our Conversation Analytic Personality Diagnostic (Chapter 3, 'You are the turns you take').

Here are some examples of 'recruiters'. They are all from email conversations. In Example 30, Glenn and Clare are both senior managers, with similar responsibilities. After receiving this email, Clare sets up the arrangement using the electronic diary to which they both have access.

Example 30: Colleague email

01   Glenn: Can we meet please.

So, rather than simply sending Clare an electronic invitation, Glenn recruits Clare to make the appointment, and she is recruited to make their meeting happen.

Here are Glenn and Clare again. Glenn has forwarded an email to Clare, about an organisation-wide opportunity. He adds one line to his email.

Example 31: Colleague email

01   Glenn: Are we doing anything about this?

In this case, rather than make a suggestion, Glenn puts the burden on Clare to drive forward the opportunity. If she responds, Clare is, again, the 'recruited'.

In a final example, Glenn leaves Clare, once again, in a position to have to respond to him, while he could have set up a meeting himself.

Example 32: Colleague email

| 01 | Glenn: | Let us find some time to discuss it. |

What I am calling 'burden' the French comic artist 'Emma' refers to as 'mental load'. 'Mental load' manifests in conversations like these.

Example 33: Heterosexual partners[98]

| 01 | Woman: | You didn't do the dishes? |
| 02 | Man: | Well, you never asked! |

Example 34: Heterosexual partners (invented)

| 01 | Man: | ((From the couch)) Do you want some help? |
| 02 | Woman: | ((Fumes silently)) No! It's fine! |

Of course, I am getting into tricky territory here, gendering a phenomenon that may or may not be ... but there is a great deal of evidence that these stereotypes are borne out in homes around the world. Emma defines the 'mental load' as 'always having to remember' and tells the following story to illustrate it.

---

98 www.theguardian.com/world/2017/may/26/gender-wars-household-chores-comic?

The fact that this load exists becomes obvious when I decide to take care of a simple chore, like clearing the table. I start by picking something up to put it away, but on the way I come across a dirty towel that I go put in the laundry basket, which I find full. So I go to the washing machine . . . and I see the vegetables that I need to put in the fridge. As I'm putting away the vegetables, I realise that I need to add mustard to the shopping list. And so on and so forth. In the end, I'll have cleared away my table . . . only to find it covered in stuff again later that evening. If I ask my partner to clear the table, he'll just clear the table. The towel will stay on the floor, the vegetables will rot on the kitchen counter, and we won't have any mustard for dinner.[99]

I will leave the (heterosexual) gender wars there, for now. I want to end with a small dedication to my partner, George, and his recruitment tactics. He is the kind of person who loses his keys, pencils, a jacket, his phone . . . and this is not a gendered phenomenon, at least in my experience. I know plenty of scatty women.

Here is a very typical scene from my house. George is downstairs, about to go out (and running late) to meet friends. Liz is upstairs, writing this book.

Example 35: At home (not quite invented)

01	George:	.HHHHHHHH ((loud sighing))
02		(5.0)
03	George:	.hhhh HHHHH pffff ((annoyed sounds))
04	Liz:	((calling downstairs)) Y'okay?
05	George:	Yeah . . . ((more annoyed sounds))

---

99 english.emmaclit.com

06		(3.0)
07	George:	Can't find that voucher for ((names the café where he
08		is meeting friends))
09	George:	Never mind. Have a nice day! ((leaves))

I realise that I probably do not come off well in this episode. I do not dash downstairs to help. I do not – slowly or reluctantly – offer assistance. In my defence, I have learned not to respond to George's sounds of irritation – because he almost always finds the thing he has lost within a few seconds.

Indeed, when I first met George, he reminded me of (a much gentler!) Bulldog – the sports radio presenter in the US sitcom *Frasier* – who frequently loses things, loses his temper, only to immediately find the thing he has lost and return to calm. In this example, Bulldog is in *Café Nervosa*, frantically patting his jacket for some sports tickets and looking around at the other customers.

Example 36: *Frasier:* **'Oops'**[100]

01	Bulldog:	Hey. Where's my tickets to the Sonics game.
02		They were here just a second ago.
03		SOMEONE STOLE MY TICKETS TO THE SONICS GAME!!!
04		THIS STINKS!
05		THIS IS TOTAL BS!
06		THIS IS- Oh – got 'em . . .
07	Audience:	((Laughter))

---

100 Written by David Angell, Peter Casey and David Lee.

Bulldog's rants, like this one, comprise one of the show's motifs. The audience laugh partly because the episode is recognisable to regular viewers, and they know he will find the tickets very rapidly. They also laugh because of the way the actor delivers the lines: Bulldog's anger escalates so quickly, and in such an exaggerated way, before de-escalating to a happy calm just as quickly.

Thank you for not helping

This chapter has explored core actions for building and maintaining human sociality: requesting and offering help. We have encountered the many ways that people can, in many different settings, offer help, anticipate another's needs, resist help, or communicate the importance of a request. Some of the examples we have analysed reveal people's tacit skills in anticipating and providing help, before others have asked for it. Other cases show how speakers fail to offer assistance when it is due or overdue, sometimes resulting in help or service being completely absent.

In the final chapter, we bring much of the book together, to build up a toolkit for having better conversations. Take a deep breath . . . and prepare to talk.

7

HOW TO HAVE BETTER CONVERSATIONS

This book is not a self-help book to improve your communication. But, by reading this book – and this chapter – you have new insights into the conversations you have. You have fresh understandings about the systematic nature of talk, and scientific ways to study it. You might even start to see your words and turns at talk, as you produce them, stream out as transcription!

To know how to have better conversations, we must first understand what *counts* as a better conversation. How do we develop communication guidance? How do we train people to communicate better? And how do we assess people's communication skills? These are the questions we will address in this chapter. As a starting point, consider the first few seconds of this telephone call to the vet's.

Imagine you have been given the task of developing (or assessing) communication skills for this type of workplace. What would you watch out for? Does the receptionist have 'good communication skills'?

Example 1: Calling the vet (simplified transcript)

01	Reception:	U-good afternoon Town Veterinary Surgery Anna
02		speakin' how c'n I help.
03	Caller:	Hi.=I just got a new puppy the other day. .hhh
04		s'wonderin' how much it'd cost t'get the jabs done.
05		please.
06	Reception:	Of course, yeah, let's have a look for you,=what
07		was um the breed o'the puppy that y'had.
08		(0.4)
09	Caller:	Oh 'e's jus' a cross breed.=collie [cross.
10	Reception:	[Ohhw::.

You may notice things about the manner in which the receptionist answers the phone. Within one turn, she does a greeting, announces the name of the vet's, her own name, and makes an offer of help. These four components – four actions – comprise the maximal way of answering the phone from an organisation or service. Call-takers may drop or rearrange actions, and we have seen many examples across the book (e.g., 'Good afternoon, Fine Bar Windows'; 'Good evening Rindley Leisure Hotels, you're speaking to Diane, how can I help?'; 'Good morning reception, Melanie speaking').

You may notice things about the receptionist's second turn, in which she immediately ('of course') gets to work answering the caller's request for information. She talks collaboratively ('Let's') with a focus on personal service ('for you'). Asking about the dog's breed is necessary to progress the call, but the receptionist also creates an opportunity to affiliate with the caller. She can now respond to whatever answer the caller gives – any dog breed is special for the owner – with an 'Ohhw::.'. This 'oh', you may remember from Chapter 6, is a 'change-of-state' token – the receptionist has gone from 'not knowing' to 'knowing'. But this 'oh' does not just register new information. By infusing it with warm and soft intonation, the receptionist also affiliates with the caller.

In terms of assessing the receptionist's skills, then, perhaps you would make a positive assessment. You may deduct marks for apparent disfluency (the little 'u' right at the start of her first turn). But you may also then remember that such sounds are generally not 'errors' (Chapter 4). And you now know how messy real talk looks when it is transcribed accurately.

In terms of developing guidance or training, you may recommend that receptionists take and create opportunities to affiliate while asking service-relevant questions, like 'what breed is the dog?' The call could have easily unfolded like the invented version below, in which the receptionist no longer says, 'Of course, yeah, let's have a look for you', or 'Ohhw::.'

Example 2: Calling the vet (invented)

01	Reception:	U-good afternoon Town Veterinary Surgery Anna
02		speakin' how c'n I help.
03	Caller:	Hi.=I just got a new puppy the other day. .hhh
04		s'wonderin' how much it'd cost t'get the jabs done.
05		please.
06	Reception:	What was um the breed o'the puppy.
07	Caller:	Oh 'e's jus' a cross breed.=collie cross.
08	Reception:	Right, the cost is (. . .)

Examining the first few turns of a service encounter has enabled us to identify a potential 'trainable' for vet receptionists: 'take opportunities to affiliate when asking routine questions about the type of animal the caller owns'. Or has it? We will return to this example later in the chapter.

Identifying better conversations by examining real conversations – and turning this evidence into guidance or training – contrasts sharply with the way the communication training field works more generally, in terms of both research and practice. Almost all communication training involves some form of simulation or role-play, which you may have participated in yourself.

The first part of this chapter will set out some problems with traditional forms of communication guidance, role-play and simulation – all underpinning the realisation of communication skills. We will address the issue of authenticity of role-played and simulated encounters, and the problems of developing and implementing written communication guidance. Towards the end of the chapter, we will consider briefly the implications of research on simulated conversation for the future of human communication, with other humans and computers. Finally, despite not being a self-help book, this chapter will end by consolidating some of the key messages about talk, with five ways to have better conversations.

The problem with communication skills

This book is about real talk. Although I have taken the liberty of inventing a few cases to illustrate particular points about conversation, if we want to understand real talk, we need to study real talk. As part of my own journey, communicating about conversation analysis to many different audiences, I decided to examine non-real talk. Non-real talk is, of course, real talk of a kind. But it occurred to me that the talk produced in training sessions – role-played, simulated encounters – might be worth examining. How authentic is simulated or role-played talk? Are the turns taken in simulated conversations the same as those that occur in the real versions? If not, what is role-play for? Is it okay to assess someone's communication skills, based on what they do in role-play? Is it okay to pass or fail them, or promote or demote them, on the basis of a simulated conversation?

Role-play and simulation are ubiquitous in the communication training world, and as methods for assessing people's apparent skills. Hundreds of companies offer 'practical role-play scenarios' to enable participants to practise 'real-life' business situations. They offer a 'diverse team of role players who can play a wide range of characters and types to create realistic scenarios and personnel reflecting your company profile'. They offer 'professional role players who can convincingly replicate any workplace scenario or personality'.

Hardly anyone has attempted to interrogate or challenge claims such as these. Instead, researchers and practitioners alike ask post-hoc questions to participants in training sessions, like 'How authentic did it *feel*?' They do not compare simulated encounters to their real counterparts.

One clear difference between real and simulated encounters is the stake people have in the talk they produce. The outcomes are quite different. Very often in simulated encounters, the goal is to pass a component of training, to get hired, promoted, qualified or not fired. In real encounters, the goal is to collect evidence, diagnose an illness, give support, or one of myriad actions done in workplace and organisational settings.

Another goal of simulated or role-played encounters is to align what you say to written guidance. Again, training manuals and guidelines for communicating are available for almost any profession – sales, police, medicine, healthcare, teaching, management. To be a successful participant in a communication training course, and pass the course, you must turn the written guidance into spoken talk. But what if the written guidance is wrong? Who writes the written guidance? Is it research-based? Is it based on what we have identified as communication myths . . .?

So far, I have raised many questions about role-play and written guidance. Let us start to answer them, beginning with a comparison of real police interviews (with real suspects) and simulated police interviews (with actors playing the part of suspects). I collected both types of recorded data. When suspects are arrested, their interviews are recorded on old-fashioned cassette tape, by law (not for research). Because simulations are designed to mimic actual interviews, they are recorded in the same way (again, not for research).

A few years ago, I decided to examine the very opening moments of real and simulated interviews.[101] What happens in openings is heavily prescribed by law – the Police and Criminal Evidence Act (PACE).[102] This means that, in both cases, the police interviewers' first job is to turn the following written PACE Items into spoken talk with the suspect.

1. The interviewer should tell the suspect about the recording process. The interviewer shall say the interview is being audibly recorded.

2. The interviewer shall give their name and rank and that of any other interviewer present.

3. The interviewer shall ask the suspect and any other party present, e.g. a solicitor, to identify themselves.

4. The interviewer shall state the date, time of commencement and place of the interview.

5. The interviewer shall state the suspect will be given a notice about what will happen to the copies of the recording.

6. The interviewer shall . . . remind the suspect of their entitlement to free legal advice.

Given this clear structure, one might wonder how differently 'reminding the suspect of their entitlement to free legal advice' could be expressed in talk. The answer is . . . quite differently.

---

101   Stokoe (2013b).

102   PACE: Police and Criminal Evidence Act (1984); PACE 'Code E' (2008: 202).

The first difference between real and simulated interviews occurred even before PACE Item 1. The interviews start with a 'squeal' made by the audio cassette, which continued until the magnetic, recordable part of the tape spooled into place. Look at the two examples below. If you can, without reading ahead, try to work out which is the real interview and which is the role-played encounter. There are two officers present in each.

Example 3: Police interview

01		((tape squeal))
02		(0.7)
03	Police 1:	>.HHH This is a< tape recorded interview in interview
04		room two at Boroughtown p'lice sta:tion?
05		(0.6)
06	Police 1:	The time is: (0.3) ten past (.) two, on the fourteenth of
07		July two thousan' an' four.

Example 4: Police interview

01	Police 1:	[((clears throat))
02		[((tape squeal))
03	Police 2:	We're in.=okay, cooking on gas now,
04		(1.0)
05	Police 1:	Right, (.) a(h)s y(h)o(h)u can see £eventually:£ ↑every
06		thin' we say is now

06   bein' re<u>co</u>rded, .hhh an' <u>at</u> the <u>e</u>nd I'll give you a notice

07   explainin:: where the tapes will be goin' an' what w'll be

08   h<u>a</u>ppenin' to th<u>e</u>:m?

The first PACE Item is that 'the interviewer should tell the suspect about the recording process. The interviewer shall say the interview is being audibly recorded.' How does this imperative statement get turned into actual words and turns at talk?

In Example 3, the first police officer says, 'This is a< tape recorded interview in interview room two at Boroughtown p'lice sta:tion?' The police officer also completes PACE Item 4 ('state the date, time of commencement and place of the interview'). But 'place' is formulated as part of Item 1.

Example 4 differs from Example 3 in several ways. First, some talk happens that has nothing to do with PACE; the first officer clears her throat, and the second says, 'We're in.=okay, cooking on gas now'. Apparently, the officers have had some trouble operating the recording equipment, which they turn into a jokey remark. And, in this example, the PACE Item is turned into quite different words: 'everythin' we say is now bein' recorded'. Finally, while in Example 3 the officer combines Items 1 and 4, in Example 4, the officer combines Items 1 and 5 ('The interviewer shall state the suspect will be given a notice about what will happen to the copies of the recording').

Have you guessed which the real interview is and which is role-played? Most audiences guess that Example 3 is role-played and Example 4 is real. In fact, it is the other way around. Analysis of both datasets revealed that PACE Items were put together in different combinations in real and simulated interviews. It also revealed that police officers said things prior to PACE Item 1 only in simulations, before getting down to business. In real interviews, the police interviewers got straight down to business. And, while in real interviews officers stated that 'this interview is being tape recorded', in simulations they stated that 'everythin' we say is now bein' recorded'. The personal pronoun 'we' helps to turn dry text into something more collaborative.

These differences were systematic across the two types of interview. In real and simulated interviews, police officers turned written guidance into spoken talk in quite different ways. And neither quoted directly from the legal text of PACE. In real interviews, the data shows that police officers have a particular way of turning PACE into talk. In simulations, police officers do it another way.

Before examining the difference between real suspects and actors-playing-the-part-of-suspects, I want to show you another example of PACE Item differences. It is perhaps not surprising that, in simulated interviews, officers spent much longer in general on these preliminaries. In particular, they took more time explaining adult suspects' rights (Item 6) in simulations than in real interviews. This is interesting because the Item states only that the police should 'remind the suspect of their entitlement to free legal advice', which is what happens in real interviews with fully competent adults. In real interviews with children or adults with special needs – in which 'appropriate adults' were also present – police officers took time to check suspects' understanding of their rights. In simulations, long conversations happened with actor-suspects – in ways that looked more typical of interviews with children.

PACE Item 2, 'The interviewer shall give their name and rank and that of any other interviewer present', revealed some particularly interesting differences. Again, try not to read ahead, and work out which is real, and which is role-played.

Example 5: Police interview

01   Police 1:   .hh ↑I'm pee cee ↓treble six eight Smith attached to

02   Boroughtown p'lice station,

03   (0.4)

```
04      Police 1:    Also present is my collea:gue,

05                   (0.2)

06      Police 2:    .pt Pee cee four two four Torball: also attached to:

07                   Boroughtown police station.
```

The police officer announces his rank and (sur)name, and also supplies his 'badge number' and affiliation, 'Boroughtown p'lice station,', neither of which are specified by PACE. While the guidelines state that 'the interviewer' should supply the 'name and rank and that of any other interviewer present' – implying one officer can introduce all officers present – in fact the two officers do this in tandem. The first officer starts this off, saying, 'Also present is my colleague...', and the second officer completes the sentence. They have, across two turns, produced a single action together, collaboratively.

Here is another way of turning the written PACE Item 2 into talk.

Example 6: Police interview

```
01      Police 1:    Um: (0.3) my name is pee cee Hargreaves, as we've

02                   >already discussed< please call me Linda?

03      Police 2:    .pt my name's uh- pee cee two three seven: .hh Tim

04                   Jensen: but- feel free to call me Tim,

05                   (0.3)

06      Police 2:    [All the way through,

07      Police 1:    [An::
```

The police officers are doing the same action – they use an announcement to identify themselves – but they design their announcement differently. First, rather than stating, 'I am . . .', they each say 'my name is . . .' Second, rather than build one action collaboratively, each officer takes their own complete turn, each starting with 'my name is'.

What is most striking, of course, is that both officers also invite the suspect to call them by their first names – Linda and Tim. Indeed, Linda reminds the suspect that she has 'already discussed' this with him. Finally, note that, in contrast to the rather more slick way that the officers in Example 5 introduced themselves collaboratively, in Example 6 there is a glitch at lines 06–07, as the second officer adds a little bit more to his invitation to 'call me Tim, . . . All the way through'. This was not anticipated by the first officer who, simultaneously, begins the PACE Item.

Can you spot which is real, and which is simulated? In real interviews, officers generally introduced themselves saying, 'I am . . .', not 'my name is . . .', and, when more than one officer was present, they worked in tandem like we see in Example 5. In simulations, officers used the 'my name is . . .' format. They each took their own full turns to introduce themselves. Remember that they are being observed as they role-play – so ensuring that the examiner sees that they introduce themselves is most likely what they want to ensure happens. And it was only in simulations that officers invited suspects to call them by their first names. In Example 6, the first officer not only invites the suspect to call her Linda, but makes visible the fact that she has already done some 'rapport-building' work with the suspect, off-tape, to establish an informal footing for the interview ('as we've already discussed').

If you are a driver, you might remember how you drove on the day you took your test. You knew all the little actions the examiner was watching out for – checking in the rear-view mirror, placing your hands correctly on the steering wheel, using the side mirrors, and so on. And so you probably exaggerated each of those actions to ensure that they were visible to the examiner.

In simulations, the same thing occurs. Speakers ensure that the 'assessable' communication practices are clearly present, to be ticked off by the observing assessor. The next example, from a role-play, illustrates this beautifully.

Example 7: Simulated interview

01	Police 1:	<Like I'said before I'm pee cee two four six eight
02		Jim O'Dowd?
03		(0.5)
04	Police 1:	Others present are,
05		(1.0)
06	Police 2:	Uh- my name's (0.3) Brian Smith, pee cee <u>o</u>ne two
07		three zero?

((9 lines – Police 1 moves on to the next PACE Item))

16	Police 1:	↑Right.=like I said my- (0.2) name is pee cee:: (0.6)
17		Jim O'Dowd, but- please jus'- refer to me as Jim if
18		that's okay with you,=it's more- (0.8) it's what I
19		prefer really,

You will have noticed that, as in real interviews, the first officer starts delivering PACE Item 2 using the 'I'm PC . . .', not 'My name is . . .' But he adds, 'Like I'said before', which is more typical of simulations. The first officer then invites the second officer to complete an introduction ('Others present are . . .'), again like real interviews.

However, after a delay, the second officer fails to complete the introductions. Instead, he starts a fresh new turn, starting in the way that we have seen in role-played encounters – 'My name is . . .' And notice the 'Uh' that initiates the second officer's turn on line 06. It is not an error. As we saw in other examples in the book, saying 'uh' marks the prior turn as inapposite. For the second officer, the upshot of what he does is something like this: 'I want to ensure that I make a full introduction on my own, not in collaboration with what you, first officer, are doing.'

Once the introductions are completed, the first police officer moves onto PACE Item 3, which is, 'The interviewer shall ask the suspect and any other party present, e.g. a solicitor, to identify themselves.' What he has not done, unlike the role-playing officers in Example 6, is invite the suspect to call him 'Jim'. This is not a requirement of PACE. It does not happen in real interviews. Suspects may call officers by their first names, most likely because introductions happen before the formal recorded interview.

In role-plays, officers invite suspects to call them by their first names. Evidence that these invitation sequences are to do with training and assessment comes from the fact that Jim's invitation is dislocated from the announcement of his name. He has already moved into the next PACE Item. Repeating 'like I said' reinstates the earlier sequence but also suggests the officer 'forgot' to do the invitation earlier and is now, with the assessors in mind, ensuring the invitation is formulated explicitly.

Other details are interesting. Jim does not ask the suspect if he would *like* to use his first name but instructs him to do so: 'please jus'- refer to me as Jim'. An instruction is arguably less rapport-building than an invitation. Jim then adds, 'if that's okay with you', which makes it less instructional and more optional.

Finally, Jim provides an explanation for inviting the suspect to call him 'Jim'. He starts saying 'it's more-', but stops himself, instead saying 'it's what I prefer really'. What could it be 'more . . .'? More informal? Officers are trained to build rapport and using first names is a 'textbook' way to do that. If they make explicit that first names are 'more informal', it undermines the very informality they seek to produce. The police officer's tiny correction gives us further evidence, then, that invitations are done for training and assessment reasons, not genuine rapport.

Amazingly, the alternative formats for doing introductions ('My name is . . .' versus 'I'm PC . . .') in role-played and real interactions are not limited to police interviews. Another conversation analyst, Sarah Atkins,[103] has shown that the same difference occurs in doctor–patient conversation. In real encounters, general practitioners introduce themselves by saying, 'I'm Dr Smith.' However, when being assessed on their consulting skills in simulations, GPs say, 'My name is Dr Smith', to pass their 'objective structured clinical examination' (OSCE).

This finding is a wonderful reason for conducting conversation analysis – but also for thinking about real and simulated interaction. Clearly, different occupations are trained to make introductions in the same way – 'My name is . . .' Doctors and police officers use this format when being assessed. But they use 'I'm X' in real encounters – with no evidence that this is less effective in 'rapport-building'. Where does the instruction to say 'My name is . . .' come from? I do not know. What I do know is that it does not come from looking at the way people actually do introductions.

Yet training for, and assessment of, communicative encounters, is often apparently designed on the basis of people's attempts to make explicit their tacit knowledge and build that into guidance and recommendations. This leads to failures in identifying the right 'trainables' or 'assessables', because people's memories of their communicative encounters are shaped by many factors, from sheer processing capacity to stereotypes and heuristics.

We see this cashed out empirically if we compare guidance for police officers to ask effective initial questions of suspects with what works in actual encounters. The guidance[104] states:

> Best-practice interview protocols advise that interviewers elicit a 'free-narrative' account of offences through adherence to non-leading open-ended questions where possible, i.e., questions that encourage an elaborate response without dictating what specific information is required.

---

103 Atkins et al. (2016).

104 Powell et al. (2010).

Example 8 comes from a role-played interview with an actor playing the suspect. The officer's first question is a close approximation of the textbook open-ended non-leading question.

Example 8: Simulated police interview

01	Police:	↑FIRstly um: (.) I'd like y't'tell me about (0.8) your day: (.)
02		from: when you woke up this mornin' until the point that
03		we ↓met.
04		(1.8)
05	Suspect:	*Uh:: got up,h* (0.6) *went t'th'toilet:* (1.4) 'ad break
06		fast: (0.3) wen' t'Tesco, (1.4) got ju:mped on.
07		(1.1)
08	Police:	Okay, .hhh um: (.) would y'care t're- to: (0.4) expand on
09		tha' an' give me some more detail.=t'describe: (0.6)
10		your day.
11		(0.3)
12	Suspect:	*Uhm::* (1.1) *got up,* (1.2) wen' toilet, h (2.5) uh:: (1.4)
13		wen' for a poo, (0.5) £.shih£ (0.4) uh: (.) wen' downstairs:
14		(1.8) uh: put toast in: toaster (0.3) uh:: got pan out, put
15		butter in the pan. Put eggs in pan Uh:: stirred that round
16		((continues for several minutes))

In the interview, the textbook question does not generate from the suspect what is sought by the police officer. Evidence for this is that the officer redesigns the question and asks it again (lines 08–11). Furthermore, the suspect, an actor, subverts the process by doing things that real suspects typically do not. More generally, I found that paid actors playing the part of suspects often did things that real suspects did not – because they could; because the consequences for them were not as they would be for a real suspect in a real interview.

Compare this to another example, this time from a real interview.

Example 9: Real police interview

```
01    Police:    Could you tell me (0.3) uh the circumstances that le:d (0.4)

02               t'[you bein' arrested.

03    Suspect:   [Uh- basically, (0.8) me an' Bob 'ad a little (0.6) ding-

04               dong we're fallin' ou:t, (0.) 'e chucked me ou:t an' I just

05               fli:pped an' I went- (0.7) I jus' (0.4) 'it his doo:r with me

06               golf club basically, (0.5) that was it,
```

In Example 9, the officer asks a markedly different kind of question to the textbook version in Example 8. It is grammatically different – it is a 'closed' interrogative formatted question rather than an open-ended imperative. It includes noun phrases and verbs from a legal rather than informal register ('the circumstances' versus 'your day'; 'arrested' versus 'met'). And it narrows the scope of the answer, rather than keeping it broad.

In the real interview, the police officer's grammatically 'closed' question generates far more than a yes or no in response; it generates the kind of account he is looking for. In contrast to the actor, the real suspect produces an account of his actions that orient to the relevant part of the day and his actions leading to arrest, rather than his bowel movements and cooking breakfast. While real suspects subvert the interview process in other ways (e.g., by responding with 'no comment'), they do not – at least in those I have studied – do what actors do in role-play.

Here, then, the communication guidance is wrong. It does not include the kind of question that works. It includes another type of question that sounds right – open-ended, non-leading. But it assumes that interrogative questions are 'closed'. This is another communication myth that we need to bust. Indeed, one motive for writing this book is to ensure that training is based on scientific rigour, rather than communication myths like open/closed questions, and others we encountered in Chapter 4. Grammatically 'closed' questions regularly generate longer answers in everyday and institutional settings. The apparently closed grammar of a 'yes/no' question is often a vehicle for an expansive action, like telling a story.

In another project, the research team[105] analysed neonatologists interacting with parents of extremely premature babies. Published guidance for such conversations recommends that doctors invoke the 'best interest'[106] of the baby in their consultations. We found that doctors used one of two approaches to initiate decision-making conversations, which either opened up or closed down opportunities for parents to participate. The approaches also differed in the amount of conflict generated.

When doctors made recommendations, which included phrases such as 'the best interests of the baby', they reduced opportunities for parents to ask questions and increased conflict. The problem with doing a recommendation is that parents can either accept it, or reject it. If they rejected a doctor's recommendation, they found themselves in the position of apparently acting against their baby's 'best interests'. However, when doctors listed options, and did not use 'best interest' in the framing of the conversation, they created opportunities for parents to ask questions. Conflict was reduced, and parents participated explicitly in the decision-making process.

Again, the communication guidance was wrong. Of course, no one intends to publish guidance that leads to conflict in highly emotional and difficult situations. But guidance is developed from . . .

---

105   Shaw et al. (2016).

106   Royal College of Paediatrics and Child Health (2004).

what? Experience, memory, authority, hunches? Recall the 'some' or 'any' study introduced in Chapter 5. Because general practitioners know that patients typically mention only one concern at the start of a consultation, they are trained to ask, 'Is there anything else we need to take care of today?' It sounds good. But we discovered that the question, in fact, places interactional constraints on patients. They are less likely to mention other concerns than if they are asked a different type of question. The guidance is wrong.

Let us return to the first conversation we encountered in this chapter – a telephone call to the vet's. I asked you to consider the receptionist's communication skills. Here is the transcript again, labelled as Example 10. This time, focus on what the caller does.

Example 10: Calling the vet (simplified transcript)

01	Reception:	U-good afternoon Town Veterinary Surgery Anna
02		speakin' how c'n I help.
03	Caller:	Hi.=I just got a new puppy the other day. .hhh
04		s'wonderin' how much it'd cost t'get the jabs done.
05		please.
06	Reception:	Of course, yeah, let's have a look for you,=what
07		was um the breed o'the puppy that y'had.
08		(0.4)
09	Caller:	Oh 'e's jus' a cross breed.=collie [cross.
10	Reception:	[Ohhw::.

The caller does not actually have a puppy. The caller is a 'mystery shopper', whose job is to pose as a customer, client, patient, or other kind of service user, to assess the quality of goods or services, with the aim of improving customer experience and satisfaction.

In the police role-plays we saw earlier, both parties – the police officers and actor-suspects – know that they are not in a real interview. In Example 10, however, the receptionist does not know she is talking to a mystery shopper. Now our question about the conversation is transformed – does the mystery shopper authentically produce a real call? If she does not, what does this mean for the skills of the receptionist?

One clear difference between real and mystery shopper calls is that, first, real pet owners do not generally ask about cost – and certainly not as their reason for calling. Mystery shoppers, however, often begin and end their calls with this as the sole topic. It does not take much imagination to see that this is quite odd for receptionists, who are ready to have an empathetic conversation about a new, or sick, animal. Cost is not the foremost concern.

Another feature of Example 10 is the caller's response to the receptionist's question about the breed of her puppy. Note the delay in responding, followed by an 'Oh' – a 'change-of-state' token which suggests that the caller is surprised that the question is asked. Yet it is a standard question in real calls, causing no difficulties for real pet owners.

I hope that you did not identify the call as a mystery shopper at the start of the chapter. The features that now seem glaringly obvious were not apparent before comparing a larger number of mystery shopper calls with real calls. Here is another mystery shopper call.

Example 11: Mystery shopper calling the vet

01	Reception:	Medivac Surgery Chloe speakin' how c'n I help.
02		(0.4)
03	Caller:	Hi: I need to get my um dog castrated, I jus' wonder'd
04		h'w >much it'd< cost me.
05		(0.2)
06	Reception:	UH: °°let's have a look.hh°°

```
07                  (0.2)

08    Reception:    #So::?# duh::, (1.7) ((typing sounds)) °Castra:te,°

09                  (0.9)

10    Reception:    Ho:w: I- much does your dog wei:gh?

11                  (0.5)

12    Caller:       Um: how much does 'e wei:gh, (0.3) oh I've no idea,

13                  (0.9)

14    Reception:    Has 'e been to us before.

15    Caller:       N:o.

16    Reception:    .hhh what breed is he?

17    Caller:       He's (jus') cross breed, (0.2) um:
```

Mystery shoppers ask about cost. They do not know how much their 'dog' weighs, and, like the caller in Example 10, their dogs are generally 'just cross breeds'. They do not know the kinds of things that real pet owners answer readily. They also do not, of course, make appointments. They do not have a dog . . . So mystery shoppers avoid making appointments – which again produces an odd contingency for the receptionist to grapple with.

Here is an example of a real call.

Example 12: Calling the vet

```
01    Reception:    Dunnetts Vets.=Highuptown, Maggie speaking, how

02                  can I he:lp.

03                  (0.4)
```

04   Caller: <u>H</u>ello there:.=um: I need t'make an appointment

05   t'bring the cat in t'get its um: updated <u>v</u>accina:tions.

The caller's reason for telephoning the vet is to make an appointment – not to enquire about cost. The real and mystery shopper callers therefore ask for different things – one is making an appointment; the other enquires about cost.

Another tiny, yet revealing difference between this call and the mystery shopper enquiry is the placement of 'um' in the overall request. The mystery shopper asked, 'I need to get my UM dog castrated'. The real pet owner asked, 'I need t'make an appointment t'bring the cat in t'get its UM: updated ↓vaccina:tions.' The real pet owner knows she is calling about 'the cat' but hesitates before asking for the required service. The mystery shopper hesitates before remembering which type of pet the call is about, rather than before the required service.

The problem with 'communication skills' is inextricably tied to the problems with the way we develop communication guidance, training and assessment. First, we develop guidance that includes normative, stereotypical things about talk, rather than what research shows is effective. While practitioners are indeed effective in their real-time encounters – as we have seen in many conversations throughout this book – they are rarely able to specify what worked, when positive outcomes turn on a particular word, intonation or question format. As Harvey Sacks,[107] the pioneer of conversation analysis remarked, 'from close looking at the world you can find things that we couldn't, by imagination, assert were there'.

Second, at the start of this section we saw that the police officers' words – as they turned PACE into spoken talk – became different from the letter of the written law. Note that the PACE instructions are not provided in the form of 'what to say' anyway, but take the form of generalised instructions about what kind of thing to say – topics, not words to say. Turning the written word into spoken talk is a challenge,

---

107   Sacks (1992: 420).

just as making a written record of speech is. Moving between speech and written text is ostensibly simple, but actually always complex, reflecting the different conventions and uses of speech and writing.[108]

Analysts have also shown that when people turn written survey questions into spoken talk – in which the aim is to replicate a validated research procedure – they often vary in subtle or gross ways from the original survey instrument.[109] When psychologists deliver diagnostic questionnaires, they subtly alter the constraints implied by the written question. When police interview victims of sexual assault, they translate guidance about interview conduct in consequentially problematic ways.[110] When researchers run experiments, they alter the wording of the set questions. Almost all of these differences are hidden from scrutiny, inside the black box of the survey, the interview or the experiment.

Third, in the previous chapter, we examined several recordings of patients calling their GP to make an appointment. If they are dissatisfied, they can record their dissatisfaction on a national GP Patient Survey on a scale of 1–10. But when the surgery examines this evaluation, what should they do if scores are low? We know that practitioners struggle to identify and action changes based on feedback alone. So thinking about what to improve is based on hunches or (mis)rememberings. Interventions can also be stereotypical ('smile when you answer the phone!') or empirically wrong ('use the patient's name to build rapport' – which we will examine shortly).

You may remember that, at the end of Chapter 5, I began to describe the development of an alternative approach to communication training based on conversation analytic research evidence and the science of conversation – CARM (the Conversation Analytic Role-play Method). CARM takes evidence about what works in real conversations – and what does not – to underpin training, across all

108 Edwards and Middleton (1986).

109 Gibson (2013); Houtkoop-Steenstra and Antaki (1997); Maynard and Schaeffer (2006).

110 Richardson et al. (2018).

types of organisation.[111] Much of the research presented throughout this book provides the basis for CARM workshops with doctors, mediators, lawyers, police officers, hostage negotiators, salespersons, and so on. In the case of GP receptionists, conversation analysis revealed two simple changes that receptionists could make, borne out of real practice. Following research-based training, patient satisfaction increased.

If communication guidance is wrong, and real people cannot role-play in authentic ways – especially if authenticity comes down to the placement of an 'um' in a request for service – can we expect computers to replicate real talk? What does the science of conversation imply for artificially intelligent, machine-learned algorithmically produced *talk*?

The future of talk

Even as I write this section of the book, conversation analysts – including myself – are starting to work with computer scientists and neuroscientists to feed their insight into the design and synthesis of robotic, virtual and other artificial systems.[112,] In January 2018, newspapers reported the development of an algorithm to enable robots to augment the human operation of emergency calls. The Danish[113] developers describe how their artificially intelligent digital assistant is able to spot symptoms in verbal communication, tone of voice, breathing patterns, while analysing other metadata. By comparing data across millions of automatically analysed calls, the software can identify important patterns in the interaction, to inform recommended action.

Developments like these are exciting and transformative. I will keep this section short, as it will be out of date by the time the book is published. However, right now, for you and me, the reality of talking

---

111 Stokoe (2011b).

112 https://rolsi.net/2018/02/16/guest-blog-talking-with-alexa-at-home/

113 www.corti.ai

with conversational agents is probably a bit less dramatic and a bit more frustrating. I have not yet managed to get my 'Alexa' to play a particular programme on BBC Radio 4, although it will play the channel live.

We are still a long way from enabling computers to talk to each other like humans, and from talking to them like humans. For a start, there is still a way to go before natural language processing – in which recorded talk is turned into text – is accurate enough for conversation analysis. Consider the many transcripts you have read in this book. As I write this chapter, I have not yet seen speech-to-text systems that are more than 80 to 90 per cent accurate for words – and talk is much more than lexical units.

Furthermore, there are no algorithms – yet – for any kind of automatic conversation analysis. There are no algorithms – yet – for producing conversation analytic transcripts. Of course, conversation analysts produce and work with far more than a basic, verbatim transcript of recorded conversation. We include detail about pace, prosody, intonation, overlap, interruption, repetition, repair, interpolated laughter, the tiniest of incipient sobs, and much, much more.

More importantly, computational classifications of things like 'sentiment', 'tone of voice', or 'personality' – common features of big data analysis of communication – do not address the actions people do with talk. They do not include the paired sequences that organise talk into social interaction, or the way inserted, pre- and post-sequences are initiated and progressed. Natural language processing systems in AI, neural networks and machine learning will remain limited until they are trained to do what I call natural *action* processing.

For now, we remain focused on humans talking to other humans. I am confident that the science of conversation presented in this book will remain current, and relevant, and that people will keep talking to each other for many years to come.

Five ways to have better conversations

In the final section of the book, I want to return to the most useful strategies that I and other analysts have identified to help you have better conversations. I will expand on some more than others, depending on how detailed an exploration appeared earlier in the book. So, here are my top five tips for talking effectively.

1. Don't build rapport

2. Listen (. . . no, really listen)

3. Check your entitlement

4. Change one word

5. Bust the myths

1. Don't build rapport

'Rapport' is a nebulous concept yet is pervasive in the communication skills and training literature. What does it mean to build rapport? And why is my first tip warning *against* building rapport?

You may recall that, from Chapter 1, the preliminary phase of a conversation between acquainted parties involves rapid, reciprocal and recurrent components. People greet and identify each other, and ask each other 'how are you?'. The 'how-are-yous' are not 'pointless filler' – when they are absent, we know that a potentially difficult conversation lies ahead.

We also saw what happens when salespeople use 'how-are-yous' too early in a conversation, with a too-smiley tone of voice, with an interlocutor they have never met. In one example, a salesperson asks, with the sound of a wide grin, 'how are you doing this morning?' The customer replies but does not reciprocate the 'how are you'. The salesperson says they are 'good thanks' even though they have not been asked. It is a rapport fail, *par excellence*.

It is even worse, then, that in Example 13, a salesperson fails to reciprocate a 'how are you' that is initiated by the customer.

Example 13: Business-to-business cold-call sales (simplified transcript)

01	Customer:	Hi Guy,
02	Sales:	.ptkhh hi John,
03	Sales:	.hhhh[h [I got] your: email through?
04	Customer:	[>You all r[ight<?]
05		(0.7)
06	Customer:	Yep,

After the initial greetings, with a pre-existing customer, the salesperson announces the reason for his call ('I got your: email through?'). At the same time, the customer asks, 'You all right<?' So, the customer has initiated a 'how are you' sequence right where it is due – after the greetings, by saying 'You all right?' But the salesperson has probably not heard the customer's words – as he talks in overlap.

At line 05, a gap of 0.7 seconds of silence occurs – go back and look at the ominous 0.7 seconds in Dana and Gordon's conversation in Chapter 1. The customer's next turn responds to the salesperson's announcement – after the delay, and with a 'yep' (not 'yes', 'mhm', or 'yeah'). The 'p' sound is all we need for a finely calibrated display of irritation.

Here is a great example of how to do a 'how are you', which I observed at the reception desk of a hotel. The customer has approached the desk to check in.

Example 14: Hotel reception (field note)

01	Desk:	Good evening.
02	Guest:	Hi – I'd like to check in?
03	Desk:	Of course. Can I take your name?
04	Guest:	Yeh, it's Janet Wilkinson.
05	Desk:	((Looking at her computer)) How are you doing this
06		evening?
07	Guest:	Fine thanks, how are you?
08	Desk:	I'm good . . . Wilkinson . . . yes, there you are.
09		You're staying two nights?

In this case, rather than packaging the 'how are you' with the greeting – like the salesperson on Chapter 1 – the hotel desk staff member included it after the check-in process was initiated, and during the search for the guest's booking. The guest reciprocated the 'how are you' – which, because it was 'out of sequence', sounded genuine rather than scripted.

Before we move to the next tip, I want to say something else about rapport-building errors. One of the most common assumptions is that it is a good idea – for rapport reasons – to announce your name ('Liz speaking') when answering the telephone. However, across all the service encounters I have studied, the most important component of the first turn is the name of the organisation, not the person taking the call. There are no instances, across thousands of cases, of callers asking 'who is speaking?' in response to the call-taker's answering turn. But they do ask, 'is that the surgery?', 'is that the council?', or 'is that the vet?' Callers need to know they are in the right place, not whether they are talking to Jane, Tom or Jackie.

For example, in the crisis negotiation below, the negotiator starts by introducing himself.

Example 15: Crisis negotiation (simplified transcript)

01	Negotiator:	Hi darling. My n- my name is David.
02	P in C:	Who are you,
03	Negotiator:	I'm just here to try and help.
04		(0.7)
05	P in C:	Yeah. Who are you.=You know from where.
06		(0.3)
07	Negotiator:	Oh- I- I'm from the police.

The negotiator introduces himself – 'My name is David'. Given our observations about introductions earlier in the chapter, saying 'I'm David' might be better. But probably not, at least on its own, because the person in crisis responds immediately to ask who she is talking to. For her, the fact that the negotiator is called David is irrelevant. She wants to know what his role is; what organisation he is from.

Second, people assume that if they say the name of their interlocutor, it demonstrates that they have listened accurately, and that using it makes the call personal, thus building rapport. This is a basic misunderstanding of the way we use names in real talk. Names are a summons. We use them to hail someone, to attract attention, or to nominate someone to speak. We have all experienced a sudden jolt in a meeting, for instance, when someone says our name. Names summon us into an encounter.

A dramatic illustration of the way names work as summons is in the crisis negotiation encounter below. The person in crisis, anonymised as Natalie, is slowly choking and losing consciousness, with a noose around her neck.

Example 16: Crisis negotiation (simplified transcript)

01	Negotiator:	Natalieↄ
02		(0.4)
03	Negotiator:	>NATALIE.<
04		(0.4)
05	Negotiator:	NATALIE.
06		(0.3)
07	Negotiator:	Throw the keys.
08	Negotiator:	Do it now.

The negotiator repeats Natalie's name three times, with increasing volume. The tacit logic – evidenced by psychologists – is that names do something to us, physiologically. Quite literally, saying our name summons us back into the interaction; back to consciousness; back to life.

Names are used at moments of incipient conflict, too. In Example 17, the radio broadcaster Jenni Murray is interviewing the food writer, Nigella Lawson.[114] The interview is, unremarkably, mostly about food. However, about a year before the interview, the media had widely reported an incident in which Nigella had been photographed with her ex-husband, Charles Saatchi, with his hands around her neck. Jenni Murray suggests that Nigella has had a tough time recently, and decides to ask Nigella about the incident with her ex-husband.

---

114 http://www.bbc.co.uk/programmes/b06fpy4m

Example 17: BBC Radio 4 *Woman's Hour*, 9 October 2015[115]

01	Jenni:	<u>W</u>hat <u>a</u>ctually idid happen outside that restaurant
02		with your iformer ihusband.
03		(0.4)
04	Nigella:	W'll I'll <u>t</u>ell you this Jenni. hh I have- you're right I've
05		had a <u>t</u>ough time >very much< in the public eye and
06		what it has made me (0.7) uh::realize is <<u>ho</u>:w much
07		I:> <u>ha</u>ve t'pre<u>se</u>rve my privacy.

Nigella uses Jenni's name in a dispreferred turn – she is not supplying an answer to a question. And, when she uses Jenni's name, she is not using it to show that she is listening, that the conversation is personal, or to otherwise build rapport. She is summoning Jenni into this interactional moment, creating that physiological jolt.

People are trained to use names to build rapport without knowing their function as a summons. In the final example, a salesperson asks their customer her name.

Example 18: Business-to-business cold-call sales (simplified transcript)

01	Sales:	Wh<u>a</u>t's your <u>n</u>ame.
02	Customer:	Denise McAndrew
03	Sales:	That's wonderful.
04		(.)
05	Sales:	Denise.

115 https://www.bbc.co.uk/programmes/b06fpy4m

The customer supplies her name, and the salesperson uses it – not quite immediately. Line 04 is a micropause of a tenth of a second. But it is just enough to sound clunky, done for a purpose, and unnatural. In fact, in this setting, the micropause almost lasts a lifetime.

The problem with 'building rapport' is that it is oxymoronic. If you have to try to build rapport, you are probably very visible in your doing of it. And this just undermines what rapport is. Don't build rapport.

2. Listen (no, really listen)

'Good listening skills' are often included as part of building rapport. A good listener engages in things such as 'active listening', 'mirroring', 'summarising', 'paraphrasing' or 'emotional labelling'.[116] Many of these skills are intuitively sensible and compelling. However, what such 'skills' look like in real talk – how they are designed and what they accomplish – is more complex. For example, 'summarising' someone else's talk can be a powerful way to demonstrate shared understandings, or to drive a conversation encounter forward. But it can also transform versions of events in ways that undermine one party or another.

When it comes to listening, we may listen for information, but also for action. We know that one speaker is able to anticipate the action of another, and prepare to respond, well before the end of the first speaker's turn. Sometimes one speaker mis-projects the end of another speaker's turn, and starts talking too soon, or too late. And sometimes one speaker misinterprets the action being done by another and provides an ill-fitted response.

Example 19 comes from a cold-call sales conversation. The salesperson, who works for a printing and copying technology company, is trying to get a prospective client to agree to meet to discuss a new photocopier contract. We join the call as the potential client – who has resisted the salesperson's attempts to set up an appointment

---

116   Van Hasselt et al. (2006).

– explains that she is happy with their current supplier. What's more, her contract does not expire for several months.

Example 19: Business-to-business cold-call sales

01	Client:	Doesn't- ↑doesn't expire until the <u>au</u>tumn,

02		(0.4)

03	Client:	A:nd it's [with] Konica,=And Konica have been VEry

04	Sales:	[Oh .]

05	Client:	very good with us:,=

The client, informing the salesperson that her contract has months yet to run, volunteers the information that the contract is with Konica. Already we can see that the salesperson is not listening effectively. Her 'Oh' is delayed – not only does it come after a 0.4 second delay, but it also occurs after the client has started a new turn. The 'oh', as a 'change-of-state' token, responds to the *first* part about the contract expiry date – the salesperson now knows something about the contract date that she did not know before.

We return to the conversation a few moments later.

25	Sales:	You were saying you w:- >you're with uh< who- who

26		is your supplier <u>currently.</u>

27		(0.5)

28	Client:	°Konica.°

The salesperson's ineffective listening reveals itself here. She asks who the client's current supplier is, despite having been told this information – and how happy the client is with Konica – only seconds earlier. The client marks her irritation by delaying her response, and uttering the answer in a low voice.

The next conversation provides a clear illustration of poor listening for the actions being done. In this crisis negotiation, a negotiator is trying to get a person in crisis to give her his name. In fact, she asks him what she can *call* him – which shows her understanding that he might not want to give his full or real name. However, the person in crisis resists answering the question.

Negotiators work in units of four. While negotiators three and four relay and gather information, and manage the scene, the role of the second negotiator, or N2, is to support the first, offering encouragement, information, and, more often than not, words to say to the person in crisis. However, they should enact their role discreetly, and not attract the attention of the person in crisis. In this episode, the N2 whispers to the first negotiator what she should say to get the person in crisis to supply his name.

Example 20: Crisis negotiation (simplified transcript)

01   Negotiator 1:   What do you want me to c<u>a</u>ll you.

02   (0.3)

03   P in C: Why should I tell you my name yeah?

04   Negotiator 1:   I told you <u>my</u> na:me↲

05   Negotiator 2:   °Say it's cos I c<u>a</u>re for you°.

06   P in C: [N<u>o</u>.]

07   Negotiator 2:   [°Cos I] care for you°.

08   (0.2)

09   Negotiator 1:   I care for <u>you</u>:↲

10		(0.4)
11	Negotiator 1:	If I didn't care for you I wouldn't be
12		[HERE. Would I.]
13	P in C:	[Why do you want to] get my NAME!
14		(0.3)
15	Negotiator 1:	You're not <LISTENING TO ME:>.

The negotiation is derailed by the second negotiator, who offers under his breath, and then insists, that the first negotiator brings his words into the conversation. So it is ironic that this episode ends with the first negotiator telling the person in crisis that *he* is not listening to her.

The person in crisis asks the first negotiator why he should tell her his name – even though this is not what she asked. Her response is a tit-for-tat explanation – she told him her name. The person in crisis says 'no'. It is at this point that the overhearing second negotiator suggests she provide a reason for asking – '°Say it's cos I care for you°.'. It is hard to see how 'cos I care for you' is an appropriate explanation. Rather, it is ill-fitted to the question.

After a short gap, the second negotiator urges the first to use his words. This time, the first negotiator complies, and says, 'I care for you.' What is the difference between what the second negotiator suggests, and what she eventually produces? The first negotiator drops the 'cos', saying 'I care for you.' The fact that she drops the 'cos' supports our assessment that 'cos I care for you' is an ill-fitted answer to the person in crisis's question. 'Cos' connects two turns together in a way that they are not. So the first negotiator has no option but to start a new sequence, disconnected from the preceding talk.

Having adopted the second negotiator's suggested words, the first negotiator elaborates further, stating that she would not be there with the person in crisis if she did not care. But he does not wait for her to finish her turn, instead reiterating his earlier question – 'Why do you want to get my name?' So the person in crisis also treats 'I care for you' as not dealing with his original question. He has to ask it again.

The second negotiator shows an inability to turn the words he is hearing into the action it is doing. Instead of supporting the negotiation, he spoils it. He has not listened. To listen effectively, ask yourself what a person is *doing*, with the words they are *saying*. Do actions with words.

3. Check your entitlement

A few years ago, the phrase 'check your privilege' came into common parlance. Roughly speaking, it is a way of reminding someone who is making a political point that they should consider the position they speak from – are they, for example, a man, white, heterosexual, able-bodied, salaried, and so on.

When it comes to conversation, check your entitlement. We spent some time in earlier chapters examining how people ask for and offer help; what constitutes good and bad service, and what makes people a 'recruiter' or the 'recruited'. When you make a request – whether in your personal or workplace life – think about how entitled you are to make it, whether or not you should do the thing you are requesting yourself, how much effort it will take for the other person to do it, and how important it is. With those contingencies in mind, design your request accordingly. Don't be a recruiter.

Similarly, if you find yourself doing things for others and resenting it, resist being recruited. To the person who asserts, 'Can we meet please', say, 'Sure – my diary is up to date – choose a slot that is convenient for you.' Reduce the conversational burden on other speakers. Anticipate needs, make offers. Help people to check their entitlement.

4. Change one word

One of the most surprising discoveries from doing conversation analysis is that one word really can change the outcome of a conversation. Of course, changing one word alters more than the lexical unit itself. It impacts the grammar, action and preferred response of the transformed turn. Replacing the word 'any' with the word 'some' in a question about further medical concerns changes the likely response from 'no' to 'yes'. Changing the word 'interested' to 'willing' in a question about participation in mediation changes the likely outcome from 'no' to 'yes'. And changing the word 'talk' to the word 'speak' in negotiations is more likely to get suicidal persons in crisis to . . . talk.

One of my favourite examples of how words change outcomes comes from David Maxfield and Joseph Grenny.[117] Maxfield and Grenny are behavioural scientists, not conversation analysts, and their frames of reference and explanations are quite different from mine. However, in one of their experiments to 'nudge' behavioural change, they start by arguing – very much like a conversation analyst – that 'Words matter. A lot. The words you choose to frame a problem powerfully influence the way you and others feel about it.'

In their study entitled, 'Does Santa Make You Selfish?', Maxfield and Grenny got two groups of children to visit Father Christmas, accompanied by another child, who was a confederate of the experimenters. In the first group, the children were asked the familiar question, 'What do you want to get for Christmas?' All children are ready to answer this question, and so they listed their responses to Santa.

Next, Santa sent the pair of children off to see his elf, to receive a present. However, when the children arrived in front of the elf, he announced that there was only one big chocolate bear left – and several small ones. The elf asked the child who was being experimented upon to choose who got which bear. Maxfield and Grenny observed that the children almost immediately grabbed the large chocolate bear for themselves.

---

117   www.youtube.com/watch?v=ywWUDgHdoSk

In the second group, the children were asked a slightly different question. Rather than Santa asking, 'What do you want to *get* for Christmas?', he asked, 'What gifts do you want to *give* this Christmas?' Many of the children could barely compute this question initially and simply responded by listing the things they wanted. But Santa persisted, and eventually the children listed some things they might give to their parents, for instance. This time, when the children approached the elf, their behaviour changed. They were more likely to offer the large chocolate bear to the confederate child, than take it themselves.

Changing 'get' to 'give' in Santa's question changed the subsequent behaviour of the children. A one-word change opens up slots for children to show their generous side, just as asking people if they are 'willing' opens up slots to say, 'I'm nice'. Words matter. Think about them. Change them.

5. Bust the myths

The aim of this book is to provide insight into the world of conversation analysis, and the study of real talk. Replace talk myth with conversation science.

So . . . throw away advice that tells you to be a good listener, or build rapport, or use body language, or that advises you to talk in a particular way to a woman (or a man).

Don't be a first mover. Think about the first turn you take in an encounter and embody the interaction you'd like to have. And if you encounter a first mover, push back, like Gordon.

Don't be a mis-greeter or a recalibrator. Pay attention to the person you are saying hello to – it's really not that hard.

Open up slots to give your interlocutor opportunities to do the things they want to do, or close down slots for conflict and misalignment.

Don't ask people you do not know how they are doing today. Ask people more than 'how are you?' when you do know them.

Don't be a recompleter; don't talk incessantly – allow others to take a turn.

Challenge the validity of role-play as a training tool. Find a conversation analyst. Embrace the science of conversation.

Now you're talking.

APPENDIX

Here is a list of Gail Jefferson's (2004) transcribing conventions.

Symbol	Definition
.hh hh	Inhalations and exhalations, respectively
Spee::ch	Colon indicates a syllable that is drawn out
To-	A dash indicates a word has been cut off abruptly
<u>Ve</u>ry	Underlining indicates stress or emphasis
(1.4)	Numbers in parentheses indicate length of pauses within a turn, or gaps between turns (in tenths of seconds)
(.)	Micropause of less than 0.2 seconds
.,¿?	Punctuation indicates intonation at the end of units of talk. A full stop indicates falling intonation; a comma indicates continuing intonation; a reverse question mark for slight rise, and a question mark for sharp rise in intonation.

[yeah]

[okay]   Square brackets represent overlapping talk

=   End of one turn and beginning of next begin with no gap/
                pause in between (usually a slight overlap if there is
                speaker change)

(words)   A guess at what might have been said if the recording is
                bad, or the words unclear

wo(h)rds   Within-speech breath-bursts (laughter)

WORD   Talk produced loudly in comparison with surrounding talk

#word#   Creaky or croaky voice

°word°   Quiet, breathy, voice

↑word   Marked shift upwards in pitch

↓word   Marked shift down in pitch

> <   Encloses speeded up talk

< >   Encloses slower place of talking

.pt   Lip smack

ACKNOWLEDGEMENTS

As someone who spends much of her time forensically analysing people's words, writing some acknowledgements is a slightly daunting task. It's often the first thing that I look at when reading other people's books. But, here goes . . .

I've dedicated this book to my PhD supervisor, Dr Eunice Fisher. Despite what some would see as a rather inauspicious start to my academic career at, as it was then, Preston Polytechnic, Eunice spotted something in me when I turned up for an interview at Nene College, for a PhD studentship. This was 1993. Eunice was coming to the end of her own career and had moved from the University of Cambridge and The Open University to set up a new degree at Nene College (now the University of Northampton). Although there are over thirty years between us, Eunice and I shared a birthday and a love of crime fiction, and our student–supervisor relationship provided the best start anyone could have in academia. She retired when I left, in 1997, with my PhD, and we have been in each other's lives ever since.

Since then, and throughout my career, first at Derby, then Worcester, and, since 2002, Loughborough University, I have had tremendous support from colleagues, many of whom became great friends. I moved to Loughborough to join a world-class Department of Social Sciences, and, within it, a world-renowned research group, the Discourse and Rhetoric Group (DARG). I never looked back. In DARG, I was lucky enough to work with my academic heroes: people who invented and transformed fields, especially the way psychologists conceive of and study conversation. Derek Edwards, Jonathan Potter, Alexa Hepburn and Charles Antaki have all been pivotal in shaping my thinking, and are wonderful mentors, colleagues, collaborators and friends.

During the past five years, I've worked as an Associate Dean for Research at Loughborough University. These years have coincided with a lot of the research and science communication I've done that underpin this book, and although the many colleagues I've worked with (other Associate Deans, Research Office and Research Committee colleagues, colleagues across my School) are not conversation analysts (but communication and media scholars, geographers, sociologists, politics scholars, designers, chemists, engineers . . .) – and might be surprised to find themselves in the Acknowledgements section of a book about talk – they are a group of brilliant people who have created a very happy workplace that I am lucky to be a part of.

One of the great things about academia is the opportunity it creates to meet and work with wonderful people. I have been to many conferences, and invited to many universities as a visiting professor, over the years. While conversation analysis has often been the starting point, I have found kindred spirits who have nourished and inspired me (whether they know it or not) along the way. Thank you especially to all those I've had the privilege to publish with, especially Bethan Benwell (with whom I wrote my first academic book); to share what we conversation analysts call 'data sessions'; or been invited by for visits, conferences and the other best bits of academic life. Along the way, I discovered special affinities with the Nordic countries. *Tack! Takk! Tak! Kiitos!*

I'm privileged to have met and supervised exceptional PhD students and post-doctoral researchers. Since 2014, I have worked with Rein Ove Sikveland, who is not just a brilliantly talented phonetician and conversation analyst, but a tremendous colleague and friend. Something that my dad (who spent half his career as a teacher) passed on to me was the aspiration for my students to be a damn sight better than me. They'd better be, or our field will not grow. Some of these students and post-docs have become great friends too, just like me and Eunice. You know who you are!

In 2012, in his role as British Psychological Society Social Psychology Committee press officer, Chris Walton recommended that *The Psychologist* feature me in their series on psychology careers. Happily, the editor, Jon Sutton, accepted the recommendation, and I was interviewed by Ian Florance. The piece turned out to be the route to an invitation to appear on BBC Radio 4's *The Life Scientific* in 2013. Having my research and biography featured on that programme – which included such luminaries as Robert Winston, Uta Frith and Brian Cox – was not just a huge honour (especially for a BBC Radio 4 addict); it led to so many other subsequent invitations to talk about talk, and . . . several emails from book editors and agents. Of course, I am indebted to the person who became my editor at Little, Brown – Andrew McAleer.

The Life Scientific spawned new research projects and helped me evolve the then-nascent 'Conversation Analytic Role-play Method' for communication training into something serious and productive. There are too many brilliant mediators, police, medical, sales, and other professionals to list, who helped kick-start projects or spread the word about CARM. But those who went above and beyond include Chula Rupasinha, Judith Scott, Lesley Saunders, Mike Shallcross, Jez Cottrill, Stephen Anderson, Mary Shaw, Paul Gadd, Juliette Dalrymple, Laura Kirkpatrick, Laura Mackay, Gail Packer, Brad Heckman, Niklas Traub, Karen Leichtnam, Barry Goldman, Paulette Morris, Colin Anderson, Rodney Wells, Austin Chessell, Wendy Brown, Paul Thorn, Carl Day, Chris Mills, Alison Lambert, Neil Marlow, Duncan Jarrett, Paul Aveyard, Graham Todd and Kurt Wilson. And the list keeps growing.

Richard Williams was the first person to help me to 'commercialise' CARM, and I am grateful for his belief in me. I am also appreciative of colleagues from the Enterprise Office at Loughborough University for supporting my endeavours, and for introducing me to Fran Collins and Joanne Wdowiak from brand and design company A Dozen Eggs. The Eggs not only challenged me to think about how I communicate about conversation analysis; we have evolved a mutually rewarding collaboration, which also spills well over from business into friendship.

Speaking of friendship, I am so fortunate to have many wonderful friends – here in the UK and around the world – who have ebbed and flowed with me across the decades. It also 'goes without saying' (there's another idiom about talk) that my family, along with my friends, are my bedrock: my parents, Lynne Stokoe and Bill Stokoe; my stepfather, Arthur Middleton; my grandparents; my brother, cousins, aunts and uncles; my recently acquired in-laws. I don't want my appreciation of them to be left unsaid. I am proud to be their daughter, sister, niece, cousin and in-law.

Finally, the men. Some people meet their partner when they are very young, and travel through life with that person. This didn't happen to me. But I've been fortunate to share years with two men who, despite being an ex-husband and ex-partner, supported me greatly in the time we were together. And we're still friends many years later. Peter Harries, who runs Boz Books in Hay-on-Wye, was my husband while I finished my PhD and worked my first two lecturing jobs. Derek Edwards was my partner, and research collaborator, throughout much of the 2000s, and we still live around the corner from each other.

But my great love is George Burdett, who I married on 31 May 2017. We occupy 'a green airy space, not locked in'.[118]

Loughborough, June 2018

---

118 Denise Levertov, 'About Marriage'.

REFERENCES

Albert, S., Albury, C., Alexander, M., Harris, T., Hofstetter, E.C., Holmes, E. and Stokoe, E. (2018), 'The Conversational Rollercoaster: Conversation analysis and the public science of talk', *Discourse Studies*, 20(3), 397-424. DOI: https://doi.org/10.1177/1461445618754571.

Atkins, S., Roberts, C., Hawthorne, K. and Greenhalgh, T. (2016), 'Simulated Consultations: A sociolinguistic perspective', *BMC Medical Education*, 16(16). DOI: 10.1186/s12909-016-0535-2.

Arminen, I. and Leinonen, M. (2006), 'Mobile Phone Call Openings: Tailoring answers to personalized summonses', *Discourse Studies*, 8(3), 339–368. DOI: 10.1177/1461445606061791.

Baumeister, R.F., Vohs, K.D. and Funder, D.C. (2007), 'Psychology as the Science of Self-reports and Finger Movement: Whatever happened to actual behavior?', *Perspectives on Psychological Science*, 2(4), 396–403. DOI: 10.1111/j.1745-6916.2007.00051.x

Beattie, G. (1983), *Talk: An Analysis of Speech and Non-verbal Behaviour in Conversation*. Milton Keynes: Open University Press.

Berger, I., Kitzinger, C. and Ellis, S.J. (2016), 'Using a Category to Accomplish Resistance in the Context of an Emergency Call: Michael Jackson's doctor', *Pragmatics*, 26(4), 563–582. DOI: https://doi.org/10.1075/prag.26.4.02ber.

Bolden, G.B. (2008), '"So what's up?" Using the discourse marker so to launch conversational business', *Research on Language and Social Interaction*, (41)3, 302–337, DOI: 10.1080/08351810802237909.

Curl, T.S. and Drew, P. (2008), 'Contingency and Action: A Comparison of Two Forms of Requesting', *Research on Language and Social Interaction*, 41(2), 129–153. DOI: http://dx.doi.org/10.1037/a0032430.

Dingemanse, M., Roberts, S.G., Baranova, J., Blythe, J., Drew, P., et al. (2015), 'Universal Principles in the Repair of Communication Problems', *PLOS ONE*, 10(9): e0136100.https://doi.org/10.1371/journal.pone.0136100.

Dingemanse, M., Torreira, F. and Enfield, N.J. (2013), 'Is "Huh?" a Universal Word? Conversational infrastructure and the convergent evolution of linguistic items', *PLOS ONE*, 8(11): e78273., https://doi.org/10.1371/journal.pone.0078273.

Drew, P. (1992), 'Contested Evidence in Courtroom Cross-examination: The case of a trial for rape', in P. Drew and J. Heritage (eds), *Talk at Work: Interaction in Institutional Settings*, pp. 470–520. Cambridge, UK: Cambridge University Press.

Edwards, D. (1998), 'The Relevant Thing about Her: Social identity categories in use', in C. Antaki and S. Widdicombe (eds), *Identities in Talk*, pp. 15–33. Thousand Oaks, CA: Sage Publications Ltd. DOI: 10.1111/j.2044-8309.2012.02103.x.

Edwards, D. (2012), 'Discursive and Scientific Psychology', *British Journal of Social Psychology*, 51, 425–435.

Edwards, D. and Middleton, D. (1986), 'Text for Memory: Joint recall with a scribe', *Human Learning*, 5, 125–138.

Edwards, D. and Potter, J. (1992), *Discursive Psychology*. London: Sage.

Edwards, D. and Stokoe, E. (2007), 'Self-help in Calls for Help with Problem Neighbours', *Research on Language and Social Interaction*, 40(1), 9–32. DOI: 10.1080/08351810701331208.

Fine, C. (2011), *Delusions of Gender: The real science behind sex differences*. London: Icon Books.

Fox Tree, J.E. (2007), 'Folk Notions of *Um* and *Uh*, *You Know*, and *Like*, *Text & Talk*, 27(3), 297–314. DOI: https://doi.org/10.1515/TEXT.2007.012

Garfinkel, H. (1967), *Studies in Ethnomethodology.* Englewood Cliffs, NJ: Prentice-Hall.

Gibson, S. (2013), '"The last possible resort": A forgotten prod and the in situ standardization of Stanley Milgram's voice-feedback condition', *History of Psychology*, 16, 177–194. DOI: http://dx.doi.org/10.1037/a0032430

Goldman, R. (1982), 'Hegemony and Managed Critique in Prime-time Television: A critical reading of "Mork and Mindy"', *Theory & Society*, 11, 363–388. DOI: https://www.jstor.org/stable/657275.

Hepburn, A. (2004), 'Crying: Notes on description, transcription and interaction', *Research on Language and Social Interaction*, 37(3), 251–290. https://doi.org/10.1207/s15327973rlsi3703_1

Heritage, J. (1984), 'A Change-of-state Token and Aspects of its Sequential Placement', in J.M.Atkinson and J. Heritage (eds), *Structures of Social Action*, pp. 299–345. Cambridge, UK: Cambridge University Press.

Heritage, J. and Robinson, J. (2006), 'Accounting for the Visit: Giving reasons for seeking medical care', in J. Heritage and D.W. Maynard (eds), *Communication in Medical Care: Interaction between physicians and patients*, pp. 48–85. Cambridge, UK: Cambridge University Press.

Heritage, J., Robinson, J.D., Elliott, M.N., Beckett, M. and Wilkes, M. (2007), 'Reducing Patients' Unmet Concerns in Primary Care: The difference one word can make', *Journal of General Internal Medicine*, 22(10), 1429–1433. DOI: 10.1007/s11606-007-0279-0

Hofstetter, E.C. (2016), 'Citizens Getting Help: Interactions at the constituency office'. Unpublished PhD thesis, Loughborough University.

Hoey, E. M. and Stokoe, E. (2018), 'Eligibility and bad news delivery: How call-takers reject applicants to university', Linguistics and Education, 46, 91–101. DOI: 10.1016/j.linged.2018.07.001.

Houtkoop-Steenstra, H. and Antaki, C. (1997), 'Creating Happy People by Asking Yes-No Questions', *Research on Language and Social Interaction*, 30(4), 285–313. https://doi.org/10.1207/s15327973rlsi3004_2

Jefferson, G. (1987), 'On Exposed and Embedded Correction in Conversation', in G. Button and J.R.E. Lee (eds), *Talk and Social Organization*, pp. 86–100. Clevedon, UK: Multilingual Matters.

Jefferson, G. (1996), 'On the Poetics of Ordinary Talk', *Text and Performance Quarterly*, 16(1), 1–61. https://doi.org/10.1080/10462939609366132

Jefferson, G. (2004), 'Glossary of Transcript Symbols with an Introduction', in G.H. Lerner (ed.), *Conversation Analysis: Studies from the first generation*, pp. 13–31. Amsterdam/Philadelphia: John Benjamins.

Karpowitz, C.F. and Mendelberg, T. (2014), *The Silent Sex: Gender, deliberation, and institutions*. Princeton, NJ: Princeton University Press.

Kendrick, K.H. (2015), 'The Intersection of Turn-taking and Repair: The timing of other-initiations of repair in conversation', *Frontiers in Psychology*, 6. https://doi.org/10.3389/fpsyg.2015.00250.

Kendrick, K.H. and Drew, P. (2016), 'Recruitment: Offers, requests, and the organization of assistance in interaction', *Research on Language and Social Interaction*, 1–19. https://doi.org/10.1080/08351813.2016.1126436

Kitzinger, C. (2000), 'How to Resist an Idiom', *Research on Language and Social Interaction*, 33(2), 121–154, DOI: 10.1207/S15327973RLSI3302_1.

Kitzinger, C. (2008), 'Conversation Analysis: Technical matters for gender research', in K. Harrington, L. Litosseliti, H, Saunston and J. Sunderland (eds), *Gender and Language Research Methodologies*, pp. 119–138. Basingstoke, Palgrave Macmillan.

Laserna, C.M., Seih, Y.-T. and Pennebaker, J.W. (2014), '*Um* . . . Who Like Says *You Know*: Filler word use as a function of age, gender, and personality', *Journal of Language and Social Psychology*, 33(3), 328–338. DOI: 10.1177/0261927X14526993.

Le Guin, U.K. (2004), *The Wave in the Mind: Talks and essays on the writer, the reader, and the imagination*. Boulder, CO: Shambhala Publications.

Llewellyn, N. (2015), 'Microstructures of Economic Action: Talk, interaction and the bottom line', *British Journal of Sociology*, 66(3), 486–511. https://doi.org/10.1111/1468-4446.12143

Maynard, D.W. and Schaeffer, N.C. (2006), 'Standardization-in-interaction: The survey interview', in P. Drew, G. Raymond and D. Weinberg (eds), *Talk and Interaction in Social Research Methods*, pp. 9–27. London: Sage.

Medhurst, A. and Tuck, L. (1982), 'The Gender Game', in J. Cook (ed.), *B.F.I. Dossier 17: Television sitcom*, pp. 43–55. London: British Film Institute.

Mehl, M.R. (2017), 'The Electronically Activated Recorder (EAR): A method for the naturalistic observation of daily social behavior', *Current Directions in Psychological Science*, 26(2), 184–190. https://doi.org/10.1177/0963721416680611

Mehl, M.R., Vazire, S., Ramirez-Esparza, N., Slatcher, R.B. and Pennebaker, J.W. (2007), 'Are Women Really More Talkative Than Men?', *Science*, 317, 82. DOI: 10.1126/science.1139940

Mehrabian, A. (1981), *Silent Messages: Implicit communication of emotions and attitudes*. Belmont, CA: Wadsworth Publishing Co.

Meredith, J.M. (2014), 'Chatting online: Comparing spoken and online written interaction between friends', Unpublished PhD thesis, Loughborough University.

Mills, B. (2005), *Television Sitcom*. London: British Film Institute.

Pomerantz, A. (1978), 'Compliment Responses: Notes on the co-operation of multiple constraints', in J. Schenkein (ed.), *Studies in the Organization of Conversational Interaction*, pp. 79–112. London: Academic Press.

Pomerantz, A. (1984), 'Agreeing and Disagreeing with Assessments: Some features of preferred/dispreferred turn shapes', in J. Maxwell Atkinson and J. Heritage (eds), *Structures of Social Action: Studies in conversation analysis*, pp. 57–101. Cambridge, UK: Cambridge University Press.

Powell, M.B., Hughes-Scholes, C.H., Cavezza, C. and Stoove, M.A. (2010), 'Examination of the Stability and Consistency of Investigative Interviewer Performance Across Similar Mock Interview Contexts', *Legal and Criminological Psychology*, 15(2), 243–260. https://doi.org/10.1348/135532509X472077.

Quaglio, P. (2009), *Television Dialogue: The sitcom* Friends *vs. natural conversation*. Amsterdam: John Benjamins.

Richardson, E., Stokoe, E. and Antaki, C. (2018), 'Establishing Intellectually Impaired Victims' Understanding about "Truth" and "Lies": Police interview guidance and practice in cases of sexual assault', *Applied Linguistics*. DOI: 10.1093/applin/amy023

Royal College of Paediatrics and Child Health (RCPCH) (2004), *Withholding or Withdrawing Life Sustaining Treatment in Children: A framework for practice*. Second edition, London: RCPCH.

Sacks, H. (1975), 'Everyone Has to Lie', in M. Sanches and B.G. Blount (eds), *Sociocultural Dimensions of Language Use*, pp. 57–80. New York: Academic Press.

Sacks, H. (1992), *Lectures on Conversation* (Vols I and II, ed. G. Jefferson). Oxford: Blackwell.

Sacks, H., Schegloff, E.A. and Jefferson, G. (1974), 'A Simplest Systematics for the Organization of Turn-taking in Conversation', *Language*, 50, 696–735. DOI:10.2307/412243.

Saini, A. (2017), *Inferior: How science got women wrong – and the new research that's rewriting the story*. London: Fourth Estate.

Schegloff, E.A. (1968), 'Sequencing in Conversational Openings', *American Anthropologist*, 70, 1075–1095. https://doi.org/10.1525/aa.1968.70.6.02a00030.

Schegloff, E.A. (2002), 'Beginnings in the Telephone', in J.E. Katz and M. Aakhus (eds), *Perpetual Contact: Mobile communication, private talk, public performance*, pp. 284–300. Cambridge, UK: Cambridge University Press.

Shaw, C., Stokoe, E., Gallagher, K., Aladangady, N. and Marlow, N. (2016), 'Parental Involvement in Neonatal Critical Care

Decision-making', *Sociology of Health and Illness*, 38(8), 1217–1242. DOI: 10.1111/1467-9566.12455.

Sikveland, R.O. and Stokoe, E. (2016), 'Dealing With Resistance in Initial Intake and Inquiry Calls to Mediation: The power of "willing"', *Conflict Resolution Quarterly*, 33(3), 235–253. DOI: 10.1002/crq.21157.

Sikveland, R.O. and Stokoe, E. (in press), 'Effective Practices for Accessing "Urgent" and "Routine" Appointments in General Practice Receptionist-led Triage', in Z. Demjén (ed.), *Applying Linguistic Methods in Illness and Healthcare Contexts*. London: Bloomsbury Academic.

Sikveland, R.O., Stokoe, E. and Symonds, J. (2016), 'Patient Burden During Appointment-making Telephone Calls to GP Practices', *Patient Education and Counselling*, 99(8), 1310-18. DOI:10.1016/j.pec.2016.03.025.

Speer, S.A. (2012), 'The Interactional Organization of Self-praise: Epistemics, preference organization, and implications for identity research', *Social Psychology Quarterly*, 75, 52–79. https://doi.org/10.1177/0190272511432939.

Stivers, T., Enfield, N.J., Brown, P., Englert, C., Hayashi, M., Heinemann, T., Hoymann, G., Rossano, F., de Ruiter, J.P., Yoon, K. and Levinson, S.C. (2009), 'Universals and cultural variation in turn-taking in conversation', *PNAS*, 106(26), 10587–10592. www.pnas.org/cgi/doi/10.1073/pnas.0903616106.

Stokoe, E. (2011a), '"Girl – woman – sorry!" On the repair and non-repair of consecutive gender categories', in S. Speer and E. Stokoe (eds), *Conversation and Gender*, pp. 85–111. Cambridge, UK: Cambridge University Press.

Stokoe, E. (2011b), 'Simulated Interaction and Communication Skills Training: The "Conversation Analytic Role-play Method"', in C. Antaki (ed.), *Applied Conversation Analysis: Changing institutional practices*, pp. 119–139. Basingstoke: Palgrave Macmillan.

Stokoe, E. (2013a), 'Overcoming Barriers to Mediation in Intake Calls to Services: Research-based strategies for mediators', *Negotiation Journal*, 29(3), 289–314. DOI: 10.1111/nejo.12026.

Stokoe, E. (2013b), 'The (In)Authenticity of Simulated Talk: Comparing role-played and actual conversation and the implications for communication training', *Research on Language and Social Interaction*, 46(2), 1–21. DOI: 10.1080/08351813.2013.780341.

Stokoe, E. and Edwards, D. (2007), '"Black this, black that": Racial insults and reported speech in neighbour complaints and police interrogations', *Discourse & Society*, 18(3), 337–372. DOI: 10.1177/0957926507075477.

Stokoe, E., Sikveland, R.O. and Symonds, J. (2016), 'Calling the GP surgery: Patient burden, patient satisfaction, and implications for training', *British Journal of General Practice*. DOI: 10.3399/bjgp16X686653.

Stokoe, W.C. (1960), 'Sign Language Structure: An outline of the visual communication systems of the American deaf', *Studies in Linguistics: Occasional Papers* (No. 8). Buffalo: Dept. of Anthropology and Linguistics, University of Buffalo.

Tracy, K. (1998), 'Analysing Context: Framing the discussion', *Research in Language and Social Interaction*, 31(1), 1–28. DOI: 10.1207/s15327973rlsi3101_1

Van Hasselt, V.B., Baker, M.T., Romano, S.J., Schlessinger, K.M., Zucker, M., Dragone, R., et al. (2006), 'Crisis (Hostage) Negotiation Training: A preliminary evaluation of program efficiency', *Criminal Justice and Behavior*, 33(1), 56–69. https://doi.org/10.1177/0093854805282328

Whalen, J., Zimmerman, D.H. and Whalen, M.R. (1988), 'When Words Fail: A single case analysis', *Social Problems*, 35(4), 335–362. DOI: 10.2307/800591

INDEX

'actions speak louder than words', 101–3, 115
adjacency pairs, 43, 47–9, 56, 74
Allsopp, Kirsty, 36–7
Amazon, 103
apologies, 73, 75–6
arms, folded, 118–19
artificial intelligence, 239–40
Atkins, Sarah, 230
Atkinson, Maxwell, 117–18
Austin, John, 102

Baumeister, Roy, 137–8
behavioural scientists, 151
behaviourism, 19, 155
big data analysis, 240
black holes, 1–2, 128
body language, 100, 115–19
breaching experiments, 44–5, 60

categorial errors, 142
category words, 146
charitable donations, 159–62
Chomsky, Noam, 2
Citizens Advice Bureau, 189
closing intonation, 5, 9
cold-calling, 25–6, 242, 247–8
collaboration, 54
committee meetings, 153
communication skills, 217–18, 220–1, 234, 237, 241
communication training, 26, 115, 158, 161–2, 217–39
continuing intonation, 6, 21, 58
'conversation' (the word), 100–1
conversation analysis, 3–31
Conversation Analytic Personality Diagnostic (CAPD), 64, 67, 92–9, 212

first movers, 20, 65, 67–8,
71–2, 92–3, 95, 98, 143,
253
'how-are-you' subverters,
94–6
mis-greeters, 93–4, 253
non-transitioners, 96–7
passive-aggressive, 98
recalibrators, 94, 253
recompleters, 97, 254
recruiters and recruited, 99,
210–13, 251
Conversation Analytic Role-
play method (CARM),
174–5, 238–9
Cooper, Dominic, 33
Cooper, Sarah, 211
crisis negotiations, 28–9, 84–6,
104–5, 129, 162–6, 173–4,
190–1, 244–5, 249–51
cultural differences, 129–32

Dingemanse, Mark, 130, 132
discursive psychology, 102
disfluencies, 133–4, 137, 219
disorderly phenomena, 2
doctors' appointments, 105–6,
185–7, 201–9, 238
doctors' consultations, 105–6,
152, 154–5, 157, 161, 230,
233–4
'do-fronting', 40
Drew, Paul, 211
Duchess, The, 33–5

Edwards, Derek, 102, 126n

Electric Light Orchestra, 22–3
emergency services, calls to,
26–7, 191–5, 239
Emma (comic artist), 213
entitlement, 251
environmental health services,
188
ethnomethodology, 44
eye contact, 116

'filler' talk, 11, 14, 25, 66, 241
'filler' words 133, 135
first movers, 20, 65, 67–8,
71–2, 92–3, 95, 98, 143,
253
first pair parts, 43, 46–50, 53,
55–6, 74, 127
flirting, 119
Frasier, 215–16
Friends, 38–43, 49–53, 58–60,
73–8, 89–90, 149–50
Frozen, 35–6, 38

Garfinkel, Harold, 44–5, 60
gender differences, 119–29,
144
gift aid, 160–2, 172
'gift of the gab', 86
GP Patient Survey, 238
GP Reception Project, 201–10
Grenny, Joseph, 252

Halcyon Gallery, 103
Hepburn, Alexa, 23
Heritage, John, 151, 155, 180
Hofstetter, Emily, 35–6

'how-are-yous', 6–14, 17, 21, 24–6, 28, 30, 93, 133, 135, 241–3
   'how-are-you' subverters, 94–6

interactional imperative, 17
interruptions, 53–8, 60
   and gender, 120–3, 128
invitations, 45–53

Jackson, Michael, 185
Jefferson, Gail, 3, 11, 142
Jefferson system, 4, 9, 20, 23, 117, 255–6

Kendrick, Kobin, 211
Kitzinger, Celia, 121–2
Knightley, Keira, 33

Lakoff, Robin, 120
Lawson, Nigella, 245–6
Le Guin, Urusla K., 102
LeBaron, Curtis, 125–6
LGBTQIA identities, 114
listening, 247–51
Location, Location, Location, 36–8
Los Angeles Fire Department, 185

Machell's Guide to Surviving Modern Life, 94–5
Marland, Jonathan, 135–7
marriage guidance, 144–5
Maxfield, David, 252

mediation, 79–82, 105–12, 140, 156–7, 167–73, 189
Mehl, Matthias, 138
Mehrabian, Albert, 117–18
mental load, 213–14
mis-greeters, 93–4, 253
Mitchell, Olivia, 118
MPs' constituency offices, 189–90
Mr Mean, 77–8
Murray, Jenni, 245–6
mystery shoppers, 235–7

names, use of, 24, 243–7
natural language processing, 240
neonatologists, 233
non-transitioners, 96–7
nudge theory, 151, 252

'Oh' (change-of-state token), 180, 200, 219, 235, 248
O'Hagan, Simon, 92n
one word, changing, 252–3
Orwell, George, 112
overlapping talk, 4, 8, 10, 54–5, 57–9, 121, 123, 127, 130, 203, 240, 242

passive-aggressive, 98
point of possible completion, 9, 60
Police and Criminal Evidence Act (PACE), 222–9, 237
police interviews, 57–8, 84, 114–15, 146–8

and simulations, 221–32,
235, 237–8
political correctness, 149–50
political speeches, 117
Potter, Jonathan, 102
preference, 36, 47, 49
dispreferred responses, 47,
51, 60, 62, 169
preference organisation, 53
preferred responses, 36, 47,
51–2, 74–5, 77, 89–91, 252
Private Eye, 11
processing time, 10
Public Order Act, 114–15

questioning intonation, 5, 39
questions, 'closed', 29, 35,
232–3

racism, 82–4, 114–15
rape cases, 112–13
rapport, 24, 26, 29, 227, 229–
30, 238
errors and warnings, 241–7,
253
'fake', 28
recalibrators, 94, 253
reciprocal greetings, 13, 18, 68, 94
recompleters, 97, 254
recruited, 99, 210–13, 251
recruiters, 99, 210–13, 251
recruitment, 210–14
Reynolds, Aaron, 103
Robinson, Nick, 135–7
role-play and simulations,
220–32, 254

Rowling, J.K., 114

Saatchi, Charles, 245
Sacks, Harvey, 3, 11, 14, 148,
237
Schegloff, Emanuel, 3, 11
Schneider, David, 135–6
Searle, John, 102
self-help, 106–10, 112
self-praise and self-
deprecation, 87–92
service burden, 195–210
Sharpe, Tom, *The Wilt
Alternative*, 103–4
sign language, 116
Sikveland, Rein, 162
silence, 33
Skype calls, 6–7
smile-voice, 7, 9, 21, 25
'so', 70
'some or any' studies, 155–6,
252
speech acts, 102
speed dates, 69–72, 92
Spencer, Phil, 36–7
'sticks and stones', 114
Stokoe, William, 116
summons and answer
sequence, 7–8, 14, 16, 30
Sunstein, Cass, 151

'talk' (the word), 100–1, 162
'talk the talk', 101, 162
Thaler, Richard, 151
'thank you' (at end of call),
209–10

Today, 135–7
transformational grammar, 40
two-second delays, 35–8, 118

'ums', 132–7, 239

vet's surgery, calling, 124, 184, 217–20, 234–7

Wittgenstein, Ludwig, 102
wobbly voice, 23
Woman's Hour, 131, 139, 246
women's register, 120

YouTube, 22, 191